KUWAIT
A NATION'S STORY

KUWAIT
A NATION'S STORY

PETER VINE • PAULA CASEY

IMMEL Publishing

© 1992 text: Peter Vine and Paula Casey

© 1992 artwork: Immel Publishing

© 1992 photographs: Individual photographers

Typeset in Times Roman by
Irish Typesetting and Publishing Co. Ltd, Galway, Ireland
and by
Icon Publications Limited, Kelso, Scotland

Design by Connemara Graphics, Ireland
and by
David & Shirley Kilpatrick

Immel Publishing Ltd
20 Berkeley Street
Berkeley Square
London W1X 5AE

Telephone: 071 491 1799
Fax: 071 493 5524

ISBN 0 907151 56 6

Jacket photograph: Black Star/Colorific!

Printed and bound in Great Britain by
Butler & Tanner Ltd, Frome and London

OTHER TITLES IN THIS SERIES

Pearls in Arabian Waters: the Heritage of Bahrain
The Heritage of Qatar
Arab Gold: Heritage of the UAE
Seychelles

Contents

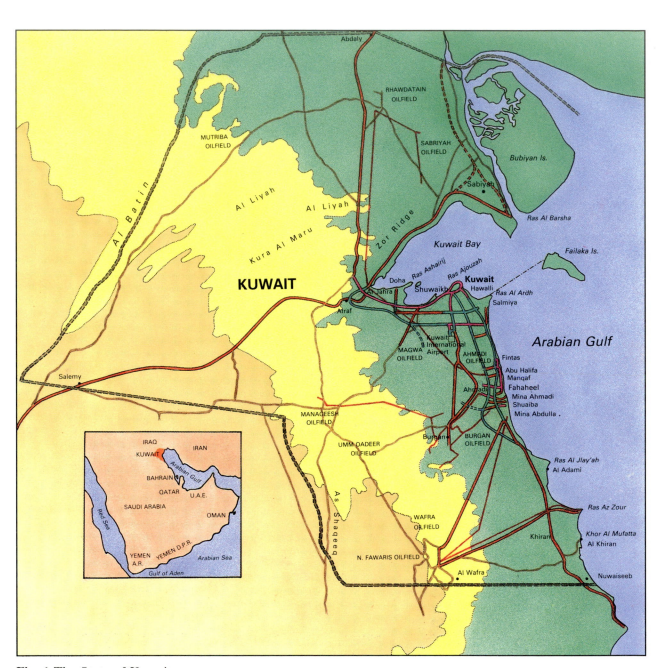

Fig. 1 The State of Kuwait

Foreword

This book was originally conceived, researched, and written in a different period of Kuwait's history, when we were enjoying the fruits of peace and the prosperity created by careful management of our natural resources. The authors travelled throughout the country, meeting politicians, administrators, scientists, business people, creative artists, teachers, doctors, lawyers, environmentalists, students, craft workers, and many others. Based upon this experience they set out to tell the story of our country, from the ancient past, right up to the present.

Their work was completed in the Spring of 1990 and production of the book began. The final stage of this process was about to commence at the beginning of August. It was halted, like everything else in Kuwait, by the invasion of our country by Iraq. For a while it seemed that the book should still be published as it was. We felt that it gave a valuable account of Kuwait's early history, its traditions, its natural environment and its remarkable progress since the discovery of oil. We were proud to talk of our growth in education and our modern health-care facilities; of our scientific progress and our work in support of the arts and in the promotion of peace and international understanding. But Iraq's impact on Kuwait became so serious that the Kuwait which we knew and loved was almost destroyed. Then we knew that the story needed to be completed.

We felt that few people really had much vision of what took place inside Kuwait to ordinary Kuwaiti citizens. For this reason we invited the senior author to return and see for himself what happened to our country. In the course of this visit he interviewed many people who lived through the horrors of Iraq's occupation of Kuwait. The authors have used many of these original interviews to tell the story of our nation through the eyes of its own people. The final two sections of this book are two more chapters in our history. They cover events and a period which Kuwaitis will never forget.

As the authors correctly point out, the experience has changed both Kuwait and its people. Today we are determined to create a peaceful future based upon justice and respect for each other. Much of what this book portrays in its earlier sections has been severely damaged or completely destroyed. As I write these words we are still struggling to put out the hundreds of fires caused by sabotage of our oil wells. Kuwait's culture was heavily targeted by the Iraqi forces intent on destroying all symbols of our nationhood. After stealing most of its contents, they set fire to our National Museum. They even burnt to the ground a beautiful 'boom', the Al-Muhalab, which was built in 1937 and was one of the finest sail-trading vessels to work out of Kuwait in this century. Today the remains of the vessel, little more than a bed of ashes and twisted nails, lie alongside the burnt out shell of the Kuwait Museum, a grim reminder of Iraq's violent efforts to erase Kuwait from the world map.

I commend the authors for their efforts to tell a true story. They have described Kuwait as it was before the invasion and have vividly portrayed the terrible consequences of Iraq's aggression. There is much in this book which Kuwaitis can be justifiably proud of, not least the courage and strength which many showed in the fight for our freedom. Their story underlines our heartfelt belief that Kuwait's greatest natural resource is its people. This is the story of their nation.

– *Professor Badr Jassim Al-Yacoub,*
Minister of Information.

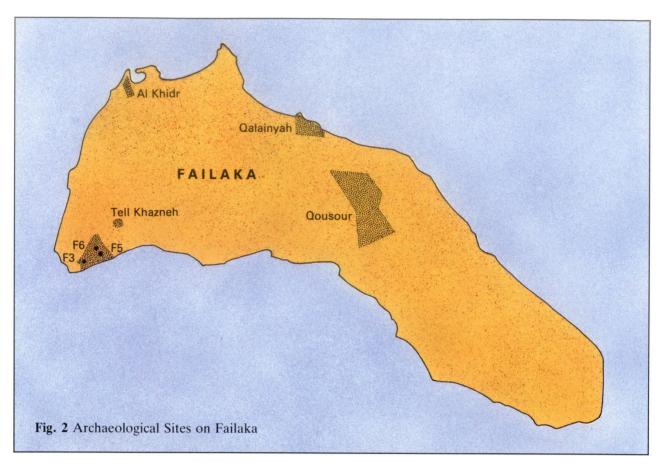

Fig. 2 Archaeological Sites on Failaka

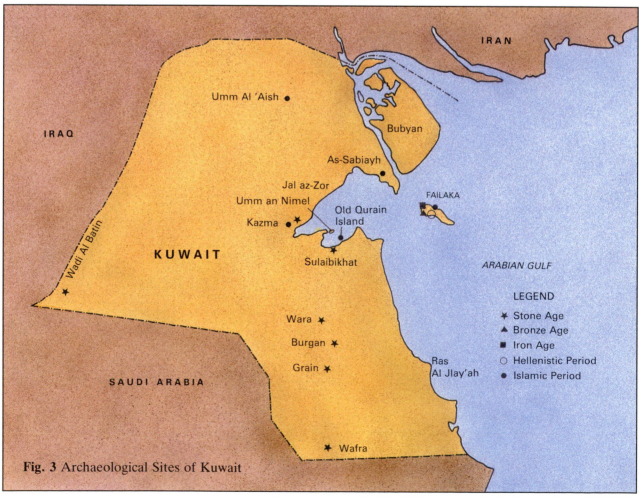

Fig. 3 Archaeological Sites of Kuwait

Unfolding the Past

A slab of limestone with Greek inscription discovered on the island of Failaka in the early 1930's hinted at Kuwait's intriguing past. Translated, it read: "*Soteles, the Athenina, and the soldiers (dedicated this) to Zeus the Saviour, to Poseidon, and to Artemis the Saviouress*", leading to much speculation as to its origins. Failaka, lying in a strategic position in the centre of Kuwait Bay and well supplied with water, seemed a likely choice for settlement in ancient times; but its story remained shrouded in mystery until the late 1950's when Danish archaeologists, fresh from an exciting run of excavations further south in Bahrain, arrived to explore the region. Their initial examination of the island, although superficial, did not prove disappointing. The twin mounds of Sa'ad wa Sa'id, the most conspicuous landmarks on the whole island, were recognised as tells—an accumulation of settlements built up over a period of time, one community building on the remains of another. Archaeologists carefully peel away the layers of settlement on a tell, attempting to date each one from the artifacts unearthed, particularly broken sherds of pottery. Here in Failaka, fragments of pottery were visible on the surface of the tell, the easternmost mound yielding sherds of glazed or red-painted bowls known to be Greek-related. It was obvious too from the shape of the mound that the archaeologists were faced with a considerable settlement—a permanent fortification in fact. But who were these Greek-speaking people that had built an extensive fort, leaving their calling card in the form of a stone slab? Had Alexander the Great's expeditionary forces inhabited the small island? Or were the Greek-related remains left by his Seleucid successors?

Two years of excavations, facilitated and supported in every way by the Kuwaitis, exposed the essentially Greek nature of the site on the eas-

Soteles stone is a piece of sandstone with Greek inscription discovered on Failaka Island in 1937. The inscription runs as follows:– 'Soteles citizens of Athens and the soldiers dedicated this to Zeus Soter the saviour, to Poseidon and Artemis Suteira the saviouress' (*ref. KM 106, Kuwait National Museum*).

Stone artifacts recovered by a team led by Dr Fahed Al Wahaibi on Umm an Nimel island, Kuwait (*photographed by the author at Kuwait National Museum*).

tern tell: a small temple bearing a remarkable resemblance to the Parthenon, albeit with marked Oriental influences, was located in a small Greek fortified town, its ramparts overlooked by corner towers and broken only by gateways to the north and south. The excavation had also uncovered a 'workshop' interpreted as a production-centre for terracotta figurines in a large brick house between the tells, yielding a range of moulds of Greek form, including a man's head in shallow relief that bore a remarkable resemblance to Alexander the Great; and, in the second year, a wine-jar handle, stamped with the rose, which was the trade-mark of Rhodes, and the vintner's name in Greek. This last article was dated to the 3rd century BC—the period when the Seleucids, inheriting part of Alexander's empire, had ruled a vast area to the north of Kuwait from Syria through Mesopotamia and Persia. Two subsequent finds were to

throw further light on the mystery. The first was a solid lump of purplish metal found outside the temple, identifiable to an expert eye even at this early stage, as Greek silver tetradrachms. The second find was even more specific: a large badly weathered rectangular slab of stone, discovered south of the altar, but clearly intended to stand on an oblong stone base outside the entrance to the temple, was engraved with a lengthy Greek inscription. In Bibby's own words: "*The interpretation seemed to be that Anaxarchos had been the local governor and had received a letter from his superior, Ikadion, instructing him in the king's name to build, or perhaps to maintain, the temple on the island of Ikaros. He had sent on the letter to the commandant of Failaka with a covering note of his own, ordering that the king's command be carried out, and that, when it was done, both letters should be inscribed on stone and set up outside the temple*". The foundation document of the temple had been found. There was no date on the stone, but it clearly identified Failaka as the island of Ikaros.

The Danes were already familiar with the beguiling picture painted by classical authors of Ikaros which was first mentioned by Strabo, writing at the end of the 1st century BC. Strabo, however makes good use of earlier sources, especially the work of Eratosthenes the Geographer who, in the 3rd century BC, chronicled the exploits of Alexander the Great's companions on their campaigns overseas. Strabo reports: *"Androsthenes, who travelled through the Gulf with his fleet, states that the navigator who comes from Teredon and who afterwards keeps the continent to his right sees the island of Ikaros where a sanctuary dedicated to Apollo as well as an oracle of Tauropolos can be found"*. Arrian, writing the Anabsis of Alexander about 170 AD, also recounts tales of the great Greek general's epic journeys, especially his sorties into the Gulf. Although his account was written 500 years after the event, he also relied heavily on contemporary sources, including the log of Alexander's Cretan admiral Nearchos. Alexander and his fleet came together at Babylon, having completed the long and arduous return from India. The great Macedonian general, annoyed because the Arabians had not sent ambassadors to pledge submission to him and encouraged by reports of vast quantities of myrrh and frankincense and cinnamon to be found in the south, planned a campaign of conquest against Arabia. Nearchos and his fleet were given the task of exploring the coast in preparation for the final onslaught. To this end Nearchos sent out three successive ships; the first terminating its journey at Tylos (Bahrain) and the last reaching the entrance to the Gulf. It was reported to Alexander that: *"There were two coastal islands at the north of the*

Stone Age implements from Kuwait. Little is known about Kuwait's Stone Age but a number of sites with flints have been located including Burgan hill; Wadi al Batin; Kazma region; Sulaibikhat and Umm an Nimel. Debate continues concerning the precise age of the various implements which have been found (*photographed by the author at Kuwait National Museum*).

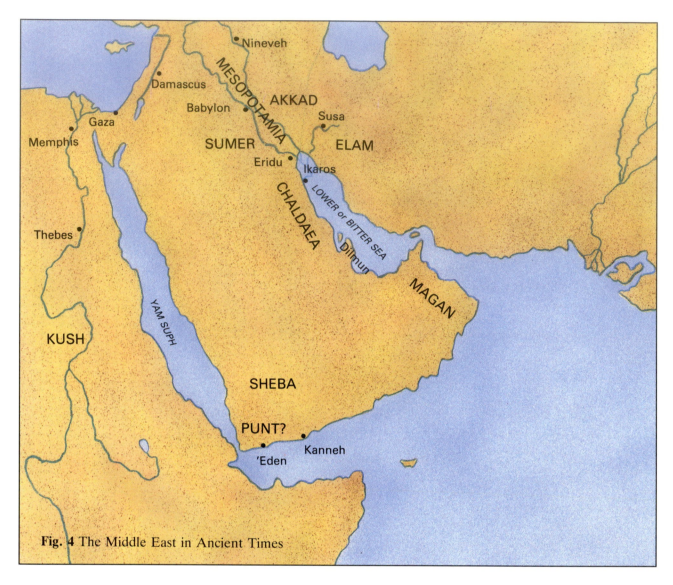

Fig. 4 The Middle East in Ancient Times

Euphrates; the first one was not far from the mouths of the Euphrates, 120 stadiums off the coast and the mouth. It was the smallest and it was covered with all sorts of trees; there was a sanctuary to Artemis too and the people who lived around the sanctuary took care of it. It was used as a grazing field by the wild goats and does which were sacrificed to Artemis. Hunting them was not allowed except to offer them to the goddess as a sacrifice; hunting was only practised in this aim, because it was not forbidden then". Arrian claims that Alexander ordered the island to be called Ikaros, *"because of the island of Ikaros which lies in the Aegean sea".* Although Alexander succumbed to a fever three days before the conquest of Arabia was due to commence and the whole campaign was aborted, the temple document was to conclusively prove that Failaka was indeed the Ikaros of Alexander's time.

Despite the significance of the find, the mystery was really only beginning to unravel. As we can see from the above translated quotation,

when Alexander named the island Ikaros there was already a shrine there dedicated to a goddess which the Greeks associated with their own Artemis. What were the origins of this shrine and who were the people that had built it? It was hoped that the western tell, excavated simultaneously with its eastern counterpart, would provide an answer to these questions. Obviously, such an advantageously situated and conveniently watered island could not have escaped the attentions of Mesopotamian seafarers, but the thin red ridged 'Barbar' pottery found on the surface of this western tell led to the unfolding of a more surprising tale. Excavations further south had succeeded in pushing back the frontiers of civilisation, confirming the theory first postulated by Sir Henry Rawlinson in 1880 that Bahrain was indeed the trading and ritual centre of the sophisticated kingdom of Dilmun during the late 3rd and early 2nd millennia BC when most of the world was in a state of savagery. Dilmun had always been a holy land in the eyes of the

A hand made giant pottery vessel of Red-Ridged-Ware similar to vessels found at the Barbar temple in Bahrain. This was recovered on Failaka island. Period 1,800 to 1,100 BC. (*Kuwait National Museum*).

Sumerians, ancient city-dwellers of Mesopotamia. The mythological tale of Enki, patron god of the ancient city of Eridu, god of the Abyss, inscribed in wedge-shaped cuneiform script on tablets of stone 4,000 years ago, but probably referring to an earlier epic, opens with the lines: *"The land of Dilmun is holy, the land of Dilmun is pure, the land of Dilmun is clean, the land of Dilmun is holy"*. Dilmun featured again and again in ancient texts. Imperishable slabs of stone inscribed in cuneiform script and stored in the library of Ashurbanipal recount the Assyrian version of the Universal Deluge. According to these inscriptions it was to Dilmun that the semi-mythical Gilgamesh had come in search of the secret of immortality entrusted to Ziusadra, whom Enki had saved from the Deluge. But Dilmun wasn't only a paradisal place. Perusal of the cuneiform texts, both temple archives and the letters of individual merchants, also show that direct trade links between Meluhha (Indus Valley), Magan (UAE) and Mesopotamia which were in place from early in the 3rd millennium were fractured by the growing importance of Dilmun as a trade centre and entrepot for the goods required by thriving Bronze Age civilisations in Mesopotamia.

Enough archaeological evidence has been found in Bahrain to identify this island with the Dilmun of myth and legend, the excavations also echoing trading patterns with the outside world already highlighted by cuneiform texts. Work at Qal'at al Bahrain, the city of Dilmun, unearthed local chain ridge ware pottery in the very lowest and oldest levels of the excavations dated to the middle of the 3rd millennium BC (2500–2200 BC). A certain amount of Umm an Nar pottery, typical of that highly organised 3rd millennium culture situated in the region of the UAE, was also found at this level, indicating that merchants

from the UAE, selling copper wrested from the Hajar mountains, were among the first trading partners of the Dilmunites. Harrappan influence emanating from the thriving cultural and commercial centre on the shores of the Indus and exhibited in the archaeological record in the form of Harappan weights and distinctive Harappan-inspired seals was evident early in the life of the city, but contact with Mesopotamia gradually intensified; the patterns on the highly typical seals reflecting this deepening Mesopotamian influence. Qala'at al Bahrain did not stand alone: late in the 3rd millennium, temples were also being built at Barbar (hence the designation 'Barbar' to the indigenous culture of this period) and so too were some of the thousands of burial mounds which dot Bahrain's island terrain.

One can imagine how excited the archaeologists were to find the same red ridged 'Barbar' pottery on Failaka over 400 kilometres from Bahrain, on an island much closer to Ur than to Bahrain. Excavation of the western tell had already begun to reveal ruins which could be

Fig. 5 Examples of Bronze Age pottery

dated to the 2nd millennium BC and numerous examples of distinctive stamp-seals, many of which were similar to those already found in smaller quantities in Bahrain. But, again, the most exciting find of all was an inscription: this time, however, it was in cuneiform writing on a fragment of a steatite bowl. Bibby, although not particularly versed in this Mesopotamian script, quickly realised that the first line was identical with the first line of an inscription found in Bahrain in 1897. It read: "*The temple of the god Inzak*", indicating that "*this bowl had been part of the inventory of an earlier temple, a temple dedicated to Inzak, the tutelary God of Dilmun*". Although it didn't answer our question as to the nature of the sanctuary already on the island before the Greeks arrived, the fragmentary inscription underlined the fact that Failaka had for many millennia been a holy island, its tradition of religious pilgrimage continuing into the present day.

Dilmun carnelian seal with double face. Diameter: 2.4 cms. Bronze Age (*Kuwait National Museum*).

Much painstaking work has been carried out since those early exciting days of discovery and much remains to be done. But, although refinements have been made in certain areas, the basic outline of the story has changed very little. Al Ubaid pottery, found in Saudi Arabia and Qatar, proves that all this region had been in contact with Mesopotamia since the 5th millennium BC. However, despite the geographical proximity of this great neighbour, a decidedly original Barbar culture developed along the eastern shores of

Arabia, at the same time profiting enormously from its trade links with those thriving civilisations further north. Towards the end of the 3rd Dynasty of Ur (approximately 2000 BC) it is thought that this Barbar culture, indigenous to Dilmun, spread north to encompass Failaka island, virtually adjacent to the borders of Mesopotamia. It has been suggested that Failaka although belonging to the same cultural area was not part of Dilmun, but a stage on the trading routes to and from that cultural religious and mercantile centre known as Agarum (as written on cuneiform inscriptions). Certainly the architectural remains (public and private buildings) and the many finds including numerous stamp-seals attest to the vitality of Failaka during this period. The location of a temple to the god Inzak—the tutelary god of the Dilmunites—confirms Failaka's religious significance as well as its trading status. Whatever its actual designation at the end of the 3rd millennium, whether Dilmun or Agarum, it is thought that Failaka became the centre of a new Dilmun displaced northwards during the period of Kassite colonialism around 1400–1300 BC.

Failaka's history during the 1st millennium BC before the arrival of the Greeks is not very clear. J.-F. Salles refutes the suggestion that a land route might have linked lower Mesopotamia to Eastern Arabia, via Kuwait, during the Neo-Assyrian period (approx. 8th–7th century BC). "*Even if it is true*", he remarks, "*it would not explain the presence of a settlement on Failaka island, for which there is, in any case, no archaeological evidence.*" During the Neo-Babylonian period (7th–6th century BC) it was presumed that the 'Dilmunite federation' of Failaka, Eastern Arabia and Bahrain, was dissolved. However Failaka was inhabited at this time since a ship loaded with a huge stone on which Nebuchadnezzar's name is inscribed cast anchor there, as well as its load! Salles comments, referring again to the suggestion that Failaka was not in fact Dilmun, that although "*Failaka should not be considered the final haven of the significant trade activities evidenced by 1st millennium BC written sources, . . . the island was an important stop on the sea-route, and . . . it would seem unbelievable that Failaka should not be part of Dilmun too . . . Moreover*", he continues, "*we would like to stress the very realistic nature of Sennacherib's proclamation after the destruction of Babylon: 'I removed its ground and had it carried to the Euphrates (and on) to the sea. Its dust reached into Dilmun'. This is a vivid descrip-*

Circular, bifacial stamp seal made from carnelian. Side A bears an old Babylonian inscription, mentioning 'Temple Egal Gula of Inzak of Agarum' (*Kuwait National Musuem*).

tion of the muddy waters which surround Failaka. Even in a royal inscription which boasts of his booty in literary style, the image cannot have applied to Bahrain island, which is too distant, but is quite appropriate for Failaka's landscape."

The quotation from Sennacherib reflects the violent struggles taking place in southern Mesopotamia during this period, as the Neo-Assyrian kings attempted to exert their control over the northern part of Arabia and the important sea-routes of the Gulf. Although the tributes paid by the kings of Dilmun right down to the reign of Ashurbanipal aptly illustrate the reality of Assyrian power, there is a question mark over the exact nature of the control they wielded in the region. Was the governor of Dilmun, mentioned under Nabunaid, a true state servant with real provincial powers or just a representative in charge of trade security? Salles disputes the theory that Failaka was the seat of a governor under Nebuchadnezzar, but he does believe that *"some kind of Neo-Babylonian power on Failaka, as part of Dilmun, must be acknowledged"*.

Although the documentation is very sparse for the Achaemenian period, Achaemenian influence (Persian of the 5th–4th centuries BC) was recognised at Tell Khazneh, excavated by the French mission, but not at other Hellenistic sites. *"The cultural and, a fortiori, political relationship between Tell Khazneh and the Achaemenian area is still unknown, but the island was inhabited in the Achaemenian period, situated at the end of an important trade route, and it was the site of a sanctuary"*. The presence of such a sanctuary at Tell Khazneh before the arrival of the Greeks, echoes the island's role during the

2nd millennium when Dilmunites, on their way by sea to Mesopotamia or Susa, broke their journey on Failaka and made sacrifices to their god Inzak. From the archaeological finds, especially pottery, we can be sure that Failaka had close contacts not only with its northern and eastern neighbours, but also with Eastern Arabia.

The Greeks are thought to have arrived on Failaka towards the end of the 4th century BC, just before Alexander's death in 323. Did Nearchus himself set foot on the island as part of his exploratory expedition through the Gulf from October 325 to March 324? Or was the island with its local sanctuary discovered by the leaders of two expeditions during the winter of 324/323, one of them being Androsthenes cited by Arrian? The dating of two coin hoards might indicate that the island was discovered around 300 BC in the reign of Seleucus I, a good twenty years after Alexander's expedition. However, Salles comments that *"the discovery of Failaka by the Greeks must be related to Alexander's time because of the evidence of the cult of Artemis Tauropolos"* and its connections with Nearchus and Androsthenes through Amphipolis (three coins from Amphipolis were also found in the hoard from Tell Khazneh). *"All these presumptions converge to accredit the discovery of Failaka to Nearchus himself."* The question remains to be answered whether Soteles, true founder of the Greek settlement (see the inscription on the original stone) was a member of the expedition.

In the centuries of Seleucid rule which followed Alexander's death Failaka apparently prospered, especially during the reign of Antiochus

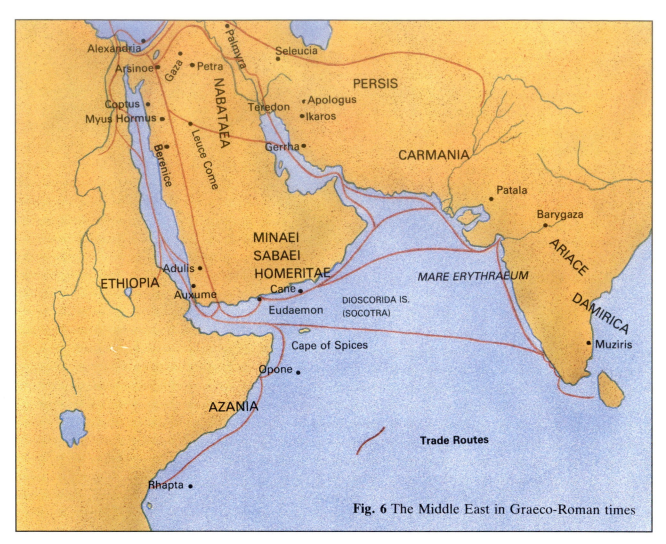

Fig. 6 The Middle East in Graeco-Roman times

III, which was a period of security for the empire as a whole. Imported terracottas found on Failaka show that Ikaros possessed mercantile connections with Susa in particular, but also with other areas to the north of Arabia. Coins from the Hellenistic sites not only reinforce these links, but throw further light on trading patterns. It is clear that Failaka was an important market place for those who transported valuable exotic goods, channelled through Gerrha, and destined for Mesopotamia or the Levant. Even though the temples within the Greek fortress seem to have lost much of their religious significance by this stage, the erection of an extra muros sanctuary reinforces the island's long history as a cult place. As this phase of security and prosperity came to an end, this sanctuary was abandoned and the fortress strengthened. At this time the Seleucid Empire was severely undermined by conflict with the Lagids and with Rome, rendering the island of Failaka dangerously vulnerable to the ambitions of Parthians and Characenians. It is likely that Ikaros was under Characene rule when that state was overrun by Mithridates II in 122 BC, thereby bringing Ikaros under Parthian control. It seems that the ruined and abandoned fortress was again occupied for a limited period from the end of the 1st century BC to the end of the 1st century AD, but, as yet, there is no evidence of occupation on the island after this period.

A Hellenistic sandstone sculpted head of a bearded man with hair combed back. Traces of red paint in nasal and oral area. Recovered by the French Expedition, in 1983, on Failaka island (*ref. KM 3451, Kuwait National Museum*).

Below: Steps and water system inside bastion of Greek fortress at Failaka (*P. Vine*).

Opposite: Remains of Greek Temple at Failaka (*P. Vine*).

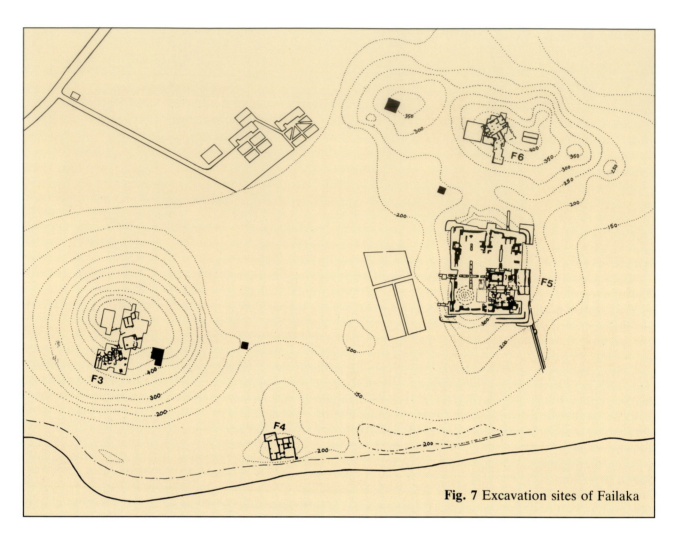

Fig. 7 Excavation sites of Failaka

THE ARCHAEOLOGICAL SITES

Bronze Age Settlements

The Danish expedition uncovered three main sites on Failaka, two of which belonged to the 2nd millennium BC. These are designated as F6 and F3. American excavations took place in the region of F6 and the French mission, with the backing, scientific and financial, of the Department of Antiquities and Museums in Kuwait, also excavated a Bronze Age building on F6 as well as a small tell (north of F6) of Bronze Age significance.

Excavations

Excavations on F6 unearthed a 'Palace' complex. This important building, 20m by 18m and oriented SW-NE with an extended main entrance on the SW side, revealed the remains of reception rooms and administration rooms to the front of the building with the residential area located to the rear. The domestic nature of this residential area is underlined by the presence of small rooms packed with medium-sized storage

jars. Carbon dating from the F6 site pinpointed a date of 1770–1870 BC. In fact Barbar, Kassite and post-Kassite occupation levels occur on both F3 and F6, although Kassite occupation is less definite on F6 than F3. Pottery from the oldest Bronze Age settlement period (Period I) has been found only in F6 and not in F3. It occurs in several trenches scattered over the whole excavation area, both inside and outside the Palace walls, but almost always at levels below the oldest floor level of the Palace, indicating that it must have been built after Period I. Three almost complete vessels in room 1 are the oldest datable pottery finds definitely belonging to a Palace context and these can be dated to Period 3A. The three vessels, like their contemporaries in F3 were probably left on the floor and covered by drift sand, after the building was temporarily abandoned. Other whole period 3A vessels have not been found in close connection with the Palace itself. In fact only rather few pottery lots from period 3A have been recovered from F6, compared to period 3B and 4A pottery, which is present in quantity. It is possible that the Palace was occupied during period 2, but further exca-

A Bronze Age rectangular brown steatite, unglazed seal of Dilmun type depicting a ship with two nude men in half sitting position. In field at top left and right, a star in crescent, a serpent (left) a monkey (right), centre a star. recovered from Field No. F6 (1242) on Failaka, by the Danish Expedition (*Kuwait National Museum*).

vation is required before the earliest palace structures can be reliably dated. Bronze Age finds from this site, including the ubiquitous circular stamp-seals, and steatite bowls are described on page 32.

American excavations in 1973 and '74 excavated a series of trenches to the west of the 'Palace' revealing what they call an 'industrial area' interspersed with small dwelling rooms. Six large circular kilns made of stone mortar and mud-brick were accompanied by storage bins containing the raw material (shells and bones) processed in these kilns, presumably to form a gypsum-organic building material. Another use for the kilns is suggested by the numerous fragments of the terracotta trays with thumb impressions used for baking bread. The abundance of metal slag, copper ingots, and a great number of metal objects also testifies to the presence of a healthy bronze-working industry. Finds included steatite stamp-seals, imported cylinder seals, an inscribed rectangular Indus seal; and jewellery of bronze, silver and gold.

The French mission in 1984 excavated on the eastern side of F6. Before arriving at the Bronze Age structures they had to dig down through layers of more recent occupation. The uppermost and newest layer on the site had been badly disturbed by a large number of pits dug either by looters looking for stones to use for building, or grave-diggers digging make-shift graves—the latest burial at this level was no more than a few centuries old. In Level II, dating to 1st millennium and Hellenistic period, stone-looters had again been in action; probably searching for stone blocks to build the fortress on F5. Despite such earlier damage to the site, the French excavators uncovered a significant quantity of Hellenistic material:- amphorae, bowls, fish-plates, and other glazed wares together with coarse pottery, some of which was found complete. The mission's report comments: "*The only evidence of occupation prior to the Hellenistic era is a unique jar burial . . . In a circular pit, a bell-shaped jar was found upside down above a flexed skeleton. The limbs of the adult body had been broken so that it could be put into the jar*". The actual date of the burial is uncertain, it could have taken place during the 7th, 6th or 5th centuries BC but it seems that the latter date is most likely to be correct since similar burials are well-known from southern Mesopotamia during the same period.

Level III revealed Bronze Age remains dated to somewhere within the 2nd millennium. Unfor-

A Bronze Age bronze scepter in the form of a human head. This would have been fixed on the end of a wooden stick (*ref. KM 52, Kuwait National Museum*).

tunately, it too had received the attentions of the stone-robbers so that all that remained architecturally were a few traces of robbed walls. Artifacts recovered included a few sherds, pieces of bronze slags, bronze fragments or objects, and a number of beads made of carnelian, agate and other stones.

Part of a large building was excavated at levels IV and V. This structure has a massive outside wall bordered by a small channel, lined by flat slabs and with a drain to the north-west. Level IV saw a reoccupation of this building in which some changes were made including the raising of the floors and the covering of the channel by the new structures: diagnostic Kassite pottery was found on the exterior floor related to this phase. Level V represents the first use of the building and a white plastered floor outside the building is related to it . Another parallel building in bad state of preservation past was also uncovered but the archaeologists doubt whether this second building was still in use during phase IV. Pottery and objects from Level V (the floor outside the

building and related loci) date to the early centuries of the 2nd millennium. "Among the more significant objects from this level is a piece of bituminous stone sculpture, comparable to pieces in the Musee du Louvre, and a fragment possibly from the same object from the Danish excavations of F6". Beneath this plastered outside floor, Level V was represented as a layer of powdery grey earth rich in finds, Dilmun seals and pottery, dated to the very beginning of the 2nd millennium BC. The pottery is very similar to that discovered at Barbar (level II) and Qala'at al Bahrain City II—red clay ridged jars. The French report comments "*This layer extends over the area we interpret as the oldest settlement in the excavated area—Level Vc—eleven Dilmun seals were found there.*"

Although the French excavations left some questions unanswered, and the team was thwarted in their desire to find evidence of settlement levels for the 3rd millennium (a few finds might suggest that Failaka was inhabited as early as the 3rd millennium: these include inscriptions and a steatite fragment belonging to

Bronze Age dagger and javelin blades made from copper recovered by the Danish Expedition (*Kuwait National Museum*).

the serie ancienne), the significance of this large building cannot be denied. *"Its size alone suggests that it cannot have had an ordinary domestic function, and it is most likely an important public building."*

G3 Excavations

G3, situated 300 metres to the north of F6, was also excavated by the French and was dated to the end of the 3rd millennium/ beginning of the 2nd millennium. In contrast to the other Bronze Age settlements in the area, G3 was abandoned thereafter. Unfortunately stone-looters had been active here also and destroyed much of the site. However two dwelling layers separated by an intermediate layer of destruction were located. Pottery of Barbar type (comparable with Qala'at al-Bahrain city II) was found in the upper or more recent layer only two walls of which were left intact; two fragments of vessels imported from Mesopotamia were also uncovered. The lower or older layer was spread over a smaller surface area, and again the stone-looters had been busy, but the archaeologists found a fireplace roughly built with irregular stones and sherds of ridged jars, containing charcoal, pieces of bones, fish bones and sea-shells. Pottery was a little more abundant at this level: in fact the small quantities of brown or red locally made pottery with fine mineral white or yellow grits from this site was made in the potter's kilns cleared out by the Danish excavators at the south of hill F3 and dated to the beginning of the 2nd millennium. Metal slags, pieces of crucibles and fragments of bronze were also found at this level. The food remains pointed to domestic activities whilst the other artifacts indicated that craft metallurgy and the working of bronze was carried on by inhabitants of this settlement. The complete absence of texts, seals, or other significant objects was somewhat disappointing.

F3 Excavations

F3 is a Bronze Age settlement, covering a small site of under a hectare composed of some private houses and various special activity areas such as Barbar period kilns. It was here that the temple of Inzak was uncovered and numerous distinctive seals (see pg. 32). Three altars stand in the yard of the temple which was rebuilt on three occasions during the Bronze Age settlement period. Poul Kjaerum has also identified four building phases in the northern part of the tell (the oldest section) and two phases in the southern part. Hojlund in his report on the Bronze Age

A steatite Bronze Age stela with carvings on both faces. Recovered in 1960 by the Danish Expedition to Failaka, in field F3 (*ref. KM 1636, Kuwait National Museum*).

Pottery of F3 and F6 comments: *"It is a characteristic feature with the F3 settlement that it does not occupy the same spot, but circulates round in the terrain from period to period. The earliest settlement, dated to period 2, lies in the northern part of the tell. After this there must possibly have been a long pause in occupation between period 2 and period 3A unless a settlement area pertaining to this period has yet to be discovered. In period 3A, a number of houses were built to the south. To period 3B belongs the Temple in F3 North, but the true occupation area must in this period be sought in the unexcavated area. In period 4A, a northern strip in the southwestern area was occupied and in period 4B, the occupied area lay at the northern extremity"*.

Hellenistic Settlements.

The most abundant remains on the island are from the Hellenistic period; the Danish mission being responsible for the excavation of two Hellenistic sites; F4, interpreted as a terracotta 'workshop', and F5: an important fortress. The French mission concentrated their attentions on B6, an extra-muros sanctuary, and Tell Khazneh which was also occupied in the pre-Hellenistic period. They also resumed work at F5.

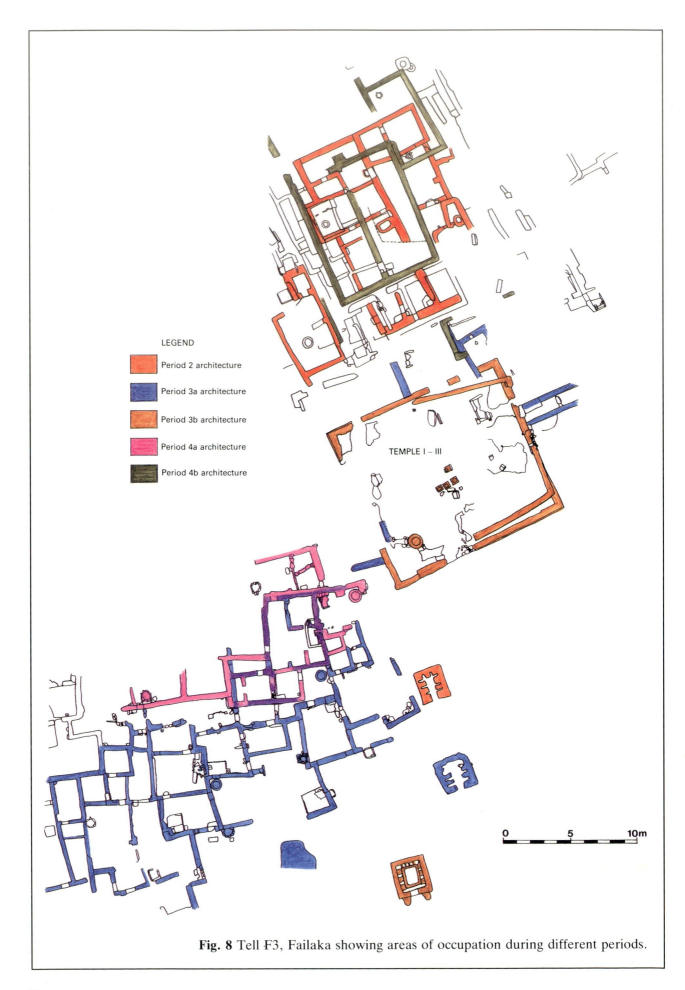

LEGEND

Period 2 architecture

Period 3a architecture

Period 3b architecture

Period 4a architecture

Period 4b architecture

TEMPLE I – III

0   5   10m

Fig. 8 Tell F3, Failaka showing areas of occupation during different periods.

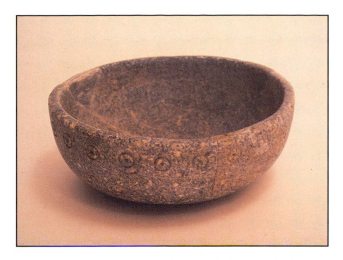

A Bronze Age concave steatite vessel, decorated with two parallel lines with circles between them. Found at Failaka Island, site F3 (*ref. KM 63, Kuwait National Museum*).

A Greek Hellenistic small jar (100 BC to 100 AD) probably used to store wine. It was decorated with two wavy lines and two parallel lines between. Recovered from F5 at Failaka (*ref. KM 83, Kuwait National Museum*).

An early Hellenistic terracotta figurine in the form of a female bust resembling Aphrodite, height 10.4cms. Recovered from trench M at F5 on Failaka Island (*ref. KM 91, Kuwait National Museum*).

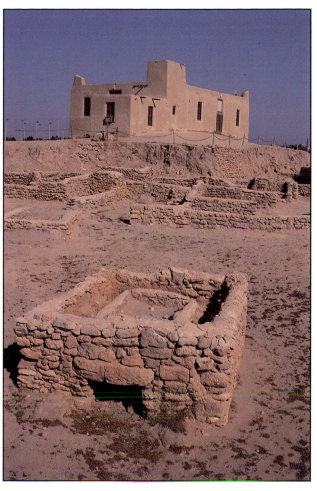

An ancient Bronze Age oven is revealed in excavations at F3 on Tel Saad, Failaka Island. The oven was used as a potter's kiln (*P.Vine*).

F5 Excavations

Excavations at this important Hellenistic site on the easternmost tell, uncovered a fortress laid out in a quadratic plan, guarded by square towers at each corner and surrounded by a wide moat, V-shaped and stone lined. Entrance was gained into the fortified area through a south door, which was later walled-up, and a north door, opened during the Parthian period. Inside the fortified walls the ruins of two Graeco-Persian temples have been cleared as well as an important number of houses. Some finds from this site, including terracotta figurines (see pg. 26) and coins (see pg. 35), are discussed under separate headings.

The fortress was first inhabited from the middle of the 3rd to the end of the 2nd century BC (Period I). An exploratory trench, 15m long and 8.5m wide, dug by the French team, to the north of the temple area, has revealed an area of private houses; the material uncovered consisting primarily of pottery and a few terracotta figurines. A description of the occupation levels exposed by the French helps to highlight the major phases in the site's development. Keeping in mind that the stages of the fortress are numbered from the base, the earliest occupation occurs at stage I which is related to Temple A and its neighbouring structures (altars, Temple B, rectangular foundation between the two altars) and to a group of two houses bound to the south curtain-wall of the rampart. *"We might assume that the first role of the fortress—or more modestly, the small fort—would have been to shelter and protect the temple or temples, with no true settlement such as a garrison or a fortified village"*. During stage II, the activity in the body of the fortress includes the construction of a few houses and the strengthening of the south-east, north-east and north-west towers. The transition from stage II to stage III is marked by the Danish discovery of the two coin hoards. (See pg. 35). During stage III, dated to the end of the 3rd/beginning of the 2nd century BC, some other houses are built inside the fortress, but more significantly, the defensive system is very considerably widened and strengthened, incorporating an impressive moat. The stela of Ikaros, the foundation document of the temple, was abandoned on the floor of stage III indicating that Temple A and its associated religious cult fell into decline during stage IV as the inhabited area

A statue of a king, probably Mithridates II, sitting on his throne, showing quite clear facial features including a moustache and beard and a Parthian crown. The terracotta figurine has been made from red/brown clay and was painted with red, blue and yellow paint. It was recovered from trench M at F5 by the Danish Expedition to Failaka in 1961 (*Kuwait National Museum*).

became more densely settled: the previously unroofed rooms are now divided by small partition walls carefully built with long, roughly dressed stone, creating smaller domestic areas. The interior defence wall is also dismantled. At the end of stage IV some rooms are abandoned, although temporarily. Stage V, the French report surmises, consists *"of a last, light occupation, on the same lay-out as stage IV. The walls are made of rubble stone, without dressed faces, and the building techniques are very rough"*.

The theory that the ruined and abandoned fortress was reoccupied for a limited period (Period II, end of 1st century BC/end of 1st century AD), as demonstrated by the finding of pottery classified as B1-ware in front of Temple A, was put forward by the Danes. Although the French only found a few isolated B1 sherds in their sounding, their observations agree with this analysis.

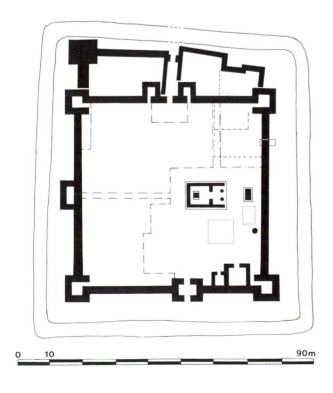

0   10   90m

Fig. 9 Plan of Hellenistic fortress at F5

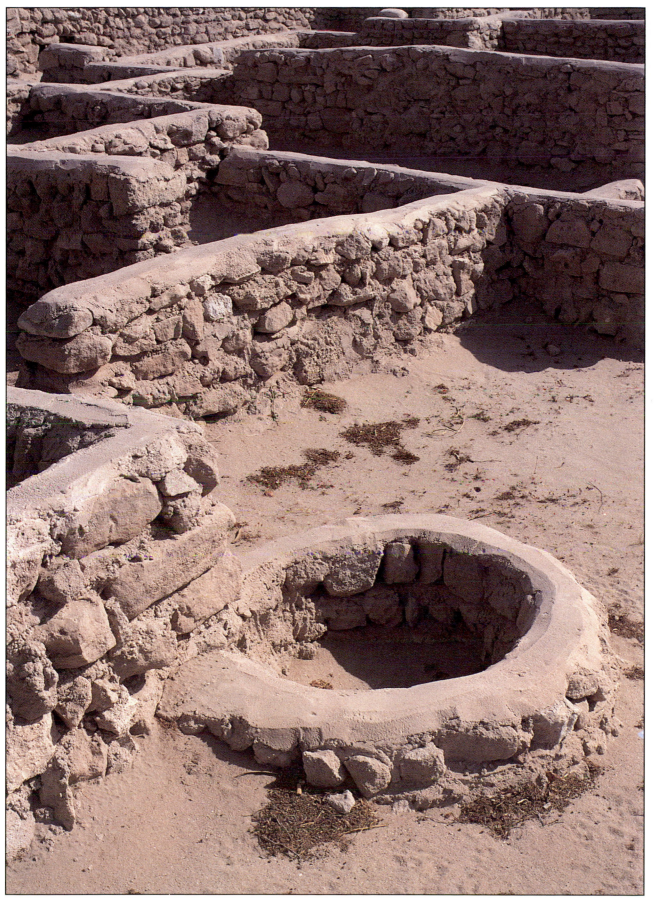

Locus H8 in the Hellenistic fortress (known as F5) at Failaka was originally excavated by the Danish Expedition between 1958 and 1963 and more recently by the French archaeological team in 1985. This particular area of the site contained private houses (*P. Vine*).

A slate plaque with bas-relief of seated Parthian man in costume holding a small object, possibly a figurine, in front of his face. Probably 6th century BC. Recovered by the Danish Expedition in Field No. F4 at Failaka Island (*ref. KM 1644, Kuwait National Museum*).

F4 Excavations

F4 was also investigated by Dr. Roussell of the Danish expedition who uncovered a rectangular building with many rooms containing a vast quantity of moulds for the manufacture of terracota figurines. For this reason it was regarded as a workshop although there is no real evidence that it was ever used as such. Unfortunately, due to Roussell's premature death, the results of these excavations cannot be published in detail. However, Hans Mathiesen studied the terracotta figurines and moulds found at F4 and at F5.

Mathiesen has divided the one hundred and twenty nine terracottas, most of which are very badly preserved, into three groups: Oriental type i.e similar to those existing in the Orient before the arrival of the Greeks, some forms of which continued during the Greek period, influenced by Greek art; Greek type i.e those following an essentially Greek pattern, although some may have been manufactured during the Parthian period; and fragments of indeterminate type including dice, gamesmen for board games etc. Both Oriental and Greek types have been dated by comparing the figurines with relevant material

found elsewhere. Mathiesen emphasises that since the Oriental types occur in Hellenized version, they cannot be taken as any indication that either F5 or F4 existed in pre-Greek times. "*Judging from comparative material those imitating Greek paradigms cover the whole of the Hellenistic period, with perhaps a certain preponderance in the late third and the second centuries BC*". Although the Oriental figurines are more difficult to date, it seems too that they were made throughout the Hellenistic period as they are found together with the Greek type at approximately the same levels. In fact one of the Oriental statuettes was found in association with a coin hoard and was therefore evidently used in a period somewhat later than the beginning of the second century BC.

Nude female figurines, possibly representing a fertility goddess; horsemen and horse statuettes, sometimes interpreted as mounted solar deities; models of boats, possibly intended as symbols for lunar deities; animal statuettes; a man's head; a relief plaque; and two Parthian figurines of seated men, probably portraits of Mithridates II; fall into the Oriental classification. The Greek group includes not only statuettes of Greek type, but also eighteen moulds for the production of statuettes. Statuettes include a head of a youthful Heracles crowned with an olive or laurel wreath, possibly a portrait of Demetrios I Soter; female heads wearing high kalathoi used as incense

Terracotta figurine statuette head with conical hat, recovered from F4 at Failaka Island (*ref. KM 116, Kuwait National Museum*).

burners ; and draped figurines. Of the eighteen moulds found on Failaka, two were probably intended for the manufacture of portraits of Alexander, one for a Nike statuette, one for a half-draped woman. There are also two moulds for male and female arms and hands; two for figurines of fishes; and four moulds copied from originals in metal. It is astonishing that none of the figurines found on Failaka have been produced in these moulds although, as Mathiesen states, *"The moulds show clearly that there must have been an intention of starting a production of terracottas on the island. A quite large range of figurines could have been manufactured from the excavated moulds alone"*. However, local production did take place to some limited extent as a number of figurines, both of Oriental and Greek type were made of a similar sort of coarse clay as the large, locally made storage jars. This local production seems to have comprised mainly types different from those imported, and may have taken place in times of emergency *"when trade relations with the outer world were interrupted for a longer period and the demand for terracottas on the island could only be met by means of locally made substitutes for imported ware"*. This imported ware seems to have come primarily from Susa, some terracottas possibly originating in more distant cities such as Babylon and Seleucia on the Tigris.

Mathiesen concludes that: *"the terracottas found on Failaka are a very mixed assortment of Oriental and Greek types which may indicate that both Oriental and Greek divinities were worshipped on the island, some of the former perhaps being confused with some of the latter . . . the complete evidence of the terracottas seems to suggest that there existed on Ikaros a fertility cult, a sun cult and a moon cult, although the figurines give no clue to the names of the divinities implied."*

B6 Excavations

This site, approximately 200 metres south-east of the fortress, was partially washed away by the sea but still revealed obvious surface remains. It was excavated by the Department of Antiquities in 1964 and by the French Mission in 1983, revealing a rectangular sanctuary exhibiting two phases of occupation contemporaneous with period I of the fortress, that is, from the middle of the 3rd century BC to the end of the 2nd century BC. Kilns were built in the ruins after the sanctuary was abandoned, but it is difficult to say when exactly they were constructed. Despite some notable differences B6 corresponds to the traditional Babylonian plan. In period 1, the oldest phase of occupation, the sanctuary is composed of two broad rooms: the remains of a stone platform were uncovered in the middle of

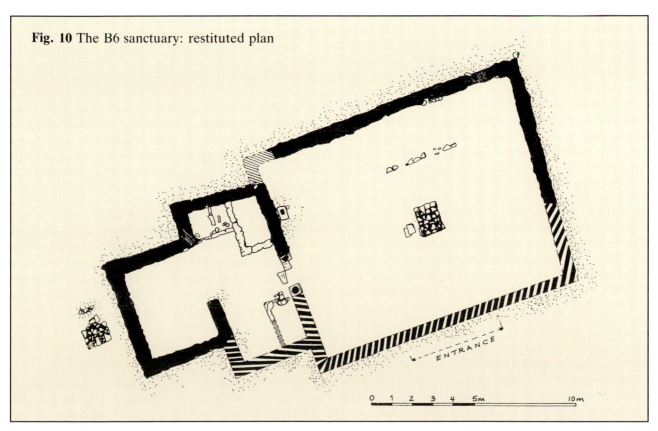

Fig. 10 The B6 sanctuary: restituted plan

ENTRANCE

0 1 2 3 4 5m   10m

A recumbent ram figurine made from grey steatite and depicting an elegant fleece pattern across the back and on the rear. This probably originated from Mesopotamia around 3,000 BC, and was recovered by the French Expedition to Failaka in 1983. The piece measures 6.5cms long with a height of 3.8cms (*ref. KM 3459, Kuwait National Museum*).

the western room or naos—this may have been the pedestal of an altar. The other room, the pronaos is longer, but approximately the same width. Inside the pronaos, two altars were located in front of a partition-wall while another stone platform behind the sanctuary may also be the remains of an altar. The entrance was flanked by two (or three) pillars standing on flat bases, but there is no archaeological evidence to suggest the height of the building.

Large locally made pottery containers, well represented in the material from the fortress, were very abundant at this level of occupation, as were glazed pottery fragments of fish-plates, bowls, pilgrim-flasks etc. Very little of the 'egg-shell' pottery, abundant in the fortress and in level 2, was in evidence here and Arab coarse red-ware produced in eastern Arabia was scarce

as well. The finds from this level include 10 bronze coins (see pg. 35); a very finely executed steatite reclining ram, probably re-used from an earlier period; the terracotta head of a woman wearing a kalathos (distinctive vegetal hair-style) with characteristic oriental features; a bronze lamp; some other bronze pieces, including a tanged arrowhead; a coral fragment associated with the altars as part of the cult; and sandstone fishing weights. It is generally agreed that these finds suggest a date of very late 3rd century BC and early in the 2nd century, and this is confirmed by the monetary findings.

During period 2, the second phase of occupation which probably lasted until the end of the 2nd century BC, the general layout of the original building did not undergo any major alterations, although the sanctuary was enlarged and reorganised. A long open courtyard was added to the eastern face of the sanctuary, substantially increasing the dimensions of the building. Two small recesses were also added to the northern face of the pronaos, and southwards, to the left of the entrance, a similar room was built. Leaning against a wall inside the pronaos, the base of a calcareous stela was sunk into the floor, at the north of the entrance. In the middle of the courtyard, a stone-platform is probably the base of an altar. Important votive material was found near the north-west corner of the courtyard, in front of the stela-base. The rich and varied findings from period 2, level 2, evidence the vitality of the building as a whole as well as this particular level of occupation. They include:–a complete two-handled flask similar to many from the Hellenistic tombs of Bahrain; 23 bronze coins; a number of terracotta lamps; bronze objects, including rings; arrowheads; iron-objects; a disc-shaped stamp-seal pierced with a hole, possibly an ancient piece reused as a pendant; bowls; cooking-pots; incense-burners of local sand-stone, main objects of the cult; the stone head of a bearded man in clearly Oriental style, probably the head of Herakles (there are many terracotta moulded figurines from Susa which show portraits of the hero rather similar to the stone-heads of Failaka); terracotta legs of a type quite widely spread in the Mesopotamian world from the Achaemenid period down to the Parthian one, quite numerous in Failaka; hand-modelled terracotta model of boats; and a yellowish sandstone altar with Greek dedication to Artemis painted in red on one of the faces,—"*for the salvation of Theokudres, . . . as to Artemis*". Deposits near the altars included many shells and some whale-bone fragments as well as a hoard of semi-precious stones. Architectural pieces included a gable fragment possibly from an acroter similar in shape and size to the acroter from the altar at Temple A in the fortress.

The French report makes the observation that amongst the Greek objects which include the Greek coins (see pg. 35) and inscriptions of B6 and the fortress, are to be found many belonging

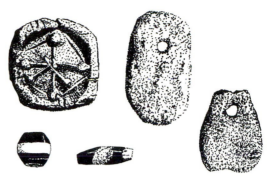

Fig. 12 Beads and stone objects from B6

to the Hellenized Oriental world. The stone or terracotta representations, Herakles's heads, naked women, and boats, all show marked Oriental influences. We are told that the figurine of a woman with a kalathos represented in B6, as well as in the sanctuaries of the fortress, is related to a tradition which is not only Mesopotamian or Susian, but more precisely Levantine or Cypro-Phoenician. "*On the other hand, the pottery, by the glaze fabric and the shapes, clearly shows a properly Oriental tradition*". However, "*the relative quantity of Arab pottery, with red or polished slip, as is found in Thadji, Ain Jawan and other sites of Eastern Arabia, in Bahrain or in the UAE, proves that the island played a leading role in the inter-regional exchanges between the Gulf and Seleucia on the Tigris or Susa. But this commercial activity was not the only occupation of the inhabitants of Failaka; the numerous jars coated with bitumen, utilised for transport of water, or the abundant fishing material, lead us to think that the daily supply remained the first occupation of men in an unfriendly natural environment*". (Some jars were also probably used to transport bitumen from its place of production; for instance, Burgan hills, at the north of Kuwait City, where spreadings of bitumen are still visible).

The miniature altar dedicated to Artemis confirms the status of this deity on Failaka, a status already alluded to in other inscriptions and in the classical texts. Three deities are mentioned in the Greek inscriptions from Failaka: Zeus Soter, Poseidon and Artemis Soteira–the Soteira mentioned on the Ikaros stela is thought to be Artemis also. The classical writers also mention Artemis several times, but it is Artemis Tauropolos along with Apollo Tauropolos, the protectors of Alexander's armies, that achieve prominence in these texts. Despite the fact that Artemis was clearly worshipped at B6, the site does not pre-date the fortress and therefore cannot have been the sanctuary described by Arrian.

Fig. 11 Artifacts from Site B6

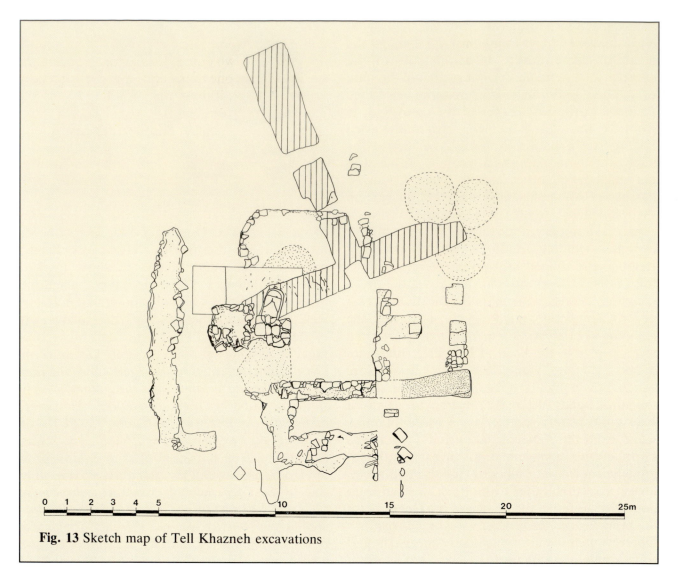

Fig. 13 Sketch map of Tell Khazneh excavations

Tell Khazneh

Tell Khazneh is a low hillock situated about 450 metres NNE of the main archaeological area in the S/W corner of the island. It is here that the stone block with a dedication in Greek by Soteles to Zeus, Poseidon and Artemis was found. An Italian archaeological mission did some work on the site in 1976 uncovering a well dug into the bedrock, in addition to heads of terracotta figurines, a seal, pieces of steatite, and a late pottery sherd, but it was Kuwait's Department of Antiquities and Museums, in conjunction with the French mission, which undertook an extensive exploration of the site in 1984.

As soon as work commenced it was evident that the area had suffered considerably from looting, destroying most architectural remains. But, despite this drawback, the team was able to study the chronological evolution of the site aided by remnants of reasonably well-preserved earthen floors. Eventually an outline of the site's history was revealed. The oldest occupation

level, level 4, was built upon a chocolate-coloured layer of natural origin. Several terracotta figurines uncovered at this floor level include horses or riders of the common oriental type as well as the figure of a woman which is not Hellenistic and the fragments of a crouching lion, the inspiration of which could be Achaemenian. Glazed pottery also occurs in Level 4, in shapes of more ancient origin, similar to pieces recovered from foundations of the Achaemenian palaces at Susa. Although the archaeologists looked to Achaemenian (5th–4th century BC) and Neo-Babylonian (6th century BC) traditions elsewhere to pinpoint the pre-Hellenistic pottery shapes uncovered at this level, these terms refer solely to chronological phases. Neither here nor at any other site does pottery produced by the Neo-Babylonian kings or by the Achaemenids exist. We are told that 'pseudo' Barbar-ware is found at this level too. This form of pottery, existing also on Bahrain, is specific to the northern part of the Gulf. A coin hoard (dated to about 290 BC) and the silver drinking set, described below, were found just above floor 4, dating this floor level to about 400 BC *"without excluding the possibility that it might have existed earlier"*.

There are some carefully dressed stones as well as evidence of mudbrick structures on level 3, but the Kuwaiti and French team found it impossible to define any architectural remains. Although the figurines of Oriental style, riders, horses and animals, are at their most numerous at this level, the first female figurines of Hellenistic style also begin to appear. Glazed pottery from level 3 shows new shapes of western inspiration, such as incurving rim bowls and plates with a central depression, but the more ancient shapes still persist. The French report, commenting on the evolution of pottery shapes states that: *"it may reasonably be assumed that during the period of level 3, western Hellenistic influences appear, coming from Mesopotamia or even the eastern Mediterranean, however some traces of the earlier period can be found too, such as Pseudo-Barbar-Ware and fine pottery of Achemenian tradition"*. This material, as well as the location of the coin hoard just below its surface, gives an early 3rd century BC date to the level 3 floor; probably at the beginning of the Hellenistic period in the Gulf.

Level 2 witnessed a considerable extension of the site. Architectural remains are most substantial at this level, (many carefully dressed stone-blocks without arrangement were found–whereas the walls in situ were built crudely, using irregular pieces of rubble) although these are still very indistinct. The structure at level 2 was probably a rectangular building, about 10 by 8 metres, oriented E-W. Inside there may have been a large, long room on the north side, and two smaller rooms to the south: the building probably had two entrances, one on the northern side, the other one to the east. The French report comments that, if their reconstruction is correct, it is reminiscent of the layout of the Achaemenian Chapel at Nippur. Several dressed-blocks and pieces of rubble were scattered on the floor, probably from the building's walls. One of these bore a fragmentary inscription in Aramaic, and two others could be fragments of a South Arabian inscription. Except for some pseudo-Barbar-ware, two fragments of pre-Hellenistic figurines and a decorated ring, most of the material from this level shows a marked degree of Hellenization and is quite similar to the finds from the F5 fortress and B6 sanctuary. Terracotta figurines of Hellenistic style are most numerous, as are diagnostic Hellenistic pottery shapes such as bowls with incurving rim, plates with angular profiled rim or fish-plates which first appeared in level 3. Level 2, dated to about 200 BC, is probably contemporary with these two sites. Level 1 is nothing but a re-use of the previous floor. Although it is difficult to be certain, this site was probably abandoned around 150–100 BC coinciding with the collapse of Seleucid power. This would agree with the remarks made about the F5 fortress and B6 sanctuary. Tell Khazneh would not then have been occupied after the end of the Greek settlement on the island.

A number of small objects of all kinds were found during excavations at Tell Khazneh; utilitarian objects such as stone basins and bronze nails, together with personal ornaments including rings, bracelets and earrings; but much less numerous than in the sanctuary B6. Several objects, directly related to the practise of a

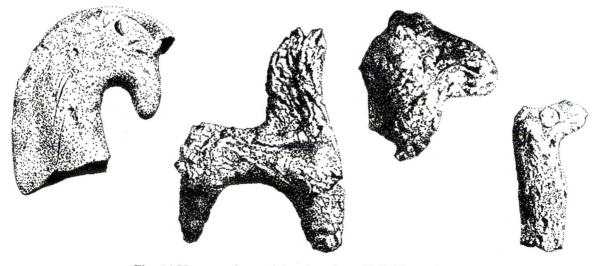

Fig. 14 Horse and camel figurines from Tell Khazneh

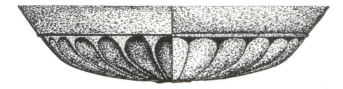

Fig. 15 Hammered silver bowl from Tell Khazneh

religious cult, such as incense-burners/miniature altars, a 'wine set', bronze bowls or spoon handles were found. We are told that the finds compare more favourably with artifacts dated to the Achaemenian-beginning of the Seleucid periods rather than the 2nd century BC. Even though many of these kinds of objects are known throughout long periods, they still lend support to the assumption that Tell Khazneh existed as early as the 5th century BC.

The wine-set is particularly interesting, it was found in Level 4, but it is an intrusion from the upper layers of the site dating after 400 BC. A stand and a spoon were placed inside a bowl, along with two small bronze rings. There are indications that the whole set was wrapped in a piece of fabric or set into a woven bag before burial. The hammered silver bowl was found in a very bad state of preservation but restoration allows for reconstruction of its rather simple shape and 'petal' decoration (see fig. 15). The bowl was probably made in the 6th or 5th century BC and reused during the Hellenistic period when the drinking set may have been assembled. A cylindrical lead object with a concave surface to fit the rounded bottom of the bowl obviously served as a stand. The spoon, belonging to a long

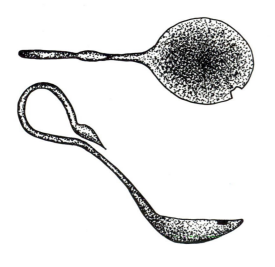

Fig. 16 Spoon with animal head handle

tradition in Greece and the near East, has a particularly elegant animal head handle—probably a representation of a swan (fig. 16).

A number of inscriptions were also found at Tell Khazneh including a fragment of pottery inscribed with three lines of Greek. The text commemorates a sacrifice performed by a group of people attesting that the site where it was discovered was a cult place, however, because of the fragmentary nature of the inscription, it is not possible to *"ascribe this small plaque to one- or more- of the gods whose cult is attested on Ikaros"*. It is quite clear that there was a sanctuary at Tell Khazneh before Greek influence arrived on the island—could this be the answer to our quest for the pre-Hellenistic temple mentioned in the classical texts? The answer is uncertain. Although the timing is correct, the written sources mention that the sanctuary was dedicated to a female goddess whereas the material found in the sanctuary at Tell Khazneh suggest a male deity.

Stamp-seals

Archaeological excavations both in Bahrain and Failaka have uncovered a great number of stamp-seals of a style unique to this area. This particular form of seal has also turned up in some far-flung regions; the distribution of the seals indicating a network of connections from Dilmun to neighbouring and more far-flung areas, such as the Indus. The finds of Dilmun seals in Eastern Saudi Arabia, however, where also pottery of Barbar type has been found, may indicate that this eastern region of the peninsula was an integrated part of Dilmun. The largest group of Dilmun seals outside the Gulf are, naturally enough, from the near-by cities of Ur and Susa and their environs. The Dilmun seal did not penetrate any further north or west.

Over five hundred stamp-seals have now been uncovered from both Bahrain and Failaka, the latter island yielding by far the greatest number. Poul Kjaerum has outlined a basic stylistic continuity from the older 3rd millennium Gulf seal tradition to major elements of the later 2nd millennium group on Failaka. Most of these stamp-seals exhibit the same basic shape: round buttons with a domed reverse. Most are unifacial, but a small distinctive group are bifacial. Unifacial domed seals are categorised by the decoration on the reverse side of the seal into two types: the type I group is limited to seals ornamented by one or two grooves cut diagon-

Circular Bronze Age stamp steatite seal, blackish-grey, glazed. It depicts a pastoral scene and was recovered from excavations (Field F5, trench Q, level 3.72)on Failaka Island carried out by the Danish Archaeological team in 1963 (*ref. KM 29, Kuwait National Museum*).

ally across the dome: in type II, designated Dilmun-type since, Kjaerum points out, this particular category is "*diagnostic for the Dilmun area in its most prosperous period—the first half of the second millennium*", the ornamentation on the reverse is accompanied by circles, usually four arranged symmetrically around the grooves or lines. These seemingly insignificant criteria for differentiation between the types are, in fact, accompanied by "*a major change in style as well as in motifs. In type I the design is dominated by animal figures and symbols of various kinds, while the Dilmun seals are characterised by ritual scenes involving people, gods, cult objects and animals. The transition to seals of Dilmun type seems to have taken place during the Ur III period towards the end of the 3rd millennium.*" Although there is some overlap between the two types of seal, especially on Bahrain, this only occurs on two Failaka seals.

There is little doubt that the Dilmun seals evolved on the islands of the Gulf (particularly Bahrain); however, it is equally clear that the imagery on the seals was influenced by contact with Mesopotamia, Syria/Anatolia and India. "*Unambiguous evidence of contact (with Indus) is found in the occurrence of Indus script on a Dilmun seal from Failaka*". Bull representations on many Dilmun seals have also been considered Indus related, but apart from a few examples they are accompanied by designs foreign to the

Indus region. "*By and large, the script is the only certain 'motif' common to the Indus and Dilmun seals, but affords in itself incontrovertible evidence of a connection between the Gulf and the Indus culture continuing until the beginning of the 2nd millennium*". On the other hand, Mesopotamian imagery is everywhere in evidence on these Dilmun seals (see fig. 17d) "*the dress and the horned crown of the gods, bullmen, monkeys, standards of various kinds, harps with taurine sound-boxes, erotic scenes and many other features, manifest not only close contact, but also a deeper, spiritual affinity.*"

Over and above this general Mesopotamian imagery the influence of the Levant is evident in a number of seals from Failaka featuring tables with a concave top, resting on a moulded column which splits into two curved legs ending in bull's hooves (fig. 17e). "*Tables of this kind may have been an article of trade and may have been part of the ritual equipment in both areas. The common themes in which they occur indicate, however, that they served the same ritual purposes both in Dilmun and Syria. Other images of a more symbolic nature, but again with a Levantine background, occur on other seals*". In addition to abstractions of animal forms, in a number of scenes, animals—usually bulls and antelopes—are placed on altars or podia, (fig. 17b) and in other ritual performances the place of altars or standard is taken by serpent monsters—single or entwined—or antelopes, which certainly must be conceived as idols (fig. 17c). Very similar themes

Dilmunite (Bronze Age) steatite seal, single face, recovered by Danish Expedition on Failaka Island (*ref.KM 999:– Kuwait National Museum*).

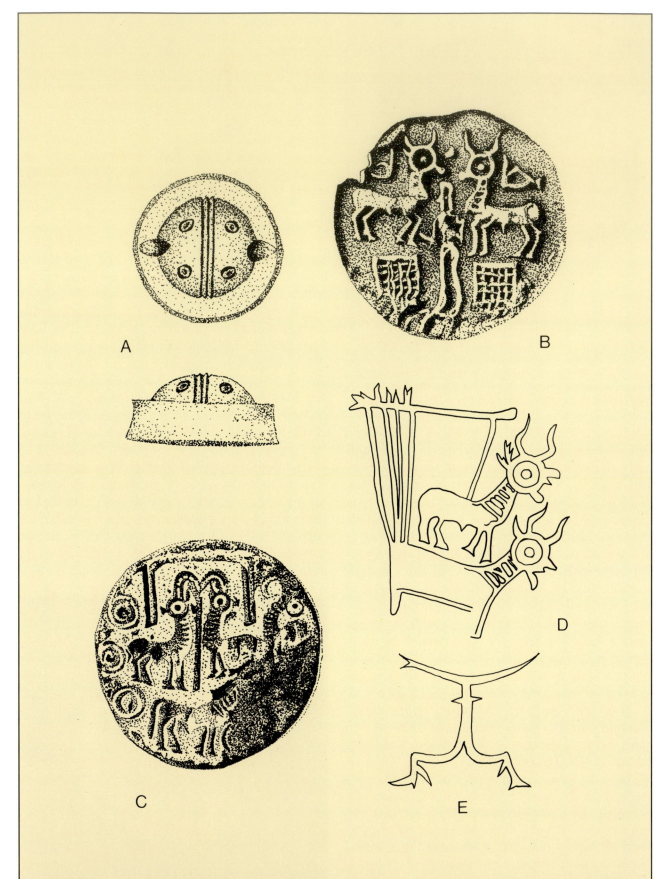

Fig. 17 a) typical shape of stamp seal from above and side; b) seal showing bulls on altars or podia; c) antelopes on seal; d) Mesopotamian imagery of harp with taurine sound box as depicted on Dilmun seal; e) Levantine influence on Failaka seal depiction of table resting on moulded column split into two legs ending in bull's hooves.

with many common elements are found in the Levant. The extent and pervasive nature of this Levantine influence leads the experts to believe that close relationships between these areas must have arisen around 2000 BC transcending *"the mere mercantile intercourse which had been carried on for several centuries before the advent of the Dilmun seals"*. This is not to say that there was any major usurption of the indigenous traditional culture of Bahrain which was transplanted in the colonization of Failaka. Kjaerum believes that: *"The imagery which dominates these seals therefore hardly reflects a massive change in the basic make-up of the population, but rather a displacement towards population groups with Mesopotamian and especially Levantine cultural background, which must have formed a powerful new ethnic element of western origin, attaining dominance in Dilmun around the turn of the millennium."*

Some of the stamp-seals carry inscriptions: the Indus script already mentioned as occurring on one of the seals has not to date been deciphered, but the cuneiform inscriptions on the seals frequently mention the god Inzak. For example, one side of a two-sided seal reads:– *"expert in seeds, Inzak of Agarum"*. Inzak and Meskilak were also the two main deities of Dilmun-Bahrain. Cylinder-shaped seals imported from Mesopotamia have also been found alongside the distinctive stamp-seals. The cuneiform inscription on an old Babylonian example translates : *"Enki Damgalnuna"*, referring to the god Enki, patron God of the ancient city of Eridu and his lover, Damgalnuna. A particularly interesting translation is included by J.J. Glassner in his catalogue of inscriptions; deriving from a cylinder-seal of the Kassite period, showing that Man's preoccupations have changed little over the intervening 3000 years, it reads as follows.

> *"He who is provided with this (seal)*
> *let him live*
> *let him be fit*
> *let him prosper*
> *let him beam with joy*
> *let him be young*
> *let him be in good health"*

Coins

As already mentioned, a coin hoard was found between the floors of level 3 and level 4 at Tell Khazneh, consisting of 27 silver coins, all tetradrachmas of Alexander the Great originating from many different mints as far apart as Greece and

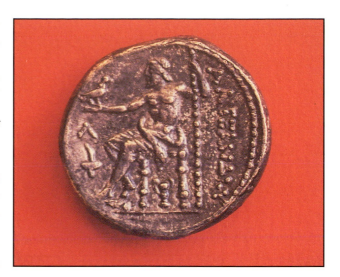

Silver tetradrachma coin of Alexander, minted in Amphipolis, recovered in 1984, by the French archaeological team, excavating at Tell Khaznah on Failaka Island. The Hellenistic coin weighs 16.32grams and has a diameter of 2.6cms (*ref. KM 4823, Kuwait National Museum*).

Media; Phoenicia, Mesopotamia and Susa. The legends mention Alexander, Philip III of Macedonia, and Seleucus I. The hoard was buried in the very beginning of the 3rd century BC, probably around 290/285. Ten bronze coins were also found in the excavation only seven of which were legible. Six of these were coins of Alexander (336–330 BC) with the head of Herakles wearing the lion skin on the obverse, whilst the reverse showed the name of Alexander in Greek with varied motif of quiver, bow and club. The seventh coin was from the time of Seleucus I (310–281 BC): on the obverse was depicted the laurelled head of Zeus, and on the reverse a thunderbolt and monogram.

Danish excavations in 1960 unearthed a mysterious lump of metal in the fortress, just outside Temple A and a little way north of the altar. This purplish mass, on closer examination, turned out to be a hoard of coins of Hellenistic origin.

Abbasid period brass coins from 157 A.H. (*ref. KM 4820, Kuwait National Museum*).

Twelve of the thirteen silver tetradrachmas in the hoard were of the same type: the thirteenth was minted by the Syrian king Antiochus III, who ruled the Seleucid Empire from 223 to 187 BC. The portrait of Antiochus III on the coin can be pinpointed to the early days of his reign (223–212 BC); the god Apollo is depicted on the reverse side of the coin. A booklet on the coins issued by the Ministry of Information in Kuwait points out that: "*The style in general suggests one of the eastern mints of the Empire, and the monograms point to Susa, which is also, as it happens, the Seleucid mint which lies closest to the place of discovery, Ikaros/Failaka*". Keeping in mind that the coin is still in such excellent preservation it can hardly have been in circulation for very many years and the youthfulness of Antiochus's portrait, the coin and the hoard with which it was buried can be dated to about 210–200BC.

The other twelve coins have a poorly-executed representation of the Greek hero Herakles wearing his lion skin on the obverse; the reverse shows a somewhat distorted Zeus sitting on a throne with the sacred eagle perched on his outstretched right hand, his left holding a sceptre. A rather crude Greek inscription and a minter's mark can be seen behind the figure indicating that the coins were minted in the name of Alexander the Great, even though approximately a hundred years had elapsed between his death in 323 BC and the date of their striking. We are informed that: "*This in itself is not unusual since Alexander's coins had such a reputation in the 3rd and 2nd centuries BC they were imitated in many places in the Greek world by cities which wished to secure for their coinage the good-will which had attached itself to this design*".

It will appear clear from the above description that the coins are rather crudely minted and the Greek inscription rather haphazardly cut. Where did these barbarianised coins originate? Eight of the twelve Alexander-coins have been struck with the same obverse die and the same reverse die also occurs in several cases. "*Such a concentration of dies in a single hoard, normally means that the coins have gone by a fairly direct route from the mint to the place of burial without having been in circulation in the interim. It indicates, too, that the place and time of burial is not far removed from the place and time of minting, even though* there can naturally be no certainty on this point. *The problem is thus to find a locality in the East which lies outside the frontiers of the Hellenistic kingdoms (where, of course, coins were struck in the name of the reigning king) but which at the same time was so closely associated with the Greek world as to make it reasonable to expect "a la grecque" minting there. It would moreover lie on one of the main trade-routes in that area for without trade there would be no coins."* Failaka itself can be ruled out since it was under direct Seleucid rule at the time. However further south from their capital Gerrha, situated on the Arabian mainland, an Arab tribe, the Gerrhaeans, dominated trading in eastern Arabia, bringing spices and exotic goods from the South Arabia and the East up the Tigris and Euphrates to the major cities of Seleucia and Susa and onto the Mediterranean through Syria and the Phoenician cities. *"There is a reasonable probability that the barbarianized Alexander-coins in the Failaka hoard originated in Gerrha."*

Subsequently another hoard of silver coins was found between two floor levels in a room imme-diately west of Temple B. According to Mork-holm these coins were also hidden about 210–200 BC. The Danish excavations also unearthed some single coins; three of which are Seleucid copper coins from Susa or Seleucia on the Tigris. The Ministry of Information pamphlet informs us that: *"One was struck by Seleucus I in the name of Alexander the Great about 310 BC, while the other two belong to the reign of Antiochus III, 223–187 BC, and are thus approximately contemporary with the silver hoards. Few as they are, these coins provide an excellent illustration of Failaka's close economic connections with the large cities of the eastern provinces of the Seleucid Empire. Connection to the south are illustrated by a modest little silver coin, a so-called drachma. For this can be attributed to the Minaeans, an Arab tribe which lived in south Arabia a few hundred miles north of the Aden area."*

Thirty-two bronze coins in very bad condition were found during the French excavations of 1983, many of which are illegible, whilst others are of uncertain origin. Six coins are from Seleucia on the Tigris mint and were struck during the

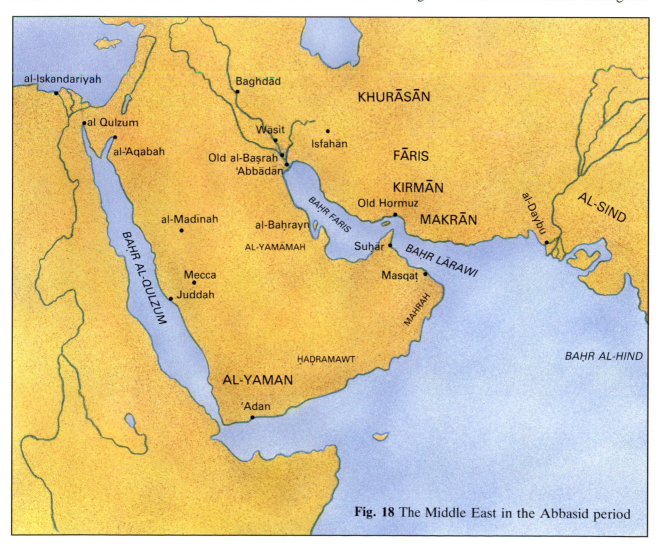

Fig. 18 The Middle East in the Abbasid period

reign of Antiochus III (220–187). Five of these have a standing Apollo, a bust of Hermes, or a head of Artemis on the obverse whilst the reverse shows the name of Antiochus. One is from an uncertain mint, but the obverse depicts Antiochus III. Two coins were struck at the Susa mint during the reign of Seleucus IV (187–175): on the obverse of both these coins is the head of Athena wearing a helmet, whilst the reverse is illegible on one and the other bears the name of Basileus Seleucus. One other coin with the laurelled head of Apollo on the obverse can be attributed to the Seleucia on the Tigris mint during the reign of Antiochus IV (175–164). Of the uncertain or doubtful attributions two could be dated from Antiochus III, one from Seleucus IV and one from Antiochus IV. Of the twenty illegible coins, seven show the same basic weight and characteristics as the identifiable ones and are attributable to the Susa or Seleucia on the Tigris mints, dated to the reign of Antiochus III or Antiochus IV. The second group of illegible coins dates from the Seleucid period—3rd or 2nd centuries BC.

Most of the coins are from the reign of Antiochus III (223–187). This is not particularly surprising since it was a period of expansion not only for the Seleucid empire, but also for the settlements on Failaka. We also know that Antiochus III led a campaign south to Gerrha and Tylos (Bahrain) with the object of ensuring that the lucrative Oriental trade of Gerrha would pass through Seleucid territory. This trade was routed up the Gulf by boat to the mouth of the Euphrates and the Tigris, on to Susa, and then by caravan to Seleucia. Trading suffered a slight decline under Seleucus IV (only 3 coins) and serious disruption under Antiochus IV (2 coins). Mints also show a predominance of the Seleucia on the Tigris mint. Taking the Danish finds into account, it seems clear that Failaka must have formed a trading post for the direct passage of the lucrative and exotic trade between Gerrha and the Seleucid empire further north.

The Middle Years:

3rd century AD–16th century AD

Commercial activity in the Gulf, disrupted by Parthian rise to power, prospered again as the second great Persian empire, that of the Sasanids, was established in 226 AD. Cargoes of copper, sandalwood, teak, blackwood and ebony, arriving from the Orient, were exchanged for Sasanian shipments of purple dye, clothing, wine, pearls, dates, gold and slaves. So far, there

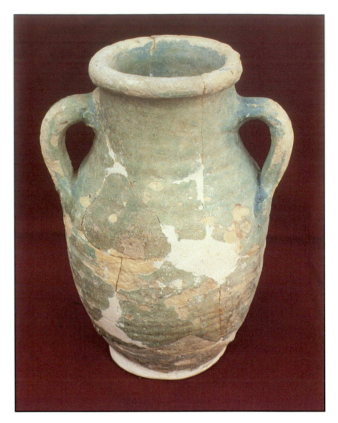

Dilmon carnelian seal with double face. Diameter: 2.4cms. Bronze Age (*Kuwait National Museum*).

is no archaeological evidence of Sasanian occupation in Kuwait, either on Failaka or the neighbouring mainland. It is inconceivable that such a well-watered island should have escaped the attentions of the Sasanians when much less hospitable environments further south were settled. The harvest of the seas, particularly precious pearls gleaned from the pearl oyster, and purple dye extracted from Murex shells, seemingly attracted the Sasanians to otherwise unwelcoming shores. By the 6th century AD, Iranian Sasanids, the dominant force in the area since early in the 3rd century, were in firm control of the Gulf; Sasanian governors exercising their influence through local rulers.

Islam swept the entire Arabian peninsula in the 7th century, overturning pagan deities previously favoured by its inhabitants; Muslim conquests eventually extending an Islamic sphere of influence from Spain to India. The Umayyad dynasty, Damascus-based rulers of an expanding empire, were overthrown in 750 AD by the Abbasids, descendants of the Prophet Muhammad's uncle. Under the latter a "medieval Islamic theocracy" flowered and prospered, acting as a perfect medium for the cultivation of music, literature, philosophy, mathematics and medicine. Abbasid relocation of its capital to Baghdad, founded in 762, had political and economic implications for the Gulf: it was inevitable that trade would benefit from the wealthy administrative and commercial centre established there to oversee the empire. From Arabic sources, we learn that the demand for pearls in Abbasid Baghdad was particularly high, stimulating, no doubt, the pearling industry on the western shores of the Gulf. Except for Oman however, there is very little written concerning the history of the western shores of the Gulf in the early centuries of Islam. Kazima near Kuwait was recorded by Yaqut al Hamawi, the famous Arab geographer who died in 1229, having compiled a 'Dictionary of Countries' listing alphabetically the names of cities and islands with a brief description, supplementing his own observations with reliable written material from the best available sources. Archaeological finds from Kuwait dated to the Islamic period (at Kazima, Failaka, Sabbiyah peninsula, Akkaz and Um al Aysh) support the textual evidence. These finds range from moulded thick glass, glazed and unglazed fragments of pottery, to foundations of architectural constructions.

There is no doubt that the Gulf was a thriving maritime highway in medieval Islamic times, the extent of this activity surpassed only by recent petroleum-backed economic developments.

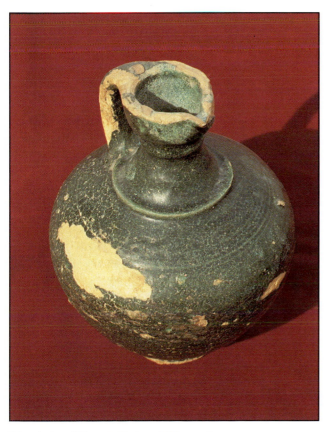

Islamic jug (*Kuwait National Museum*).

Trading extended as far as China whilst the settled coastal communities wrested from the sea both a livelihood and a commodity in the form of pearls which could be traded far and wide. This phase of mercantile expansion culminated in the kingdom of Hormuz in the 15th and 16th centuries. The arrival of the Portuguese at the beginning of the 16th century was to change both the balance of power and the pattern of trade in the region. They came not just as traders but as conquerors; Hormuz falling to Albuquerqe in 1514. Even though the principal trade routes from East to West had been deflected further south since the Portuguese, with Arab aid, had discovered the sea route to India in 1498, the Gulf was still of major significance to the western powers attempting to establish a foothold there. Hormuz straddling the entrance to the Gulf, acted as the base from which the Portuguese, throughout the 16th century, held sway over the Gulf waters as far as Bahrain; their maritime supremacy challenged, albeit unsuccessfully, by the Ottoman Turks who had succeeded in reaching the head of the Gulf overland in 1536.

The task of maintaining control over Indian Ocean routes stretched maritime resources to the limit. In 1622 the great Safavi ruler of Persia, Shah Abbas I, allied with the superior naval expertise of Britain, captured Hormuz from the Portuguese. Around this time too the Ya'ariba of Oman, realising that Portuguese power was in decline, began to press them very hard, capturing fort after fort from the foreign invader, finally expelling them from Muscat in 1650. Challenges to Portuguese hegemony in the Gulf, and its trade monoply to the East, had already begun early in the 17th century. On the 31st December 1600 Queen Elizabeth I granted the Royal Charter under which the English East India Company was incorporated while the Dutch East India Company was formed in 1602. In contrast to Portuguese commercial activity monopolised by the crown, 17th century Gulf trade was dominated by "merchant adventurers" from England, Holland, and eventually France. By the middle of the 17th century English trade in the Gulf had been overshadowed by that of the Dutch and the English East India Company gradually assumed a more political role to further its trade prospects. Following the collapse of Portuguese supremacy at sea and Safavid control on land early in the 18th century, local rulers began the process of reasserting their independence, disturbed only the brief rule of Nadir Shah in Iran.

Early Days in Kuwait

The town of Kuwait, visited at night by a refreshing west wind wafting from the desert, was originally a summer resort of the shaikhs of the Bani Khalid, who held sway in eastern Arabia since the Ottoman occupier was driven from the region in the 16th century. Based at the fertile oasis of al Hasa, the Bani Khalid controlled Indian and Far Eastern trade which was channelled through al Qatif and al Uqair to central Arabia and along the desert route by camel caravan to Mesopotamia. A small fishing village was located around a *kut* or fortress at this summer resort, hence the name Kuwait, it being a diminutive of the Arabic *kut*, but the town was also known to European travellers of the 18th century as 'Grane', a derivative of *qarn* or small hill. Although drinking water of very poor quality had to be transported from a well outside the town, a relatively mild climate and a wide sweeping bay with good deep anchorages apparently led to a more permanent settlement.

The absence of historical data on Kuwait town itself makes it very difficult to determine exactly when it was established, although it is generally assumed to have come into existence sometime before the 18th century. The date of the arrival of the Utub, a federation of Arab families who were to eventually attain control in Kuwait, is also rather obscure, local historians disagreeing with both oral tradition and official archival material of the British Empire in India. All authorities are in agreement, however, that the Utub were part of a sub-division of the Anaza, an Adnani Arab confederation who inhabited Najd before spreading eastwards. Local tradition intimates that the Utub lived in al Aflaj district in Central Arabia until the drought which beset that area in the second half of the 17th century forced them towards the coast and Qatar.

Eighteenth Century

Having attained maritime skills in Qatar and al Hasa, the Utub families scattered into the various ports of the Gulf littoral before settling in Kuwait. The date of this event cannot be pinpointed exactly, but it probably occurred at the beginning of the 18th century. Although the Bani Khalid were officially in control of the area, the authority of the Al Sabah was quickly established among the local communities; their chief, Sabah bin Jabir became the shaikh of Kuwait in the 1750's. Local traditions, though again not entirely sure of the date relate that Sabah was chosen by the inhabitants of Kuwait in the tribal manner to administer justice and the affairs of the thriving town. As early as 1758, Sabah's authority seems to have been well established in Kuwait and the surrounding area, Utub suzerainty extending at least as far north as Jahra village where the wells were superior to those of Kuwait. Nearby islands like Qurain, Umm al-Naml and Failaka were also ruled by the Shaikh. The security engendered by Sabah's rule, coupled with its unique geographical position, ensured that Kuwait became a thriving commercial success and an important port-of-call for desert caravans carrying goods from southern and eastern Arabia to Aleppo in Syria. Kuwaiti merchants also benefited enormously from the handling of exotic goods imported from India by Kuwaiti vessels. The Dutch factory at Kharaq Island, in operation from 1753 to 1765, routed most of their merchandise through Kuwait because of the difficulties they encountered with the Pasha of Basra. Although much of the trade through Kuwait was in transit, rice, coffee and Indian spices were also carried for local consumption. According to the Danish explorer Carsten Niebuhr, Kuwait, in 1764, had a local population in the region of 10,000. Listing pearl fishing as another source of wealth for the pros-

Photograph by D. Clayton

perous Kuwaiti's, Niebuhr states that over 800 small boats sailed south to annually exploit the rich pearling beds off Qatar and Bahrain.

Other Utbi families besides Al Sabah, shared in the prosperity generated by trading and pearling. Abu Hakima, the noted Arab historian states that: *"Among the first families mentioned in local traditions and in the records of the Bombay Government are Al Jalahima, Al Khalifa, Al Zayid, Al Ghanim, Al Badr, Al Rumi, Al Khalid, Al Qinaat, Al Saif and others. Apparently these families settled in such a way that made every section of town take one family or more. The town was thus divided into* Hayy-Sharq *(People of the East),* Qibli *or* Jibli *(the West, because this is the direction of Makka), and the* Wasat *(centre). Al Sabah lived in the central quarter"*. Local sources differ greatly on the date of Shaikh Sabah's death, but he did leave five sons: Abd Allah, the youngest was chosen as his successor for his qualities of bravery, justice, wisdom, and generosity. Abu Hakima, to whom we are indebted for recording much of the early history of Kuwait, fixes 1762 as the date in which Abd Allah came to power. It has been suggested that Abd Allah's succession rather than that of his cousin from the Al Khalifa, who were shaikhs at Kuwait before Sabah bin Jabir, prompted the latter to emigrate to Zubara in Qatar in 1766 to be followed by other Utbi families, such as the Al Jalahima.

The Utbi settlement of Kuwait continued to flourish under the rule of Abd Allah eventually attracting the unwelcome attention of rival powers in the Gulf. The Persians and the Ottomans were not as yet in a position to fetter Kuwait's growth: the Persians had neither the sea-power nor the internal peace to control even their own coast of the Gulf and the Ottoman Turks were more or less in the same position in occupied Iraq. As far as European powers were concerned, the English East India Company was now coming to the fore in the intense competition for trade between the English, Dutch and French. The English Company established a factory at Basra in 1723, this Residency being recognised by the Porte in 1764 as a Consulate. The Company's increased share of trade in the Gulf was also at the expense of both Indians and Arabs. Lorimer's Gazetteer of the Gulf yields much useful information on the activities of the East India Company in this and later periods, however it is important to remember that this comprehensive account of the Gulf was, in fact, written at the beginning of this century as an

Photograph by D. Clayton

"apologia for the long history of British colonialism in the Gulf". Serious omissions and historical inaccuracies occur in the text, primarily because its method of compilation was highly selective.

The most powerful Arab maritime powers on the Persian littoral at this time were the Bani Ka'b, based at Dawraq; the Arabs of Bandar Riq; and those of Abu Shahr. Bani Ka'ab raids at sea had already caused considerable problems for Utbi sea trade. The Bani Ka'b also threatened the East India Company's goods destined for their Factory at Basra. Karim Khan Zand, the Vakil of Persia, tried unsuccessfully to subdue Shaikh Sulayman in 1759, and an Anglo-Ottoman expedition against the capital, Dawraq, in 1765, yielded little or no results. In fact many historians cite continuous Utbi disputes with the troublesome Bani Ka'b as the main movitation for the movement of al Khalifa south to Qatar, although others explain the emigration by stating that the Al Khalifa wished to be nearer to the lucrative pearl fishery situated off the coast of Bahrain and Qatar.

Despite these difficulties, Utbi fortunes continued to flourish at Kuwait and Zubara, the latter's policy of free trade drawing considerable business. Kuwait did apply dues although they were much less compared with those demanded

41

by the Government at Muscat. Heavy duties were also collected by the Government of Basra on all imported goods by sea from Baghdad, in addition to all goods exported by sea or through Aleppo, the only exceptions being provisions and European goods. As a result Utbi ports were much used for the carrying of goods from India and Arabia to Syria and other ottoman territories. The state of affairs in other areas bordering the Gulf also proved beneficial to the growth of Kuwait and Zubara. The Bani Khalid, for instance, were much too preoccupied with the threat from Najd, where those who espoused the orthodox Islamic doctrines promulgated by Shaikh Muhammad bin Abd al Wahhabi had gathered under the leadership of the Al Saud. The Persian capture of Basra, in 1776 also diverted much trade further south to the benefit of the Utbi ports. All the Indian trade with Baghdad, Aleppo, Smyrna and Constantinople was channelled through Kuwait between the years of 1775–1779.

Official British contact with Kuwait was initiated during these years when British desert mail from the Gulf to Aleppo was despatched from Kuwait instead of Zubara from 1775–1778. In 1783 the Utub of Kuwait joined with their compatriots from Zubara in conquering the island of Bahrain in retaliation for an attack made on Zubara by the island's Persian-affiliated overlord, aided and abetted by the ever envious Ka'b and the Qawasim. Although Zubara suffered a decline after the establishment of the Al Khalifa at Bahrain, this new conquest served to increase Utbi prosperity in Kuwait. There was, however, one repercussion from the recent battle for this island which was to have long-term consequences for both Utbi families controlling Kuwait and Bahrain. A simmering dispute over division of spoils caused an acrimonious split between the Al Jalahimah and Al Khalifah. Rahmah ibn Jabir, son of Shaikh Jabir former leader of Al Jalahimah, fired with an undying hatred, waged an unrelenting war of attrition against the Al Khalifah and all who supported them for more than forty years. Rahmah's fate was to be intimately linked with the struggle taking place in central and eastern Arabia at this time, a struggle which was to have major ramifications for the whole Arabian peninsula.

From 1793 to 1795 the British Factory originally based at Basra was temporarily translocated to Kuwait because of difficulties experienced with Turkish officials at Basra. Despite fierce opposition from the Bani Khalid, Saudi rule had been established in Najd and in 1793 a great force led by Al Saud and fired by religious zeal, surged towards al Hasa and conquered the stronghold of the Bani Khalid. Although strictly speaking under orders to maintain a neutral stance, the British Factory aided the Kuwaitis in repelling an attack by Saudi forces, a not infrequent occurrence at this time. Lorimer records that: *"During the soujourn of the factory at Kuwait the Wahhabis were at war with the place, which they were anxious to reduce to submission; and they frequently showed themselves in the neighbourhood, causing incessant alarms. The town was at this time poorly defended by a mud wall, which, in the rainy season, frequently crumbled down in large breaches to the great alarm of the inhabitants; but the courage of the people was sustained by their confidence in Shaikh 'Abdullah-bin-Subah, described as a venerable old man of commanding appearance, whom they regarded more as a father than as a governor. In general a Wahhabi attack did not amount to more than a temporary seizure of the wells by a party of ten or twenty Bedouins, whom the matchlockmen of the town ordinarily succeeded in dislodging after a bloodless skirmish at very long ranges . . . During the stay of the East India Company's servants at Kuwait only one serious attack in force, which was easily repulsed, was made by the Wahhabis."* Although official reports are remarkably reticent about the facts it now seems likely that the guns from the British cruiser at anchor in the bay, and the sepoy guard of the Factory, combined with the Kuwaiti force, succeeded in repelling a Saudi force estimated at 2,000 camels, each camel carrying two men, the front rider armed with a gun and the other with a lance to protect his companion while reloading.

Towards the end of the 18th century, the English East India Company was having some difficulty maintaining its trade levels in the Gulf, partly due to the expansion of commercial activity by Arab and Indian traders. But the Europeans weren't the only ones experiencing inroads into their trading activities. Oman, under the Al Bu-Sa'id, soon to become allies of the British, was also apprehensive about its traditional mercantile role at the entrance to the Gulf. However the Utub of Kuwait stood firm with those of Bahrain and Qatar in the face of Oman's attempts to expand and consolidate its control in the Gulf. Sultan ibn Ahmad of Oman declared war against the Utub of Bahrain in 1799 and, on his second attempt in 1800, succeeded in forcing the Al Khalifa to yield and agree to pay him tribute. It appears that Sayyid Sa'id of Muscat, together with his fleet, sailed as far north as Kuwait to remonstrate with Kuwaitis for granting asylum to the Utbi leaders he had driven from Bahrain. There is however no record of an attack having taken place. Kuwait during this period benefited considerably as a consequence of disputes between the Saudis and their subjects in al Hasa: Kuwait and Basra supplanted Qatif and Oqair as ports of entry for the interior.

1800 to 1841

The repudiation of their agreement with Oman in 1801 provoked further attacks on the island of Bahrain. Al Khalifa won assistance from the Saudis in return for recognition of Saudi authority and an agreement to pay tribute but the Kuwaitis repulsed a Saudi attack in 1808 and subsequently refused to pay the tribute that was demanded; Saudi plans for a naval attack on Kuwait and Basra by the Qawasim never materialised.

The British, hoping to weigh the balance of power in favour of Oman, attacked Ras al Khaimah in 1809, supposedly in revenge for alleged attacks of 'piracy' by the Qawasim on British shipping. Al Qasimi in his book, The Myth of Arab Piracy in the Gulf, points out that at this time "*animosities were rampant on all sides and that instability and internal troubles were the state of affairs in all lands bordering the Gulf*". Many of the attacks against shipping that ensued were labelled as piracy by the British, adopting an entirely eurocentric approach to the question of legitimate warfare which, in itself, had many grey areas concerning privateering and the rights of neutrals. In addition British officials ensconced in India took little trouble to understand the complex web of relationships in the Gulf and the fiercely independent nature of the people who lived there. Over and above the question of hostilities, ignored entirely was the customary place of the *ghazu* or raid in the everyday life of the indigenous population struggling to eke out the meagre resources of his harsh environment: 'piratical' attacks were sometimes nothing more than the *ghazu* carried onto the sea. There is no doubt too that the English East India Company took advantage of the uncertainty to promote its own position. As Sultan Al Qasimi rightly points out: "*Its obvious intention, in the face of increasing competition, was to use 'protection' as an excuse to employ the force of the Bombay Marine to squash the competitors . . . Having secured the cooperation of the Persians and Omanis, the British then turned their attention to their more*

persistent competitors the Qawasim who had been carrying on a vigorous and profitable trade by sea".

Rahmah ibn Jabir remained untouched by this outpouring of righteous retribution although orders were issued from Bombay to proceed against him. The Al Khalifah in Bahrain had, by this time, incurred the displeasure of the Saudis who, aided by an embittered Rahmah ibn Jabir together with a fleet of forty dhows, forced the Al Khalifah to submit in February of 1810. Rahmah was forever resolute in his hatred of all things Utbi, but Saud was soon preoccupied with the considerable activity on his western flank: the Sultan of Turkey had despatched Muhammad Ali Pasha of Ottoman Egypt in 1811 to regain the sacred cities of Mecca and Medina, recently overrun by the Saudis.

Shaikh Abdullah of Kuwait died in 1812 *"much regretted by all on account of the mildness of his rule, which favoured commercial development, and under which the population of the town had increased very greatly".* The powerful and independent Sabah line continued with the succession of his son Jabir-bin-Abdullah and in 1813–14 Kuwait was reported to be free of Saudi influence. In fact, Wahabbi power was to collapse in Central Arabia in 1818, but not before the Al Khalifa again sought their protection in the face of Omani belligerence. Rahmah, implacable in his hatred of the Al Khalifa, now joined Saiyid Sa'id in an unsuccessful attack on Bahrain and Qatar—an allegiance which was to signal the winding down of the old warrior's tempestuous career. Evasions, half-truths, unsubstantiated allegations and downright lies propagated by self-justifying, trigger-happy 'Company' Commanders culminated in the British launching another attack on Ras al Khaimah in 1819. Certainly attacks on shipping had occurred but, as Qasimi points out, *"the pirates and privateers were not all Arabs and the Arabs were not all Qawasim"* . . .

In 1820, the year the General Treaty of Peace was signed by Britain and the shaikhs of the lower Gulf (Britain thereby formalising its military and political imperium in the Gulf) Kuwait, dependent for its water supply upon the island of Failaka, was reported as containing an armed population of 5,000 to 7,000 men. Lorimer reports that: *"In 1829 the authority of the Shaikh of Kuwait was partially acknowledged by the Bedouin tribes upon the coast as far to the southward as Ras Khafji; the annual imports of Kuwait were estimated at $5,000,000, the exports at nearly $1,000,000; and the place, which was flourishing in consequence of the peaceful policy of its ruler, was credited with the possession of a mercantile marine of 15 Baghlahs from 450 to 100 tons, 20 Batils and Baghlahs from 120 to 50 tons, and 150 other boats from 150 to 15 tons. In 1831 the town extended one mile along the shore with a depth of quarter of a mile, and the streets were wider than those of Masqat or Bushehr; but the only defence was a wall less than a foot thick on the side towards the desert, outside of which was a trench; and two honey-combed pieces of ordnance protected each of the three gates."*

In central Arabia Turki ibn Abd Allah, a cousin of the legendary Saud, succeeded to the leadership in 1824 but was driven out of al Diriyah by the Ottoman forces. Turki established himself in al-Riad in 1824 and Muhammad Ali's troops withdrew from Najd to the Hijaz.

The changing nature of the British presence in the Gulf was in uneasy juxtaposition with fluctuating Ottoman influence. Ever since the conquest of Iraq by the Turks, Kuwait, because of its geographical position, had been in danger of absorption by this regional power, but the Sabah leadership had succeeded in maintaining their independence. On account of difficulties with the Turkish authorities, the British Residency at Basra was transferred for a short while in 1821–22, to an "island" off Kuwait, probably Failaka, indicating that Kuwait was not at this time under the authority of the Ottoman Turks. Around 1836 Shaikh Jabir assisted the Turks to reduce the rebellious town of Zubair to submission; but his part in the operations was confined to a blockade Zubair's water supply. On the fall of the town one of the Zuhair family of Zubair, named Ya'qub, took refuge in Kuwait, subsequently selling his estate of Sufiyeh in the Ma'amir district on the Shatt-al-Arab.

In 1838 Muhammad Ali sent troops into Najd where they defeated Faisal bin Turki and took him prisoner to Cairo. The occupation only lasted two years but, in the meantime, the Ottoman-Egyptians sent an agent to reside at Kuwait, supposedly to purchase supplies. It was believed, however, that his real functions were those of a political emissary, a role which did not altogether meet with the approval of the British. Some consideration was given to the question of establishing a British naval and military settlement in the vicinity of Kuwait in 1839, but such plans never materialised. In fact, for the 30 years following the withdrawal of the Egyptian forces from Eastern Arabia, Kuwait had a close politi-

cal relationship with Turkish Iraq, at the same time maintaining friendly but informal relations with British representatives in the Gulf. In 1863 complimentary presents of dates were sent to Kuwait by the Turks in token of their own suzerainty, and as payment for the protection by the Shaikh of the mouth of Shatt-al-Arab.

1840–1871

The relationship between Kuwait and the Saudis which had already undergone transformation from a position of antagonism to one of uneasy alliance established itself on a firmer footing during this period of revival following the withdrawal of Egyptian troops from Arabia. In 1841 Abdullah bin Thanayan, a relative and competitor of Khalid, the de facto Saudi Amir (both cousins of Saud) took refuge at Kuwait, where he stayed for a very short time; but before the end of the same year, Abdullah, who had meanwhile returned to central Arabia, obtained the upper hand while Khalid, in his turn, sought asylum in Kuwait. In 1843 Faisal bin Turki escaped from Egypt and returned to Najd, eventually regaining control of al Hasa. Friendly relations existed between the Shaikh of Kuwait and Faisal bin Turki, but no tribute was paid by the former to the latter.

After the death of Faisal in 1865 the second great Saudi state suffered from the dispute between his sons Abdulla and Saud. Partly as a result of their intense rivalry, but also as a consequence of the opening of the Suez Canal, the Ottoman forces arrived back in western Arabia and in 1871 seized the northern part of the Arabian coast of the Gulf.

In Najd Rashid and his supporters (also followers of Abd al Wahhabi's teachings but less fundamentalist than the Saudis) were gaining the upperhand over the Saudis and by 1884 the Shammar Amir Rashid became the dominant power in Najd. Abd al Rahman (youngest son of Faisal bin Turki), accompanied by his son Abd al Aziz, went into exile in Kuwait in 1891, having suffered a major defeat in Najd at the hands of Rashid and his supporters.

During the greater part of this period (1840–71) Kuwait was ruled by Shaikh Jabir, who died in or about 1859 and was succeeded by his son Shaikh Sabah II. Lorimer recounts that: "*The Government of Shaikh Subah, who in 1863 was described as a fine, stout, hale old man, more than 80 years of age . . . was patriarchal; and he sat daily at the gate to superintend the affairs of his subjects. In the town of Kuwait there was little interference by officials with the life of the people,* *and punishments were seldom inflicted; political authority was exercised by the Shaikh, but judicial power belonged to the Qadhi alone; there were no customs or other taxes, the revenue for public purposes consisting of about $20,000 a year which was voluntarily contributed by merchants and others. Kuwait's population had declined somewhat since documented by Niebuhr, but the 1860's witnessed a return to its original strength. Shaikh Subah, at his death in or about 1866, was succeeded by his eldest son Abdullah."*

In 1866 some controversy arose over the possession by Shaikh Sabah of Sufiyeh, the estate on the Shatt-al-Arab bought from a member of the Zuhair family of Zubair about 30 years earlier. This property was now sequestrated by a Turkish Qaim-maqam in consequence of claims made by the Zubair family. Turkish officials were strongly in favour of the Zubair claimants, but eventually , in the face of the steadfastness of the Kuwaitis, the dispute was settled by the Wali of Baghdad in favour of the Shaikh of Kuwait. The British Agent at Basra, in reporting the matter, remarked that *'rather than submit to a Turkish Government at Kuwait the people to a man would abandon the place.'*

Last Decades of the Nineteenth Century

The visits of British merchant steamers to Kuwait were regarded with extreme jealously by the Turkish authorities in Iraq, and the latter appeared to be collecting statistics to prove that the prosperity of Kuwait was injurious to Basrah. In order not to provoke the Turks the British suspended the service. Shaikh Abdullah had in fact established very close relations with the Turks and had even used his good standing with the Turkish government to request support for Abdullah bin Faisal the displaced Saudi leader. Somewhere between 1872 and 1874 Faisal, was granted permission by Shaikh Abdullah to take up residence at Kuwait. Subsequently, the town was threatened by Sa'ud, but Abdullah very quickly dispelled the attackers. In 1892 Shaikh Abdullah was succeeded by his brother Muhammad who was *"invited by the Turks to co-operate in restoring order in Hasa, where in 1892 serious troubles had broken out; and in March 1893 Mubarak bin Subah arrived in Hasa for this purpose with a large force of Bedouin, having marched all the way by land from Kuwait"*.

Shaikh Mubarak bin Sabah, a proud, austere and independent desert leader assumed control on the assassination of Shaikh Muhammad and his brother Jarrah. Mubarak, who later became

known as Mubarak the Great, was to steer an autonomous Kuwait on a clear and decisive path into the 20th century. But, in the meantime, the disgruntled sons of the dead Shaikh and his brother had received support in their trouble-making from a maternal relation, Yusuf bin Abdullah, in Turkish Iraq. A decidedly unsuccessful naval expedition was launched against Kuwait in June of 1897: it retired without firing a single shot on finding the town well defended. Mubarak's nephews attempted to involve the Turks in their quarrel, at the same time trying to inveigle the British to intercede. The latter declined to intervene whilst the former took up a position of neutrality for much of the period. The Turks, however, began to make threats against Kuwait's independence. In February of 1897, they sent a sanitary official to Kuwait, and Shaikh Mubarak requested an interview with the British Resident or his agent, ostensibly to ask for British cooperation in dispelling this threat. A meeting took place in September 1897 at Kuwait in which Mubarak stated that he and his people, in order to prevent the annexation of Kuwait by the Turks, who had shown themselves grasping and unreliable, wished to establish the same treaty relationship with the British as the Shaikh of Bahrain and the Shaikhs of Trucial Oman. In support of this request he pledged that, if this were done, he would assist the British Government with all the force at his command in maintaining law and order in his part of the Gulf. His request was turned down by the British although the Government of India were of the opinion that Kuwait was, in fact, a centre of 'piracy'—an allegation stoutly denied even by Lorimer who indicated that confusion must have arisen between Kuwait and the Shaikh's estates in Turkish Iraq. Lorimer states categorically that: *"At no time before or since have there been complaints of piracy by the inhabitants of Kuwait"*. The Secretary of State for India intimated that as far as he was concerned *"there was nothing in the political situation of Kuwait to hamper naval officers in bringing home to the Shaikh his responsibility for piratical acts"* and consequently no advantage would accrue to the British in involving themselves any further than was necessary in Kuwait's affairs. Shaikh Mubarak again repeated his request for British cooperation in 1897 but to no avail.

The British were forced to reassess the situation in 1898 since they had reason to believe that the Russian Government wished to establish a coaling station at Kuwait and *"attempts were*

House of the original Political Agent to Kuwait, H.R.P. Dickson, remains a landmark on Kuwait's corniche, and at the time of writing was still occupied by his widow, Dame Violet Dickson (*P. Vine*).

being made to obtain from the Porte a concession in favour of Count Kapnist, a Russian subject, for the construction of a railway from the Mediterranean to the Persian Gulf, a scheme which, in the absence of any arrangement between the British Government and the Shaikh, might end in the creation of Russian territorial rights at Kuwait". Rumours were also circulating concerning the imminent despatch of Turkish forces from Basra by sea to Kuwait.

Turn of the Century: 1899–1900

An agreement was signed on 23rd January 1899 by Shaikh Mubarak, whereby the British attempted to achieve their objective of thwarting Russian, Turkish and French designs on Kuwait's strategic position at the head of the Gulf whilst at the same time avoiding any real committment towards Kuwait. Under this agreement, Mubarak undertook on behalf of himself and his heirs *"not to receive the agent or representative of any foreign power or government at Kuwait, or at any other place within the limits of his territory, without the previous sanction of the British government; and not to cede, sell, lease,* *mortgage or give for occupation, or for any other purpose, any portion of his territory to the government or subjects of any other power without the previous consent of the British Government"* . . . a letter was then given to the Shaikh by Colonel Meade, in which, on behalf of the British Government, he assured the Shaikh, his heirs and his successors of the good offices of the British Government, so long as they on their part should continue to observe the obligations of the Agreement. In this document the secret character of the Agreement was emphasized, and payment was promised of a sum of Rs. 15,000 which had been fixed as the consideration for its execution. (Good offices was a term used frequently by the British in their treaties—a term which they interpreted narrowly or otherwise: as self-interest dictated).

Despite the secrecy surrounding the pact between Britain and Kuwait, Turkey must have had some knowledge of the event since in the months following the agreement, the Porte renewed its efforts to assert its position in Kuwait. In the face of Mubarak's intransigence, relations became so strained between the Turks and Kuwaitis, that a naval attack seemed imminent. In response the Government of India stationed H.M.S. "Lapwing" nearby to preempt any such action. In May, Shaikh Mubarak, anxious to assert his independence, established regular customs at Kuwait and began to realise an enhanced duty of 5 per cent on all imports, including those from Basra and other Turkish ports. On the 2nd of September a Turkish harbour-master, with five soldiers, arrived to take charge of the port of Kuwait; but the Shaikh declined to receive him.

Constantinople, however, instructed Basra that the matter should not be dropped. Next it was reported that the Turks intended to establish a customs house at Kuwait and to connect Fao with Qatif by a telegraph through Kuwait, and that the Turkish military authorities were demanding forcible action against Kuwait. As a result of this aggressive Turkish policy, a warning was in September 1899 conveyed to the Porte by the British ambassador at Constantinople under the instructions of Her Majesty's Government. In summary, it stated that the British Government, while they entertained no designs on Kuwait, had friendly relations with the Shaikh; and that, if any attempt were made to establish Turkish authority or customs control at Kuwait without previous agreement with Her Majesty's Government, a very inconvenient and disagreeable situation would arise. The Turkish Minister for Foreign Affairs, in reply, gave assurances that the reception of a harbour-master by the Shaikh would not be pressed any further; that there was no intention of establishing an Ottoman custom house at Kuwait; and that no military expedition against Kuwait was contemplated. Apparently, although operations had been proposed by the Wali of Basra, the Sultan had withheld his sanction.

Mubarak succeeded in having the Wali of Basrah replaced with an official who represented Kuwait's position to the Porte in a much more favourable light. As a result, he was able to safely visit Turkish territory, receive an official Turkish decoration from the Sultan, and even make inroads into the territory of Ibn Rashid of Najd, who was at that time a Turkish vassal. Before these events took place however, a German Commission paid a visit to Kuwait in search of a suitable terminus for the proposed Baghdad Railway. The British, secure in the exclusive agreement they had made with Mubarak, although they saw fit to underscore it with a warning conveyed by the Commander of H.M.S. "Melpomene", were much relieved that they were able to prevent such a prejudicial event from taking place—prejudicial that is to Britain. Mubarak, over and above his obligations to Britain, was not at all in favour of a railway

terminus within his jurisdiction, and as he conveyed this message to the Commission he took the opportunity to reiterate to its members that *he* was in charge in Kuwait, *not* the Porte. Since the promoters of the railway had intimated that they would deal directly with Turkey over the acquisition of about 20 square miles of land at the head of Kuwait bay, it seemed that the time had come to state the British position to Kuwait vis a vis Turkey and the German Government. On the 15th April 1900, the British Ambassador at Constantinople, whilst meeting with the Turkish Minister for Foreign Affairs, reiterated that the British Government was primarily interested in maintaining the status quo in the Gulf and would not *"view with indifference any action which would alter it or give to another power rights or privileges over territory belonging to the Shaikh of Kuwait"*. On the same day the German Ambassador was left in no doubt by his British counterpart that Shaikh Mubarak could not grant any territory to the members of the Baghdad Railway Commission without the express agreement of the British Government.

In the meantime, as well as adroitly balancing the major powers to ensure Kuwait's independence, Mubarak played a significant role in regional affairs. Ibn Saud, grandson of Faisal bin Turki and rival claimant, with Ibn Rashid, to the leadership in Najd, took up residence in Kuwait in 1897 under the protection of Mubarak. Ibn Rashid's obvious resentment at the Kuwaiti extension of refuge to his enemy was further stirred by Mubarak's trouble-making nephews and their ally Yusuf of Dorah. Ibn Saud, having left Kuwait in 1900 and achieved much success in the interior, called on Mubarak for reinforcements. However, Sa'dun Pasha, from his base in Turkish Iraq raided some tribes dependent on Ibn Rashid, prompting the latter, at the end of October 1900, to show up at Samawah on the Euphrates with a large following demanding redress for the injuries inflicted on his subjects by Sa'dun and satisfaction from the Shaikh of Kuwait, as well as the reinstatement of Mubarak's troublesome nephews. Ibn Rashid threatened to attack Kuwait if his demands were not met. Shaikh Mubarak joined forces with Sa'dun and it looked as if a clash was imminent. The Wali of Basra achieved a temporary peace, but Mubarak was only biding his time and, on the 18th of December 1900, indicating that he could no longer remain quiescent whilst Yusuf was under the protection of Ibn Rashid, he gathered his forces and marched against the enemy.

Early Twentieth Century

Although suffering a minor setback at the beginning of February 1901, Mubarak's central Arabian expedition was an unprecedented success: Qasim was occupied; the son of Ibn-Sa'ud was appointed titular governor of Riyad; and some members of the family of Ibn Rashid entered into negotiations with the triumphant Mubarak. However, since heavy losses were incurred by both sides in a battle which took place on the 17th March at Sarif, Shaikh Mubarak decided to return to Kuwait.

The Wali, taking advantage of the situation, visited Kuwait and attempted to persuade Mubarak that he had need of a Turkish military garrison at Kuwait. Mubarak again declined the offer and turned to the British for support. His overtures were rebuffed since the British already had an exclusive agreement which served their needs for the time being, and there was no further advantage in embroiling themselves in Kuwait's affairs and upsetting their relationship with the Turks. Mubarak astutely managed to evade the Turkish demands, but Ibn Rashid was again becoming somewhat of a problem. His activities in the hinterland of Kuwait in Sep-tember of 1901 encouraged thousands of Bedouin along with their livestock to come to the town for protection. This resulted in a huge camp being formed on the outskirts of Kuwait, but, as the threat receded, the Bedouin merged back into the desert as quickly as they had come. Shaikh Mubarak, nevertheless, still remained somewhat apprehensive about Ibn Rashid's intentions. As a result, he looked to the British for help. This time, owing to the seriousness and local nature of the threat, several British gunboats were held in readiness at or near Kuwait and the naval authorities were empowered by the Government of India to use force to repel any attack.

However, by the middle of November 1901, Ibn Rashid was ensconced on the frontier between Turkish Iraq and Kuwait and the Wali of Basra was reported to be renewing his efforts to persuade Mubarak to admit loyalty to the Sultan, an event which raised storms of protest in diplomatic circles. A Turkish sloop-of-war once more made an appearance in Kuwait harbour, on 1st December, this time with the Naqib and a brother of the Wali on board. An ultimatum was presented to the Shaikh requiring him either *"to receive at Kuwait a Turkish military detachment—*

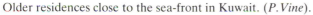

Older residences close to the sea-front in Kuwait. (*P. Vine*).

Photograph by P. Vine

which, it was promised, should be under his own orders—or to leave Kuwait and retire to Constantinople and its neighbourhood". Shaikh Mubarak, waiting for official British support for his stance against Turkey, stalled for a time. When it finally arrived, the official British response to the Wali stated: *"Since the Naqib's action was directly contrary to the understanding between Turkey and Britain (to maintain the status quo), the British Government would support the Shaikh and would not tolerate an attack by Turkish troops or ships on Kuwait, that the Shaikh should not leave Kuwait, and that he should continue to observe his engagements with the British."*

Although Constantinople was quick to repudiate the actions of the Naqib in Kuwait, Ibn Rashid, stationed near Basra, was still receiving much support from the Wali; support which seemed to be officially sanctioned by the Porte. A combined attack on Kuwait seemed imminent. Lorimer reports that: *"Dispositions were instantly made by the British naval force at Kuwait to co-operate in the defence of the town; two Nordenfelts and two Maxim were temporarily placed in the Shaikh's fort at Jahrah near the foot of Kuwait bay; and on the 1st of January 1902 the*

'Fox' and 'Perseus' were ordered from Bombay to join the 'Pomone', 'Sphinx' and 'Redbreast' which were already at Kuwait, with extra guns". This display of strength by the British combined with the fighting forces of Mubarak was too much for Ibn Rashid who retired to his own country. The Turks, however, did not relinquish their ambition to control Kuwait, but adopted new tactics to achieve their objective. Safwan, Umm Qasr and Bubiyan Island were occupied early in 1902, heralding a new policy of gradual encroachment on Kuwaiti territory. Shaikh Mubarak responded by placing a garrison at Haqaijah (Hijajah) in order to preempt further action by the Turks. It was reported at this time in Constantinople that Khor Abdullah was now being considered as the possible terminus of the Baghdad railway. The Turks used every means in their power to harass Shaikh Mubarak. Raids into Kuwaiti territory by Bedouin supporters of Ibn Rashid also continued well into 1902; at this point Ibn Rashid himself was experiencing some success in Najd.

The British Government, much to his disappointment, refused to reinforce Mubarak's fort at Jahrah with additional guns, but instead pledged to defend his territory adjoining the bay of Kuwait as long as the Shaikh himself remained there and did not rush to Najd to aid his ally Ibn Saud. It was however a well-armed expedition launched by Yusuf bin Abdullah of Dorah and headed by Mubarak's nephews which posed the greatest threat in the autumn of 1902. H.M.S. Lapwing, discovering in Khor Abdullah two of the large dhows belonging to the expedition, gave chase and captured the boats after shots were exchanged. One boat was the personal property of Yusuf bin Abdullah who subsequently escaped to Najd in order to join Ibn Rashid.

Serious attempts to undermine Mubarak's authority in Kuwait were gradually beginning to wind-down as Turkish attention was distracted by the conflict in central Arabia between Ibn Rashid and Ibn Saud. The former made one last sortie into Kuwaiti territory in December of 1902 but was repulsed by Shaikh Mubarak's forces. The Shaikh then proceeded to reinforce Jahra but was dissuaded by British fears of involving the Turks from any further action against Ibn Rashid. In any case Ibn Rashid's star had declined: Abd al Aziz ibn Abd al Rahman al Faisal al Saud, who was to eventually found the Kingdom of Saudi Arabia had captured al Riyad. It is reported that Abd al Aziz, accompanied by his brother Muhammad, visited Kuwait in March of 1903 to confer with Mubarak. Lord Curzon, Viceroy of India, paid a ceremonial visit to Kuwait in November 1903.

In the light of this successful visit, the British Government decided to take advantage of what seemed a convenient opportunity of securing, by a single measure, the improvement of postal communication with Kuwait, the establishment of a medical station, and an increase in the efficiency of British political representation with Shaikh Mubarak. The plans for a post office never reached fruition and were, in fact, supplanted by a scheme to appoint a British political officer to Kuwait in the light of Turkish activity in Central Arabia. Captain S. G. Knox arrived in Kuwait in August 1904 with instructions to pay particular but "unobtrusive" attention to Khor Abdullah and the waters adjacent to Bubiyan Island and Umm Qasr. He was joined at a later date by an Assistant-Surgeon. The Turkish Government objected to the appointment of the Political Agent as an infringement of the status quo and since the British did not want to jeopardise negotiations that were already taking place with the Turks over Aden, it was considered expedient to remove temporarily the political officer as soon as this could be achieved without loss of British prestige.

Settlement was achieved after much delay in the dispute between Shaikh Mubarak and his

---

Shaikh Mubarak's work schedule is encapsulated in an interesting account, written by Barclay Raunkiaer, an enterprising young Dane who visited Kuwait in 1912. Zahra Freeth and Victor Winstone paraphrase this description in their book on Kuwait: "*At that time the property of the ruler and his family formed an imposing complex of buildings on the hill running back from the seafront in central Kuwait. The Shaikh's own private residence lay on the slope of the hill, connected to other buildings by a bridge over a narrow street at the back. The serai or government building stood on the seafront itself—part of it still stands today, a yellow brick edifice west of the new Seif Palace.*

"*Shaikh Mubarak's daily routine followed an established pattern. Accompanied by a bodyguard of about fifty armed men, he came every morning to the serai, and in pleasant weather would sit on a veranda facing the sea where a secretary read his official correspondence to him, and the Shaikh dictated his replies . . .he enjoyed looking at ships or dhows in the bay. Mubarak permitted only British steamers to call at Kuwait, and had turned down the request of a German shipping firm to open an agency there.*

"*After dealing with his correspondence, Mubarak went to the Mahkama or administrative building in the bazaar, driving in his carriage drawn by two black horses. In front of the carriage walked a group of beduin guards, and behind, riding a white horse, came a tall negro in blue robes carrying a loaded Mauser rifle. In the Mahkama, a two-storeyed building with glazed windows on the upper floor, the ruler sat to discuss business matters and gave judgment in lawsuits.*

"*When he had taken his midday meal Mubarak retired to his private quarters for the time-honoured siesta. During this time silence fell over the whole town as shops were shut, pack animals were still, and all the inhabitants slept. The siesta ended about 3 pm when the ring of the coffee mortar in the palace signalled that the household was astir once again, and shortly afterwards Shaikh Mubarak returned to the serai to hold audience for an hour in one of the reception rooms whose ceilings were decorated with female portraits. Apparently only favoured individuals were granted audience in the palace itself, ordinary citizens came to him in the Mahkama, where he went for his second daily session in late afternoon.*

"*According to Raunkiaer, Mubarak's authority and control were apparent everywhere in Kuwait; he described the Shaikh as having the power and will to break all opposition, and for this reason public security prevailed.*"

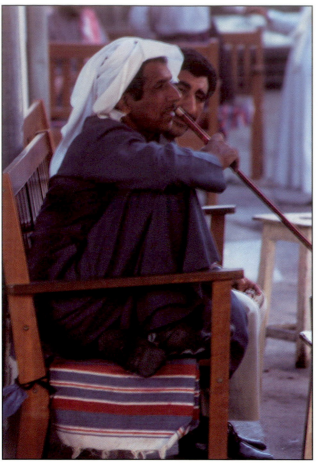

Photograph by P. Vine

nephews concerning the family estates situated in Turkish territory on the Shatt-al-Arab. Lorimer comments that: "*The general effect of the settlement was to confer on Shaikh Mubarak undivided ownership and possession of the whole property at Fao*". Mubarak also acted as intermediary between the Turks and Ibn Saud in the light of active Turkish support for Ibn Rashid, arranging and escorting two meetings between Ibn Saud and Mukhlis Pasha, Wali of Basra. As a result, Mubarak's relations with the Turks took on a friendlier disposition. Mubarak also attempted a reconciliation between Ibn Saud and Ibn Rashid after Yusuf bin Abdullah's death in 1906.

Despite the renewal of friendly relations with the Turks, the British continued to occupy a special position in Kuwaiti affairs, taking advantage of their situation to make detailed surveys of Kuwaiti territory on both land and sea from 1904–07. Kuwait continued to be ruled in an orderly and efficient manner by Shaikh Mubarak. Lorimer comments that: "*It appeared that no one could be more competent than Shaikh Mubarak of Kuwait to manage his own affairs . . . the tribal affairs of the Kuwait principality were ordinarily so well managed that nothing was heard of them, and opposition to the*

wishes of Shaikh Mubarak was rare on the part of the tribes subject to his influence." In 1914 the population of Kuwàit was estimated at about 35,000. The town was said to contain about 3,000 houses, 500 shops, three caravanserais, six coffee houses, three schools, four mosques and numerous warehouses and stores. The town's wealth was derived from its trade, shipping, shipbuilding, fishing, pearling and, to a small extent, camel breeding. Some 500 boats with crews averaging from 15 to about 50 men were engaged in pearl fishing and 30 to 40 larger vessels regularly sailed to India and Africa on trading voyages. Boat-building provided a livelihood for about 300 skilled carpenters with most of the timber being imported from India.

Shaikh Mubarak died in 1915, having skilfully steered his country with a firm and patient hand through a difficult political period in its history. Mubarak was succeeded by his eldest son, Jabir, who unfortunately died in 1917, Mubarak's second son Salim assuming the leadership. Relations had been strained for sometime between Ibn Saud and the Kuwaitis, primarily because of disputes over tribal allegiance and resistance by the powerful Ajman to Saudi overlordship. This delicate situation was exacerbated by a British imposed naval blockade of Kuwait early in 1918. The British embroiled in the First World War, were under the impression that supplies were reaching their enemies, the Turks, through the port. Kuwait, in turn, was convinced that Ibn Saud bore a heavy responsibilty for the spreading of these false rumours to the British. The blockade was lifted after the war ended, but it was feared that Ibn Saud's resentment might take a more concrete form. Kuwait were particularly concerned about any alterations to the unratified Anglo-Turkish agreement of 1913 which had set its boundaries and defined the territory under indirect Kuwaiti control, ie the area in which the Kuwaiti ruler had the power to levy tribute. Tension mounted. Skirmishes took place between Kuwaiti forces and the Ikhwan army of Faisal al Duwish whose religious zeal Ibn Saud had harnessed to bolster his rule. Fearing for the safety of their town, the entire population of Kuwait, despite the scorching summer heat, quickly built a new defensive wall five miles in circumference and 14 feet high to help keep out their fierce opponents.

On the morning of 10th October 1920, Faisal and his forces attacked the village of Jahra which occupied a strategic position on the route from Kuwait to Basra. The stronghold of the Kuwaiti

The Red Fort at Jahra was site of a key battle in the defence of Kuwait and has been preserved as an open museum (*P.Vine*).

defence was the Red Fort at Jahra—the Qasr al Ahmar- now preserved as one of Kuwait's links with the past. Faisal's bedouin troops launched attack after attack against the fort, but were held at bay by Shaikh Salim and his men who were well aware that the fate of Kuwait rested in their hands. Inflicting severe losses on the assault force, the garrison defeated Faisal's army, checking the invasion before it could reach Kuwait town. The Battle of Jahra is commemorated to this day in Kuwait, the old fort standing as a monument to the courage and steadfastness of the country's defenders.

Shaikh Salim died in 1921 to be succeeded by his nephew, Shaikh Ahmad al Jabir al Sabah, the popular eldest son of the former ruler, Shaikh Jabir al Mubarak. Under his wise and peaceful rule Kuwait began to recover from the turmoil of the preceding few years. Foremost among the town's activities was its flourishing shipbuilding industry, Kuwait dhows being famous for their seaworthiness. Cargoes of Basra dates and other re-exported commodities were traded far down the coasts of India, Arabia and East Africa.

Pearling, too, played a prominent part in Kuwait's prosperity since some of the finest pearls were to be found in the Gulf and Kuwait had become a major centre for the lucrative pearl trade. The Uqair Conference of 1922, orchestrated by the British, was to be of major significance both for Kuwait and the whole Arabian peninsula. Attempts were being made to set internationally recognised boundaries. Britain, however, continued to be enamoured by Ibn Saud and to placate the Saudi leader; Kuwait was deprived of two thirds of her declared territory which was granted to Najd. Frontiers were the ostensible subject of discussion at the conference, but it is clear that oil, which had been discovered in Persia, was never far from the thoughts of the participants. A New Zealander by the name of Major Frank Holmes, a mining

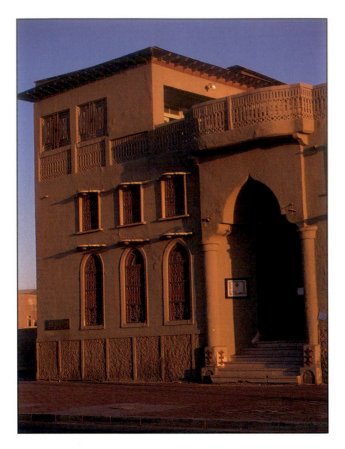

Sadu House, Kuwait city, is now run as a trust for preservation of traditional crafts, particularly weaving. It is itself one of the few preserved examples of traditional local architecture of the pre-oil era. The original house, built from mud was demolished in 1936 when it was rebuilt using stone, but preserving it's traditional lay-out (*P. Vine*.)

engineer and ex-Royal Marine, turned up at the proceedings of the conference and was to prove a familiar figure in the area in the years to come.

Before the decade came to an end Kuwait experienced a further spate of raiding by Faisal al Dawish and his forces, this time acting without Saudi support. But the Kuwaiti use of cars for speedy transport proved instrumental in dispelling the threat to their territorial integrity and, by 1930, Faisal's struggles were at an end. Acute economic depression, however, had hit Kuwait. This was primarily due to the collapse of the pearl trade, but the Saudi blockade of Kuwait following the Uqair conference which prevented the Bedu from revictualling in the town, further exacerbated the problem. The demand for rare and beautiful natural pearls had plummeted due to a world economic recession and the commercial production of cultured pearls by the Japanese. This was an extremely difficult period for Kuwait since almost every family in the town was involved in one way or another in the commercial activity surrounding the harvesting and selling of the pearls.

There was some hope that the severe economic problems experienced by Kuwait might be relieved by the production of a new commodity for the world-market—oil. Exploration for oil was already underway in neighbouring Bahrain,

Saudi Arabia and Iraq and the Anglo-Persian Oil Company had begun production in Iran. This company sent its representative, Mr A.H. Chisholm to Kuwait to negotiate a concession, but Major Frank Holmes had already recognised the oil-producing potential of Kuwait and was pursuing an option to explore further. Major Holmes transferred his rights to the American-owned Eastern Gulf Oil Company and the concession was pursued with vigour. The British-controlled company considered themselves to be in a superior position because of Britain's special treaty relationship with Kuwait. But, according to the British Political Agent in Kuwait, the trusted and well-liked H.R.P. Dickson, "*the tide had turned against APOC because of the Shaikhs grievances with Britain whom he felt could have prevented the Saudi blockade and the failure to exempt his date- gardens in Iraq from taxation*".

APOC, themselves, were both half-hearted and tardy in their approach. In any event, negotiations were extremely long and protracted as draft agreement after draft agreement was prepared, submitted to the Shaikh and sent to the Foreign Office in London for vetting. The contrast between the chief actors in the negotiations with the Shaikh epitomised the dichotomy between the two protagonists: Holmes, the stocky ebullient extrovert representing the vigorously commercial open-door policy of the Americans whilst the rigid, upright and extremely correct British representatives were mainly intent on maintaining British Imperial prestige. In order to break the deadlock, the Kuwait Oil Company was formed in 1934 and registered in London as a joint enterprise between the Anglo-Persian Oil Company (now British Petroleum) and Gulf Oil Corporation. Despite the intervention of an exclusively British third party (Traders Ltd.) in the negotiations, on 23rd of December 1934, the Kuwait Oil Company was granted an exclusive concession to search for and produce oil in the territory of Kuwait by Shaikh Ahmad. None of the parties were fully aware of the enormous resources waiting to be tapped.

Following the successful conclusion of the concession agreement, Shaikh Ahmad visited London in 1935, bringing with him a generous gift for Queen Mary which provided a link with

Kuwait's past as the State stood on the threshold of new prosperity. The Shaikh presented a perfectly round and flawless pearl, the largest ever found in the Gulf, to the Queen. Dickson, resigned his position as Political Agent and, with the encouragement of Shaikh Ahmad, became the Chief Representative of Kuwait Oil Company in February of 1936. Despite some initially disappointing results, on February 22, 1938, the drillers at Burgan found a gusher. Kuwait Digest paints a graphic picture of that exciting discovery: "*Under enormous pressure, oil burst through the wellhead valve and in an uncontrollable cascade soared into the hot desert air. An emergency was created. There was insufficient drilling mud to block the hole. Finally, a 60-foot pole was run to earth in the bazaar of old Kuwait town, quickly shaped to the dimensions required and plunged into the wellhead as a temporary stopper. It worked. Burgan Number One—still in production today—had been brought in. It was 11 a.m. on a rainy Thursday.*"

The outbreak of World War II, however, caused a temporary suspension of drilling activity, although the results of further exploration had been very promising confirming the presence of extensive oil resources. The war itself, with attendant political problems in Iraq and the arrival of a large number of troops in the Gulf, brought a good deal of hardship to Kuwait. After the hostilities had ended, Kuwait Oil Company greatly expanded its operations in a frenetic burst of building. Pipelines and pumping stations were constructed to carry the crude oil from the wells to the first improvised gathering centre where the gas was separated off and the oil pumped to two storage tanks from which it fell by gravity to the coast. To transfer the liquid from shore to tanker was another matter: a submarine line was required to reach water deep enough for tankers to berth. This sea-loading terminal was sited at Dhahan ridge, later to be renamed Ahmadi in honour of Shaikh Ahmad's role in developing his country's oil industry. On the 30th of June 1946, Shaikh Ahmad al Jabir al Sabah ceremonially inaugurated Kuwait's oil terminal and sent its first crude oil export on its way thereby starting in motion the export of the commodity which was to quickly assume the pivotal role once played by pearling and seafaring in Kuwait's economy.

Shaikh Ahmad died in January of 1950 having diligently and astutely guided his country through one of the most formative periods of its history, at the same time remaining a loyal friend

Photograph by P. Vine

to his Arab neighbours. Shaikh Ahmad, although fully aware of the the need to develop the country's oil resources, also regretted the upheaval that would follow the acquisition of wealth and the inevitable loss of some of the old customs. However, he firmly believed "*that the end result would benefit every inhabitant of the country—a conviction that has been justified by Kuwait's affluent democracy today*". Shaikh Abdullah al Salim al Sabah was chosen as the new ruler of Kuwait, having played a leading role in domestic political affairs. By the time of his succession, the oil company had created a technical base from which production could proceed with increasing volume, efficiency and profitability; it had set up the world's most advanced and effective tanker loading facility and commissioned an oil refinery capable of meeting local needs. Fresh water supplies, previously dependent on brackish desert wells and water ships from the Shatt al Arab, had improved considerably due to the installation of a distillation plant. An electricity supply system had also been set up, emanating from a new generating station at the oil port. The provision of housing, schools, and a hospital (supplementing the facilities of the first hospital founded by American missionaries) to a steadily-increasing population (150,000 by 1950) had been the primary concern of the state.

Kuwait's traditional souk (*P. Vine*).

In a remarkably short space of time, the injection of capital from petroleum revenues (rapidly increasing because of nationalistion of the Persian oil industry in 1951, and a new agreement with the oil company which granted a greater share of the profits to Kuwait) began to transform the country. Almost overnight, Kuwait was changed from an old-style dhow port into a modern metropolis and its people began to experience a new standard of living. Regular air services were established to connect the State with all parts of the world; paved roads were built to carry ever-increasing motor traffic; the life of the community was revolutionised by the easy availability of water and fuel and the extension of the electricity supply, enabling air-conditioning to be installed. Benevolent educational and health policies were pursued with new vigour. Despite this metamorphosis, much of the old Arab cultural traditions, firmly rooted in the deeply-held Islamic faith, remained as a stabilising and moderating influence.

Under Shaikh Abdullah's guidance Kuwait became a fully sovereign democratic state with all the freedom to play an independent role in both regional and world affairs. These developments were facilitated in 1961 by the Treaty of Independence which abrogated the 1899 agreement with Britain and replaced it with one based on contractual military support. In fact, the term 'Treaty of Independence' is a misnomer since Kuwait was never anything but autonomous as far as its internal affairs were concerned. Kuwait's first steps towards democracy had actually taken place as far back as 1921 when Shaikh Ahmad formed a 21-member consultative council chaired by Hamad Al-Saqr, a leading Kuwaiti businessman. Although this first council was short-lived, general elections in 1938 resulted in the formation of the first elected Legislative Council which was composed of 14 members. The time had now come to formalise this democratic process and lay down the institutions which would govern the newly-emerging state. The Constitution of Kuwait was drawn up by the mutual consent of a constituent assembly composed of 20 elected members and 11 ministers. Preparation and discussion of the Constitution lasted about six months and on 11 November 1962 Shaikh Abdullah Al Salem Al Sabah ratified the draft constitution without any amemdment. It became valid on 29 January 1963 when the first National Assembly of Kuwait convened following a General Election in which male Kuwaitis over 21 participated.

The constitution stipulates the democratic, sovereign and Arab character of the State, the pre-eminence of Islam and Islamic law, the priority of Arabic as the official language, and the obligatory use of flag, emblems, national anthem and other symbols of nationhood. The constitution embodies the positive aspects of both presidential and parliamentary systems prevalent in advanced democratic societies. The head of the State is the Amir who alone enjoys constitutional immunity. He assumes his authority through his ministers in whom the executive authority of the State is vested. Ministers are accountable both to the Amir and to the National Assembly. The constitution states that the Amir is the Supreme Commander of the Armed Forces. No law may be promulgated unless it has been passed by the National Assembly and sanctioned by the Amir. The constitution also states that Kuwait is an hereditary Amirate: "*the succession to which shall be through the descendants of the late Mubarak al-Sabah*". The Crown Prince or heir apparent must be designated within one year at the latest from the date of accession of the Amir, and his designation shall be effected by an Amiri decree upon the nomination of the Amir and the approval of the National Assembly. The constitution guarantees certain fundamental human rights, both collective and individual, which, up to this point had not been articulated so clearly on the Arabian peninsula. Personal liberty, the freedom of the press, of association and of assembly are guaranteed ; discrimination on grounds of race, social origin, language or religion invites severe penalties. Economic and social rights are also covered in a section entitled "Basic Constituents of Kuwait Society" governing the care and protection of the young and old. Many of the rights and obligations laid down so clearly by the constitution were already common to traditional Arab societies, but their articulation and development in a binding instrument, complimented by new norms, was in line with developments in the rest of the world. An independent judiciary are the guardians of the constitution.

When Shaikh Abdullah died in 1965 Kuwait had made the transition from a tribal state of limited regional significance to a modern industrial democracy with a major part to play on the world stage. In July 1961, Kuwait became a member of the Arab League thereby confirming its independence and sovereignty throughout the Arab world. Full international status was accorded by membership of the United Nations in 1963. Shaikh Sabah al Salim al Sabah took over in 1965 and in the Sabah tradition of administrative wisdom consolidated Kuwait's impressive progress both at home and abroad. In 1966 the Neutral Zone, created by the boundary conference, was partitioned equally between Kuwait and Saudi Arabia and on 13th of May 1968 Kuwait freed itself from all external obligations when it cancelled the agreement of 19 June 1961 with Britain. In March of 1975, the government acquired full ownership of Kuwait Oil Company.

Shaikh Sabah died on the 31st of December 1977 and H H Shaikh Jabir Al Ahmad Al Jabir Al Sabah, Crown Prince since 1966, was proclaimed Amir of the State of Kuwait–the thirteenth Amir from the Al Sabah family. Under his careful tutelage, progress has continued unabated despite the drop in oil prices, which has made severe inroads into Kuwait's revenue-earning potential, and the deleterious effects of the Iran-Iraq war. On 25th of May 1981, Kuwait signed the Articles of Association of the Gulf Cooperation Council. With the establishment of the GCC, Kuwait and its fellow Gulf countries have created a united platform for voicing their aspirations, fostering and furthering cooperation in the face of international threats, and dealing collectively with Gulf problems, while retaining their integral Arab character and independence.

Photograph by D. Clayton

Traditions

Arab culture and traditions, anchored by Islam, are the secure foundations upon which the modern state of Kuwait is built. Even though the process of modernisation has made serious inroads into many traditional aspects of life such as housing, occupations and handicrafts, the basic structure of society centred on Islam, the family, mutual help and hospitality, has changed remarkably little with the impact of economic prosperity. There is also a heightened awareness of the value of traditional occupations and handicrafts and much is being done towards their preservation. The traditional way of life in pre-modern Kuwait varied considerably whether one lived the precarious wandering existence of the desert bedouin or the slightly more predictable and comfortable lifestyle of the settled community. But the demarcation between bedu and townspeople was considerably smudged and, as we shall see, these two groups had much in common—the differences lying more in nuances of behaviour dictated by environmental factors.

Desert life

The nomadic way of life has existed for millennia. Mesopotamian clay tablets cite intrusions by desert nomads into the life of the earliest civilisations. Much later, around 650 BC, an attack by camel-borne desert-raiders is recorded on a carved relief in the palace of Ashurbanipal at Nineveh. Honed by the inhospitable climate, the bedu who roamed the deserts' empty wastes were renowned for their independence, pride, honour, courage, endurance, highly disciplined

austerity and patience. But the desert demanded a high price for the shaping of this rare breed—the harsh and difficult lifestyle meant that infant mortality was very high, up to 50% of children dying before the age of six. Only the fittest were left to learn the ways of survival in the scorched landscape. Most of the bedu occupying the Kuwait hinterland up till the 1940's belonged to the great tribes of east and central Arabia. The men, spare and wiry in physique, faced the world with all the stoicism and quiet deliberation demanded of a desert-dweller as they tended their camel-herds, protected their extended family, and honoured tribal allegiances. Bedu women wore

Above and opposite: Sheep have been raised in Kuwait for thousands of years, providing their keepers with a mobile source of fresh meat and the raw material for weaving a wide range of rugs, bags, cushions, tents, men's cloaks and other goods. These two scenes depict a shepherd and his herd in the northern region of Kuwait and sheep being sold at Kuwait's livestock market (*P. Vine*).

ankle-length robes, their heads draped in black, faces hidden except for the eyes by a *burqa*, remaining veiled even when attending to the cooking or household tasks. At the approach of strangers they normally retired to the confines of their tent, especially if male members of the household were present. However, if alone at camp, the elaborate social code of the desert, allowed women to offer hospitality to male strangers, as long as they were Arab.

The rigours of desert life have dictated the importance of hospitality and other customs which ensure a man's safety in the harshest of natural conditions. The relationship between tent-owner and guest brings into play a deeply-held obligation of the host to ensure his guest's safety; the same sort of relationship existing between a man and his *khowi* or travelling companion. *Dakhala* or sanctuary entitles a man pursued by an enemy to claim the protection of a third party by uttering a time-honoured and totally-binding formula. Desert hospitality knew no bounds, even the poorest of hosts would kill his last animal to feed a guest. The character of the man was everything to the bedu, obedience to religious and social laws being of paramount importance, dearer often than life itself.

The black tents in which the bedu lived were long and low, woven by the women from the wool of their own sheep and goats. In a recent article on the subject, published by Al Sadu House, Dame Violet Dickson D.B.E. comments as follows:–

"The upkeep of the black wool was one of the many tasks done by the wife of a Bedouin tribesman and her companions in the desert. The 'Bait Shar' (or hair tent as it was called) was woven from the black wool of the Kuwaiti sheep. When we had decided to own a black tent, Salim al Muzaiyin suggested that he could purchase the hand woven strips in Iraq where goat hair was

used to strengthen weaving. This he did, and we were very pleased with our new tent. Shearing of the sheep took place in March or April by men. The black wool was taken to the sea shore later by the women and well washed before spinning. As they also took care of the sheep and goats when out grazing, they took a bundle of black wool with them which they spun on a light wool spindle as they guarded the flocks.

"When summer came, tents moved nearer to the town of Kuwait, outside the city walls in the Shamiyeh area near water wells. Now one could see the loom stretched out in front of the women's portion of the tent.

"According to the length of the strip to be renewed, the black wool was stretched out round a horizontal pole, supported by two large stones or old tins. Then one metre from the near end the alternate wool threads were raised on a piece of wood or higher tins. With her spun wool she passed it across from right to left, then alternating the threads, back again to the right pulling down the threads with a flat piece of wood—or a gazelle horn, this made a tight weave. One strip from the centre of the tent was renewed each year, and the discarded centre would be used for the back— "ruag"—of the tent.

"About fifteen years ago, the news was suddenly spread among the desert people—obviously by means of their portable radio sets—in Arabic, that they could now buy in the bazaar of Kuwait, well made black wool tent strips by the metre, which had only to be cut according to the length required. It was now no longer necessary for the women to weave any more, and their hands which had become hard and rough would soon be smooth and beautiful once more. It worked miraculously."

On these and accompanying pages we tell how this fascinating traditional craft is undergoing something of a revival as a result of the efforts of the Al Sadu Society, based at Sadu House.

SADU HOUSE

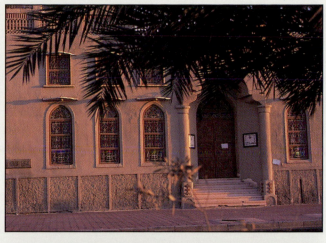

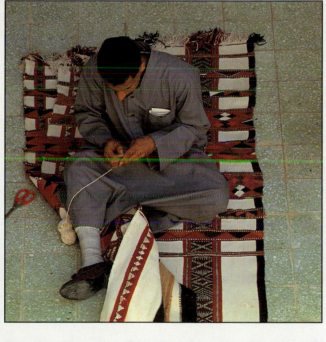

In 1979, a few concerned Kuwaitis formed themselves into a group termed 'al sadu' with the objective of working actively to resurrect a part of the heritage of the desert, and to protect bedouin culture, particularly the bedouin crafts, from total extinction in the wake of the rapid changes brought about by modernisation.

The weaving of wool is the oldest and most traditional craft practised by the bedouins of Kuwait and the Arabin peninsula. The weaving process is known as 'al sadu', a term also used for the bedouin loom. In 1980, the activities of the Al Sadu Society became centralised in the Sadu House located on the Gulf Road in the Qibla area.

The craft of weaving requires a high degree of dexterity and skill. It is a craft which has always been associated with the desert. The designs of bedouin rugs reflect the austerity of the natural environment of the desert and are governed by the wider principles of Islamic culture. (*caption text:– Al Sadu House; photographs:– P. Vine*).

The rug-weaving process involves manual dyeing of wool. Although synthetic dyes have to some extent taken over in recent years, dyeing with natural ingredients, extracted from desert herbs, is still practiced at Sadu House (*P. Vine.*)

The tents were segregated into separate compartments for men and women, the men's section was distinguished by the ever-ready coffee-pots poised by the brushwood fire, whilst the women were often accorded more privacy by the drawing of a partition to form an enclosure. There was no room for the clutter of a consumer society in the highly-mobile bedu lifestyle. Possessions were limited to the simplest necessities; a tent, a few rugs, some bed-covers, a camel-saddle for the husband and a cane-framed *maksar* or camel-litter for the wife, as well as water-skins, cooking utensils and saddle-bags to carry these goods. In addition, most men carried a rifle and cartridge belt for ammunition. It must be mentioned that the male members of the camp often went on long trips equipped with nothing but camels and rifle, disdaining tent or other cover, sleeping on the desert sand, insulated from the cold night air only by personal clothing and surviving for long periods on camels' milk and dates.

Traditional life was rich with a wealth of folktales, parables, poetry and song; this channelling of creative inspiration into oral expression, being entirely dictated by the nomadic lifestyle of the bedu. Arabic singing probably originated in the expressive lyrical oral vernacular poetry we now know as Nabati poetry. Saad Abdullah Sowayan explains how this form of creative expression was to be found in all walks of life. "*In premodern Arabia there was considerable reliance on the well-developed and highly stylised idiom of Nabati poetry as a means of communication, especially on solemn or formal occasions. Tribal chiefs and town amirs as well as relatives and friends communicated with one another in poems. Tribal territories, grazing areas, water holes, desert roads and stations; grievances, threats, battles, and other events, large and small—all were recorded and described in poems.*" Verses were also recited and sung to encourage and entertain travellers on long camel caravans. In Kuwait, in particular, the dialogue between the desert (the yellow labyrinth) and the sea (the blue labyrinth) proved a fruitful source of inspiration.

Bedouin singing is neither simple nor monotonous as the uninitiated might be led to believe.

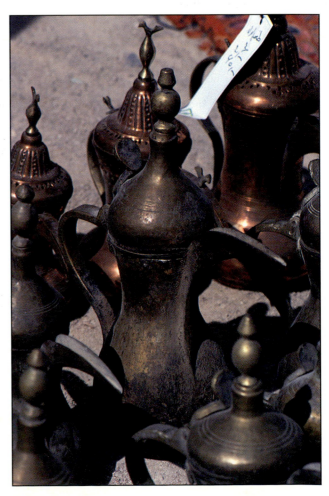

Traditional coffee pots on sale at the Friday market on the outskirts of Kuwait city (*P. Vine.*)

NATIONAL MUSEUM

Adjacent to Al Sadu House, and attached to the National Museum, is a centre for various handicrafts such as ceramics, carvings, sculpture, jewellery-making etc. Regular classes are held in the different art forms and workshops take place there, encouraging many people to enhance their skills. The pictures illustrate the buildings, peaceful courtyard together with a few of the red clay ornaments been made there by students (*P. Vine.*)

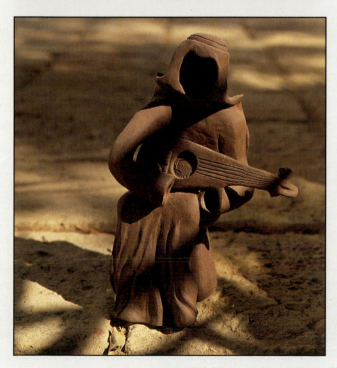

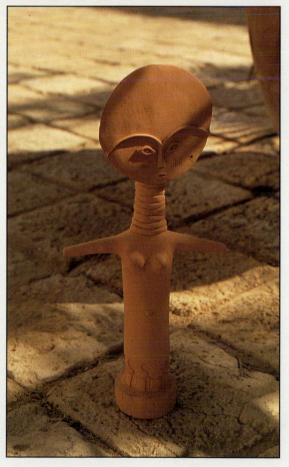

Traditional musical instrument, the oud, for sale at a Friday market in Kuwait (*P. Vine*).

The rich and varied lifestyle, enjoyed by these desert inhabitants, has produced a wide range of singing styles, some lending themselves to musical accompaniment through exposure to other cultural influences. Short rhythmic songs, both lyrical and war-like, were the domain of the bedu. Music and and dance accompanying these songs also had an important ritualistic and social function as exemplified by male ceremonial war-dances and women's song and dance performances, usually performed at weddings.

Camels

Livestock, especially camels, were the wealth of the desert. The average bedouin of a good tribe might have possessed half a dozen camels and thirty sheep, but for a tribal chieftain and his family several hundred camels was the usual complement. The great *sharif* or noble tribes of Arabia invested almost exclusively in camels, keeping other livestock only as an immediate food supply. A separate shepherd tribe of lower standing would be employed to take care of the sheep or goats. The camel was, and still is, the pillar-stone of Arabian traditional life, gracing the windblown sands with its haughty but pon-derous presence. It was everything to the bedouin, the very essence of life itself. Not only did it provide, milk, meat, wool, skin for water containers, belts, sandals and dung for fuel, but it was often the only means of transport through the soft laborious sands. Long, winding, camel caravans crossed the desert, as they have done for millenia, carrying goods such as firewood, charcoal, agricultural products and livestock to the towns; and returning with much needed supplies to the desert camp or small villages. Camels were also the main means of transport for pilgrims visiting Mecca on the Haj.

The formidable ability of the bedu to survive the harsh rigours of the arid desert environment are only outstripped by the legendary capacity of their noble beasts of burden. During cool winter months, camels may travel for as long as 30 days without drinking freshwater. As the temperature rises these periods between water intake shorten. On arrival at a water source, after a few days of abstinence, they may drink as much as 100 litres in one go. To achieve these incredible feats of endurance, camels possess an interesting range of adaptations concerned with maintenance of water balance. In order to minimise loss through evaporation they frequently group together, achieving a position which exposes the least body surface towards the sun. Even breathing is care-fully controlled, avoiding intake of sand, and moistening inhaled air within the nasal cavity, while exhaled air is cooled prior to release, thus reducing water loss. Body temperature can rise to six degrees above normal before a camel begins to sweat. The hump is essentially a food store and after a long arduous journey, a floppy hump may betray a camel's poor condition.

The long hot summers were spent camped around a suitable well, but vast areas were often traversed during cooler winter months, in search of grazing. The utmost care was taken to ensure that the camel was provided with all necessities, often at the expense of the bedu themselves. On arrival at a water-hole, the needs of the camel-herd were attended to before anything else, water being drawn from the depths of the brack-ish wells to quench their thirst. In summer, this could be a long and arduous process depending on the size of the herd and the depth of the well. In the daytime, the camel was left to roam herded by young men who would return with the livestock to the encampment at night. On oc-casions, camels wandered far from their tempor-ary home base, but disputes regarding ownership were avoided by branding.

Camels (*D. Clayton*).

Camel herds are extremely well guarded during the rutting season, great care being taken at that stage to control which animals are kept together; most herds comprising one rutting male for twenty to thirty females. The male or leading female is tethered, encouraging the rest of the camels to stay close by. Courtship and mating generally occurs from December to March, the males becoming extremely aggressive, grinding their teeth, salivating and blowing the dulaa or skin bladder out of their mouths. Calves are born from January to March, and remain with their mothers until they are about four years of age.

It is not surprising then, considering the central role it played in life in the desert, that as far as the bedu were concerned, the camel took on an almost mystical significance: a rare prize if captured in battle, but a bitter humiliation if lost in defeat. No one will deny that the life of the bedu has changed dramatically in recent years. Motorised vehicles have taken over the role of desert transport and the much lauded but extremely ardous nomadic existence has been largely abandoned for the comfort of settled houses in towns and villages, but the camel still commands the same respect, affection and admiration.

Bedouin Society.

The nomadic way of life also dictated the tribal structure of bedouin society, where loyalty to family, tribe, and confederation, was accorded in that order. A powerful leader could, of course, command the allegiance of a number of tribes. Traditionally, every bedouin tribe has had its own *dira* or home territory, across which it roams in winter and spring, and where there are wells which it uses in summer. Sometimes, friendly agreements between neighbouring tribes will allow for the sharing of *dira* which often stretch across political boundaries. The main tribes whose traditional grazing grounds are to be found around, and extending into, Kuwait are: Mutair; Awazim; Ajman; Sbei and Sahul; Harb and Shammar; Dhafir and Muntfiq. In addition, Kuwait has traditionally been the supply town for the Mutair, Harb, Shammar, Awazim and northern Ajman. Among smaller tribes, the Rashaida, renowned for their skilled hunters and beautiful women belonged specially to Kuwait and were traditional retainers of the Shaikh.

Although each tribe recognised one paramount shaikh, such leaders were regarded as no more than individuals chosen by their peers because of their outstanding qualities of leader-

ship. The most suitable candidate within the ruling family thereby succeeded to the position on the death of the previous shaikh.

Settled communities

Most townships along the Gulf are sited for obvious reasons on the coast, the inhabitants of these littoral communities traditionally following a different lifestyle and pursuing separate occupations to the true desert-dweller. This is not so surprising when one contemplates the altogether contrasting demands of the settled environment. The earliest colonisers of these towns were of course nomads, but once they had put down roots, they developed skills suitable to the surroundings in which they found themselves. Kuwait, blessed with a sheltered bay and a long, gently- shelving foreshore, eminently suitable for building boats, very soon after its inception earned a reputation for the high quality of its shipwrights and sailors. The bedu who had so successfully tamed the desert were, in many ways, uniquely equipped to exploit the sea. The shaikh and the founding families, although they ruled a community of merchants, mariners and pearl-divers, maintained their roots firmly in the desert.

For this blend of desert and sea to prosper, a balance had to be maintained between the inter- ests of both environments, requiring a strong shaikh who could act as a unifying and directing force. In the interest of the merchants who employed the mariners, the shaikh had to command the good will of the surrounding tribes or the trading caravans of the town were at their mercy. But the tribes were also dependent upon the good will of the shaikh, who could deny them access to essential water-wells, or prevent them entering the town to buy supplies. As we have seen from the historical section, the Al Sabah shaikhs achieved an equilibrium in Kuwait which allowed the town to thrive.

Kuwait in the early 1930's

A picture of old Kuwait town, vividly reflecting its distinctive character, has been painted by Mrs Violet Dickson, a resident of Kuwait since 1929. The following description draws heavily upon an account published in Zahra Freeth and Victor Winstone's book entitled: Kuwait, Prospect and Reality. The publishers are indebted to George Allen & Unwin for granting permission to quote from this source.

In 1930, the town, supporting a population of about 60,000, stretched four miles along the seashore and about two miles inland at its densest central part. A fortified wall to the south offered some protection. Inside the confines of

This page and opposite: On Kuwait's seafront, close to the main majilis building, a folk-park has recreated much of the atmosphere of the old town, including many small shops selling traditional goods. The park, which also has recreational facilities for children, is a popular place for Kuwaiti families to visit in the afternoons, particularly at weekends (*P. Vine*).

the wall, in an open space to the east, small market gardens grew radishes, tomatoes and cucumbers. Nearby, the ground was pitted with holes where clay had been dug for building or where gypsum had been uncovered and burned to be excavated for plaster. On the south-eastern fringe were many walled *hautas* or gardens which were used by men of prosperous families as their places of recreation, amid the scant greenery of a few sidr trees. Two Arab cemeteries and a small Christian one were also situated inside the wall. The town itself, built primarily of mud-brick, was a tawny ochre colour contrasting with the vivid blue of the sky and blending well with the gold of the desert. Apart from a rare tamarisk tree, it was unrelieved by any splash of greenery. There was little formal planning: houses were built at random; sandy winding roadways coming into existence where convenient access paths were needed for the donkeys, horses or camels which passed constantly to and fro carrying goatskins of fresh water, dried palm-fronds for firewood, charcoal and other merchandise.

Private dwellings, primarily single storied, shaded and sheltered courtyards, but here and there a single upper room would rise above the general level of the roof-tops. Behind high windowless walls, whose blank exterior was broken only by projecting wooden water-spouts, the life of each family went on in the enclosed courtyard. In the affluent household, the housewife, her children, serving girls, and perhaps unmarried female relatives, occupied one courtyard whilst in a second courtyard the head of the house could entertain his friends, segregated from the women's quarters. As in the desert, in this male *diwaniyah* or meeting place, coffee and tea were always available and benches were placed outside the gate where the men could sit to catch the

Scenes from Kuwait city's Friday market where one can buy almost anything from a wedding dress to a television set (*P.Vine*).

evening breeze. These houses, although primitive by modern standards, were built to shade their occupants from the intensely hot climate, and this they did most admirably without the aid of air-conditioning.

The traditional dress worn by the men of Kuwait town in this era was also admirably adapted to the twin requirements of religion and climate, but, unlike the housing, it has not been relegated to the realms of folklore and is still the norm in modern Kuwait. Men usually wear an ankle-length, cool, loose-fitting and supremely comfortable garment, (*dishdasha*), complete with a high neck and long sleeves whilst a headdress, comprised of a skull-cap covered by a long cloth (*gutra*) usually white, all secured by a wool rope *aqal* wound round the crown, protects the head and neck from the blistering sun. The bisht, a sleeveless flowing black or beige cloak trimmed with gold, is sometimes worn for ceremonial occasions. The fact that this form of traditional dress is still worn with minor variation throughout the Arabian peninsula is a sure tribute to its comfort and suitability for the difficult desert climate, even though this is now alleviated by extensive air-conditioning. But it also points to the pride people have in their Arab identity, supported and reinforced by Islam.

At the western end of old Kuwait the Naif and Jahra gates, set into the fortified wall, provided access for traffic from the desert. It was on this side of Kuwait that townspeople and tented communities dwelt in close quarters, for there was a large encampment of black tents immediately outside the wall, and some tents were even pitched within the town's precincts. Just inside the Naif gate stood a rectangular walled fortress with corner turrets, the Qasr al Naif. This was the headquarters of the Shaikh's men-at-arms and contained their arsenal of weapons, mostly rifles. Although now dwarfed by towering modern buildings, it still stands as a reminder of times long past. The desert dweller entering the town from the Naif gate and passing the fort quickly reached the wide open square of the *souk* or market-place. Here camels and sheep were sold and caravans were loaded with goods for the interior. To the north of the *souk* shops catered specially to bedouin needs. Heavily-veiled women mingled with the crowds in the street, traditional black cloaks enveloping their figures from head to toe. In one covered alley off the square was the women's souk staffed by women shopkeepers selling clothes and trinkets.

Kuwait's principal business quarter was concentrated in the main market area where a covered thoroughfare lined by shops ran directly through the town centre to the customs wharf on the seafront. In the web of bustling alleyways forking away from the main street were the workshops of the skilled artisans, as well as the premises of merchants selling richly-patterned carpets, tumbling bolts of cloth, cascades of shining gold and milky-white pearls, pungent aromatic spices and utilitarian glass and enamel utensils. Nearer the seafront, wholesalers of rice, coffee, tea and sugar had their large warehouses.

One of the most evocative and picturesque scenes in the old town was to be found along the road between the houses and the beach where boats in all stages of construction jostled for space on the seashore. By the waterside stood steel capstans and wooden water-tanks crowded by masts and spars and piles of timber. Where the road was wide enough, white sails were spread on the ground for the sail-makers to sew. On every side abounded the industry and craftsmanship which had made Kuwait the finest boat-building centre in the Gulf. Master-builders had originally come from Bahrain and, having handed down their skills from father to son, they continued to live in a separate quarter in the old city, forming a close community known as "Baharna". Boats of all shapes and sizes crafted

Basket-weaving is a traditional craft in which synthetic materials have found a place (*P. Vine*).

Kuwaitis love all kinds of birds from falcons to budgerigars and they have regular bird markets where a wide variety of species are traded for different purposes (*P.Vine*).

Perfumes, derived from a wide range of natural products, are much loved by both men and women in Kuwait. Some of the special essences can cost thousands of pounds per small bottle. The traditional perfumery store is very much a part of Kuwaiti traditional life (*P.Vine*).

Al-Muhalab is a stately Kuwaiti "boom" built in Kuwait in 1937 on behalf of Thunnayan Al-Ghanim and his older brother Muhammad, both prominent merchants in Kuwait. The builder, Hajji Muhammad Abdullah, had a high reputation for his work, himself a student of that legendary Kuwaiti boat builder: Hajji Ahmed Al-Ashram. Her maiden voyage, described by Yacoub Al-Hijji in his booklet on the vessel, consisted of collecting 6,400 packages of dates (each weighing 82 kilos) from Basra, then to India to unload before receiving a clean and maintenance prior to returning to Basra with timber and other items. At least two major voyages were made each season and the vessel continued to work in this deep sea trade for fifteen years, commanded until 1949 by Nohhada Hussain. The vessel was presented to the Departmentof Education by the Thunnayan family in 1960 and was remarked upon by Captain Alan Villiers in his book Sons of Sinbad when he wrote:–

On the waterfront was one last boom,
hauled ashore on the sand, not working
but put there as a memorial to the
great sailing days of the sheikhdom's
city-port, now gone for-ever.

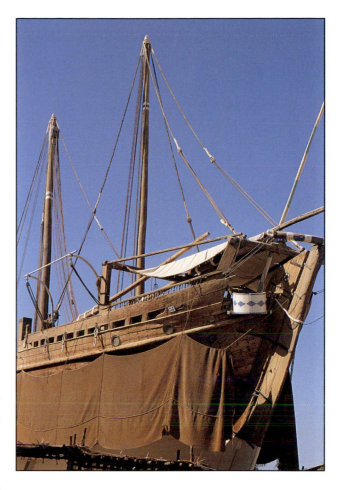

by these accomplished masters sailed in and out of the line of small harbours all along the front: small local boats used within the confines of the harbour; medium-sized *boums* which carried Kuwait's freshwater supply from the Shatt al Arab; and lighters bringing cargo from the British India steamers anchored in the bay.

But most impressive of all were the large ocean-going *boums*, some as big as three hundred tons. These dhows, the pride of local ship-builders, spent six to eight months during the winter north-east monsoon on a lengthy annual trading voyage or *sifr* in the vastness of the Indian Ocean. Leaving Kuwait in the early autumn and collecting a cargo of dates from Iraq they sailed one of two traditional trade routes. The first took them down the Gulf, along the coast of Baluchistan to Karachi, and then southwards to Cochin and Calicut, where they took on board timber for the return journey. On the second route they kept close to the Arabian coast, visiting ports and selling dates along the way, until they reached Aden. There they loaded up with salt, cloth, incense, and ghee, before continuing across to east Africa and Zanzibar to sell their cargo. Mangrove poles, used for roofing houses in Kuwait, were then taken on board and transported home.

The sailors on the *sifr boums* were among the most expert in the east, learning the trade from the age of ten or eleven as they accompanied their fathers on the sea voyages. Like the bedu in the desert, they were familiar with with every current and shoal in the Gulf, and were at one with wind and weather. Although most *boums* carried a compass and binnacle, navigation was primarily by the stars in the Indian Ocean. Returning from Africa they sailed close-hauled almost against the wind, using all the skill and seamanship for which they had earned their reputation. Kuwait's enterprising merchant families such as Al Ghanim, Shahin, Qitami and Saqar financed the building of the ships, loaded them with cargo and often sailed on their own craft. In many such families the household was left without a man for six months of every year, and there was always great rejoicing in the spring when husbands and kinsmen were welcomed home at the end of the *sifr*. When the great *boums* were laid-up in the harbour for the summer, held upright on their keels by supporting poles lashed to their sides, their masts were dismantled and a protective awning of matting was built over them to shade the decks from the summer sun. The hulls were cleaned, and the timbers above the water-line were treated with shark-oil until they shone a rich golden brown."

Boat-building

Surprisingly, in this era of super-tankers, the construction of dhows is still very much a valued tradition, although as a consequence of its reduced significance it is now restricted to Doha

Bay. However, the dhow-building art is on the brink of extinction since sons no longer accompany their fathers to the boat-yards to learn their trade, and once the old masters have retired, there will be no-one to replace them. The same simple materials and tools have been used for centuries to fashion these wooden vessels, both small and large. Hammer, saw, adze, bow-drill, chisel, plane, plumb-line, and caulking iron are all that is required to produce such a sophisticated and graceful end-product. Teak for planking, and for the keel, stem, stern and masts of the larger boats has traditionally been imported from India; for the naturally grown crooks used to form ribs and knees from India, Somalia, Iran, and Iraq; rope from Zanzibar and the sail canvas made locally. Mango was also imported from India to make the smaller boats and dug-outs.

Once the keel is raised and stem and stern posts fastened using the simple tool known as *hindasah*, the planks are fitted. This method of shell construction where the planks are put in place before the ribs contrasts with the European system of forming a skeleton of ribs prior to planking. Boats are all carvel-built with planks laid edge to edge: hundreds, sometimes thousands of holes are hand-drilled to avoid splitting the wood and long thin nails, wrapped in oiled fibre, are driven through to secure the planks to the frames. All the construction work is carried out without the aid of plans and drawings, measurements being made solely by eye and experience; templates are, however, used to shape the hull planking. Although it appears that accuracy depends solely on the instinct of the boat-builders, in fact a highly experienced master-craftsman (ustadh) usually oversees the calculations. The building of a large vessel could take up to ten months, while a smaller one would be finished in one to four months. Each one was both beautiful and utilitarian, streamlined and seaworthy.

In the pre-Portuguese era in the Gulf, Arab vessels were double-ended, their planks sewn together with coconut fibre; European influence over the centuries finally giving rise to a whole range of dhows with square sterns. But the double-ended form persists in the *boum* and *badan* among others. As we have seen, the nailing of planks together has also supplanted the less robust method of sewing, but the the lateen sail remained unchanged. Different types of vessel falling under the collective western title of 'dhow' are individually named according to their particular hull shape. *Baghlah*, *boum*, *sambuq*,

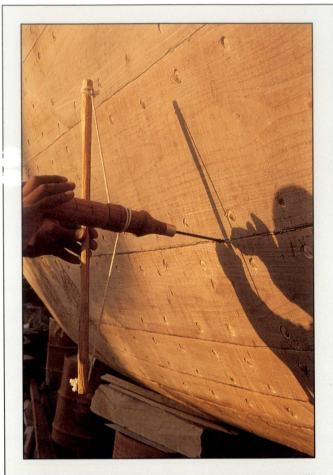

BOAT BUILDING

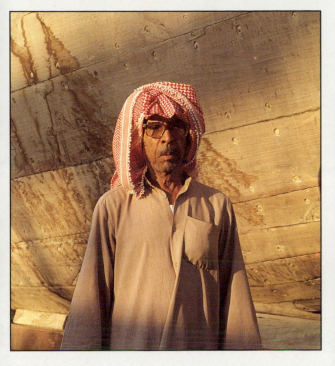

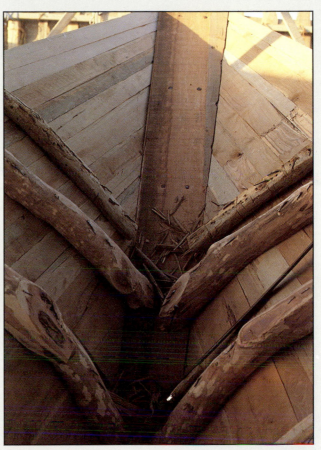

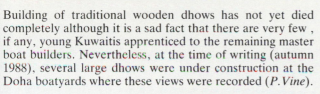

Building of traditional wooden dhows has not yet died completely although it is a sad fact that there are very few , if any, young Kuwaitis apprenticed to the remaining master boat builders. Nevertheless, at the time of writing (autumn 1988), several large dhows were under construction at the Doha boatyards where these views were recorded (*P. Vine*).

The traditional hull shape of the boom has been adapted for the motorised wooden fishing vessels which have been popular in the Gulf for many years. Despite the disadvantages of wood, traditional views have held sway, and the convenience of being able to construct and repair such boats locally, without sophisticated equipment, has been a key factor in resisting a change to fibreglass or steel (*P.Vine*)

shu'i, *batil*, *baggarah* and *jalibut* and, to a lesser extent, the huri and *shashah* were all common in the Gulf at one stage or another. Varieties on which it is inconvenient or impossible to modify hulls to accommodate engines have, by and large, fallen into disuse and are no longer being built except for museum purposes. Sterns of all suitable types have been adapted and ribs extended to make way for modern inboard engines while outboard motors are now fitted on large numbers of dug-outs or huris and other fishing craft. Sometimes, however, one can observe a new functional and streamlined hull form, not corresponding to any traditional classification, developed specifically to accommodate an engine.

The double-ended *boum*, is now the largest of all Arab vessels in the Gulf, attaining a length anywhere between 15 to 30 metres. Easily distinguishable by its high, straight stem-post protruding into a kind of planked bowsprit decorated with a simple design in black and white, it has superceded the ornately decorated square-sterned, high-pooped *baghlah* as a trading vessel.

Many smaller fishing boats are now made from fibreglass and are driven by powerful outboard motors, making it possible to cover considerable distances during a single day's fishing (P.Vine).

The sambuq, boasting an infinite variety of sizes, used to be one of the most common Arab vessels of the Gulf and is still very much in evidence. A low curved, scimitar-shaped stem-piece and high square stern lend elegance and grace to the lines of this practical boat. The length of the stem-piece underwater and the resulting short keel allowed for easy manoeuvrability on the sand banks, making this a most popular pearling vessel. It is also used for trading and fishing purposes. Shu'i, basically small sambuks, rarely over 15 tons, but sporting a straight as opposed to curved stem piece are commonly used as fishing vessels.

Pearling

Pearling, an ancient occupation, was vitally important to the economy of Kuwait and other Gulf states especially at the end of the last century. In the 1930's this lucrative trade, already devastated by the Japanese introduction of the cultured pearl, experienced a severe drop in demand as a result of economic depression in Europe and America. Before the First World War Kuwaitis worked as many as 700 boats, which would have required crew and divers totalling from 10,000 to 15,000 men. Since Kuwait could not provide this labour force an annual influx of bedu from Iraq and Najd came to chance their luck in the pearl diving game. The average annual value of pearls exported from the Gulf at the turn of the century was estimated at £1,434,000 and £30,439 was earned from the export of mother-of-pearl.

Pearling was not merely a trade or a means of subsistence, but an entirely integrated social system which has left a rich heritage of traditions to be enjoyed by an indigenous population now benefiting from the security engendered by oil. The general term for the pearl fishery is *ghaus* (literally diving) and all the classes that took part in the active operations are included under the common denomination (*ghawawis*). The method used in harvesting the pearl oyster was much the same throughout the region and probably hadn't

Pearling was once the mainstay of Kuwait's economy. Scenes such as these of pearlers and their craft are an extremely rare sight in the Arabian Gulf of today (*Arab Gulf States Folklore Centre*).

altered radically in thousands of years. The Kuwaiti boats traditionally worked in an area about a hundred miles south of Kuwait, where the depth of water was around twelve metres. All the boats departed for the pearl harvest at the beginning of June in one great picturesque swoop of sail. Depending on the preference or particular strategy of the captain, a pearling boat might anchor for the entire season at one pearl bank or move from bank to bank. Short trips were made ashore for replenishment of drinking-water, rice, dates, coffee and tobacco.

Sambuks were mostly employed as pearling

Net basket used by divers for gathering pearls underwater. The bag was pulled to the surface by assistants on board the pearling dhow (*Arab Gulf States Folklore Centre*).

boats, but *batils*, *baqgarahs*, *shu'ais* and *zarqahs* also had a place in the industry. The normal complement of crew for the average pearling vessel was 18–20:– 8 divers , 10 haulers or *siyub* and a young apprentice boy who fished, cooked, cleaned and took care of the coffee. However, the larger boats carried as many as 200 men.

Diving commenced about an hour after sunrise, the divers having breakfasted lightly on coffee and dates, and proceeded right through until an hour before sunset, except for prayers and sometimes coffee and a short rest at midday. The hard-working diver, nose pegged with clips of turtle shell and ears plugged with wax, plummeted to the bottom with the aid of a stone attached to his foot. This was subsequently pulled up by his attendant hauler on board ship. Fingers protected by leather caps, he quickly filled an attached basket with as many shells as possible whilst his breath lasted, finally signalling by a tug on his rope that he needed to be hauled to the surface. Resting briefly in the water, clinging to his rope in characteristic pose, his basket was emptied into the communal heap on deck and he, again and again, descended to the deep. All day long, the blazing summer sun shone relentlessly on those remaining on deck.

Singing was the main source of comfort for the crew, helping them to bear the rigours of life on board pearling vessels, compounded by long and painful separation from their families. There was a specific singing form attached to each particular task: hauling the anchor, manoeuvering the oars, extending the jib sail, raising the mainsail, and the actual pearl diving. *Al naham* was the the leading performer and coordinator of all the pearling songs, but his role was much more than that of mere virtuoso, he was the one who consoled and entertained the crew, attempting to lighten both their hearts and the arduous tasks ahead of them through the ecstasy of rhythm. Crew members repeated all the refrains whilst the *tabl* (a longitudinal drum with two skins), the tas (a tin bowl) and hand-clapping were used to accentuate the long, contemplative rhythmic cycles of these unique work songs. After an evening meal of fish and rice, complemented by dates and coffee, the crew attempted to settle down for the night on board the crowded deck, vainly hoping to catch a cooling breeze . It wasn't until early morning that the pile of oyster shells were opened to reveal the day's catch. This all took place under the watchful eye of the captain who took a record of any particularly big pearls that might be sold individually.

The Shaikh's arrival on the pearl banks towards the end of September gave the signal for the fleet to hoist sail and return to port together; the throb of drums and the waving of banners welcoming them home. Some *nukhada* may have already sold the season's catch to an intermediary who visited the pearl banks from time to time while the diving was in progress, some made direct contact with wholesale pearl merchants on arrival at port, whilst others had already contracted with a financier to sell the pearls at a prearranged price. The profits were then distributed in a set manner between the crew and the *nukhada* depending on the type of work each individual performed. Sometimes the *nukhada* owned the boat and had financed the trip, sometimes the money had been borrowed from an entrepreneur, in either case the expenses were paid back before the profits were divided. If the season had been a particularly bad one, the debt accumulated and could be a crippling burden on both captain and crew. Very strict rules and regulations governed both the sale of the catch and the payment of pearling debts.

Despite much nostalgic reflection on the stamina and endurance, courage and audacity of the divers who wrested riches from the sea-floor, and on the communal spirit encountered in pearling, there is no doubt that life was extremely hard and the rewards sometimes elusive for all who actively participated in the trade.

Traditional Sports

Some traditional sports grew out of the activities of the desert. Falconry for instance, for long an integral part of desert life, arose from the necessity to supplement a meagre diet of dates, milk and bread, eventually evolving into a major sport enjoyed by rich and poor alike. Hunting parties originally pursued their quarry on horseback or camel but powerful four wheel-drive vehicles are fast replacing traditional modes of transport. It is difficult to supplant the captivating image of a desert horseman:- arm outstretched to support a motionless bird of prey, man, bird and horse at one in dignity and bearing; with the lurching, fume-filled presence of the cross-country vehicle.

The Saker (*Falco cherruq*), and Peregrine (*Falco peregrinus*), are the two main species used for hunting, the former being the most popular since it is well suited to desert hawking. The female Saker, larger and more powerful, is utilised more frequently than the male. Sakers, brave, patient hunters with keen eyesight, are less fussy feeders and better able to cope with the stress and rigours of camp-life than the temperamental Peregrine whose brittle feathers tend to get broken. Female Peregrines are also preferred to the male for hunting purposes. The Lanner (*Falco biarmicus*), regarded as the beginner's hawk, was much favoured by the bedu but has lost a certain amount of its popularity.

Wild falcons are trapped during their autumn migration and trained in readiness for the hunting season, beginning in late November. Both haggards or adult birds and passagers (first year birds) are trained to hunt, the training period lasting up to three weeks. Some falcons are released in the spring when the hunting season has ended, for them to continue on to their breeding grounds. Many are kept through the long hot summer for a further season of sport, although illness is always a high risk during the extreme heat. Captive-breeding is a debatable solution to these problems: captive-bred birds often lack the instinct of the predator and therefore seldom match the performance of their wild counterparts. Over and above this difficulty, the young hatch in May or June facing into the

Fig. 19 Peregrine falcon (*U. Klinger*).

stresses of the summer months and, since females are preferred for hunting purposes, male hatchlings pose a problem—captive-bred birds cannot be returned easily easily to the wild, especially those that are totally foreign to the local habitat, as is the case of Australian Peregrines. Hybrid species, powerful and infertile, can also cause pressure on local species by competing aggressively for breeding areas.

Training begins with the falconer or handler getting to know his own bird, frequently giving it an individual name. A soft leather hood is laced over the head and gathered together at the back with the leather traces. Slowly but surely the falcon learns to accept food from the trainer's hand, gradually becoming used to both the touch and sound of his master. During this learning process the falcon perches on a mushroom-shaped wooden stand or on the trainer's hand which is protected from her sharp talons by a leather glove. The bird is held by a pair of jesses, usually braided cotton or nylon attached to a swivelled leash to allow the bird a certain freedom of movement.

Fig. 20 Saker falcon (*U. Klinger*).

Fig. 21 Hooded falcon (*old engraving*).

When the falcon has become accustomed to its handler, the hood is removed so that visual contact can be established, a bond of dependence being slowly forged as the bird accepts food. Still leashed, the falcon is allowed to jump from hand to perch, at which time she is considered to be tame and the next training session takes place in the desert, in the late afternoon or early evening. The hooded falcon remains perched on the hand of an assistant attached by string to the jesses or the end of the leash, while the trainer walks away for a short distance. Turning towards the falcon he swings a lure, usually dried houbara wings tied to a fresh piece of meat. On hearing the trainer call, the falcon is unhooded and immediately flies towards the familiar sound: the lure is lowered as the bird approaches so that she may bind to it just off the ground. As soon as the falcon swoops and brings the lure down, she is coaxed onto the trainer's hand for the expected reward of meat.

During initial training flights the lure gives way to live pigeons thrown into the air as the falcon is released. Gradually, the distance the falcon is encouraged to fly increases up to several hundred metres, such patience being well rewarded when the hunting season begins. The main prey are houbara, stone curlew (*kiriwan*) or hare (*arnab*).

Excitement and expectancy coupled with sheer enjoyment of the chase are the predominant emotions as the quarry is sighted and the hood removed from the falcon. The chase begins. The stout dumpy Houbara (*Chlamydotis undulata macqueenii*) are strong expert fliers, twisting and turning at great speed, but a well-trained falcon can bring down four or five bustards during a single hunting session. It is the chase itself that impresses and excites, the prey no longer required to fill the larder. Both Sakers and Peregrines kill in the air and on the ground. The Peregrine in pursuit of prey flies very fast to get above its victim and then makes a sudden headlong swoop at tremendous speed. Although the Peregrine is extremely fast over short distances, the Saker has more stamina.

As the shadowy evening light descends, the hunting party clean their booty and, while it is cooking over the open fire, sit and discuss in a timeless fashion the day's chase, each extolling the skill and courage of their best falcon, arguing their victories and defeats of the day: a disparaging remark about a bird can reflect on the honour of the falconer. The pleasure of the hunt is shared equally by ruler, minister, merchant or tribesman, all experiencing companionship through a sport that has been practised since time immemorial.

Camel-racing

We have heard how much the bedouin loved, respected and admired his camel, it is not so surprising then that they wished to pit their best beasts in informal camel-races. This ancient sport has been revived with so much enthusiasm in recent years that, over and above informal desert tracks, there are now several official ones. Certain slender, finely—formed breeds are more suitable for racing. Camel-training commences at about six months, entrance for official races beginning at about three years. A racing career, for the male at least, ends at about ten, but the female may race until she is at least twenty years. As in all racing animals, exercise, in the form of walking and galloping, and diet are particularly important: racing camels are usually fed on oats, bran, dates and cows milk but quantities are much reduced shortly before the race itself. The weight of the jockey is also crucial to the success of the venture, so very young boys, sometimes no more than six years of age, are used as mounts, riding either perched on the camel's hump or, in bedouin style, behind.

Fig. 22 The Arab horse (*old engraving*).

Horse-racing

The Arab horse is a legendary creature invoking images of grace stamina and strength, silken mane and tail streaming as it flies across the sand. The most ancient of all tamed horses, it has a distinctive appearance with a short back, small head showing a concave profile, large intelligent eyes and tail carried high. All Thoroughbred racehorses are descended from the three Arabian stallions, and, having been bred for centuries to win races, these are now the swiftest of all horses but cannot rival the smaller, pure-bred Arab for endurance. The Arab's fame has spread throughout the world where it is cherished and admired not only for its own qualities, but as a means to lighten and improve heavier breeds. This beautiful animal is no less cherished on its home territory. Bedouin have bred Arab horses with dedication over the centuries, particularly as a fast and agile mount for battle in regions where the terrain is not too soft. The Arab horse was always prized and especially welcomed as a gift between shaikhs and nowadays both pure Arabians and Thoroughbreds are reared and raced. Gambling, of course, is not acceptable, but generous prizes are awarded to those who participate.

TRADITIONAL FISHING

A traditional method of fishing, particularly associated with Kuwait and Bahrain, employs traps made from strung together reed poles, driven into the shore in the form of a long straight wall proceeding from the inshore end, perpendicular to the shore-line, towards low-tide mark. Towards its offshore end the wall enters an enclosure formed by a curved line of similar stakes. In some cases this has a smaller offshoot arising from it, accessed by an even narrower gap than that into the main enclosure. Fish, which move in across the shore as the tide rises to submerge the intertidal, seek to depart with the tide when it starts to fall. As they swim along the shore they meet the obstacle of the long wall of reed poles and therefore turn to swim out along the fence towards deeper water. In so doing they are eventually guided by the fence into the enclosure. Seeking to escape from this enclosure they encounter one small gap through which they swim into the even smaller enclosure which holds them until the tide has fallen completely and the Hadra trap's owner walks out across the shore to collect fish from within the trap (*P. Vine*).

Natural History

The territory we now call Kuwait has not always existed as it does today, as a primarily desertic region at the head of of the Arabian Gulf. If we could put back the clock and step into the past, say, for example around one hundred thousand years ago, in the middle of the interglacial period of the upper Pleistocene, it would probably have been necessary to employ a small raft, perhaps built by tieing bundles of reeds together, in order to traverse much of the shallow sea which then covered the region. Glacial periods on the other hand brought a lowering of sea-level and we may conjecture about how this area looked during the ancient glacial periods, for example between 30 and 50 million years ago or even during the last glacial period, ending as recently as eleven thousand years ago, when most of the Gulf was above sea-level, forming, presumably, a fertile, swampy area of reeds and grasslands through which the mighty Shatt Al Arab, fed by the Tigris and Euphrates, flowed into the sea as far south as the Straits of Hormuz.

For evidence of these tidal fluctuations and ancient maritime history we need only look at the sediments and fossils which were deposited then and are revealed today upon the surface of much of the Kuwaiti desert. In such a superficially uniform area, the least variation in landscape topography draws one's attention and the various ridges or depressions which pattern the area are indeed reflections of the underlying geology. In geological parlance, Kuwait is situated at the north-eastern border of the Arabian Shelf whose sedimentary sequence is primarily comprised of sandstone and carbonate formations. The oldest exposed rocks are along the Al-Ahmadi Ridge where Eocene limestone of the Damman Formation outcrops. Throughout the rest of Kuwait these older strata are overlain by a sequence of terrigenous sediments.

Strangely enough, it is the sea, and marine life, which has played the greatest influence in Kuwait's geology. It provided the raw materials which were later decomposed and gradually transformed into oil. Kuwait's oil resources lie, for the most part, in Middle Cretaceous sandstones while some oil is also held in Lower Cretaceous limestone. The classic oil bearing structures are doubly plunging anticlines and domes forming huge natural underground reservoirs where oil collects and remains stored until discovered and exploited by Man. It has been recently estimated (Schlumberger, 1986) that Burgan (containing the second largest onshore oilfield in the world) has recoverable reserves in excess of 87 billion barrels! Prize for the world's largest offshore oilfield is also claimed locally, by the Safania-Khafji field situated in the neutral zone between Saudi Arabia and southern Kuwait. This has proven reserves of 37 billion barrels.

Continental drift, the gradual movement of plates forming the earth's crust, also had a major role in shaping the geological picture since the Arabian Shield was once part of the African

Opposite, clockwise from top left: water run-off; dust storm; freshwater pool; sand dunes (*D. Clayton*).

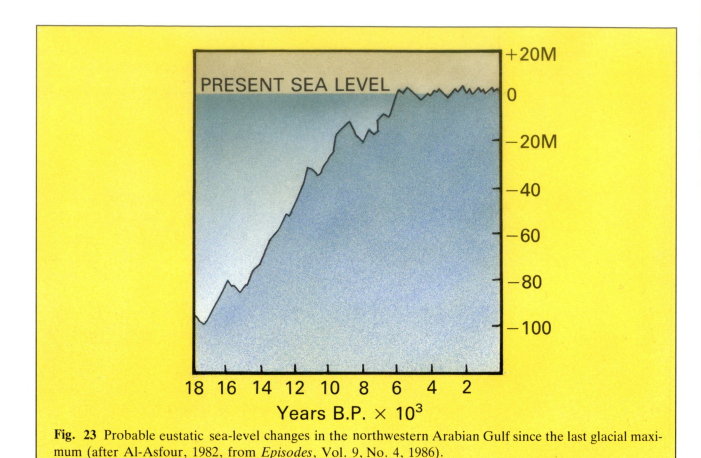

Fig. 23 Probable eustatic sea-level changes in the northwestern Arabian Gulf since the last glacial maximum (after Al-Asfour, 1982, from *Episodes*, Vol. 9, No. 4, 1986).

plate but its inexorable drift eastwards and away from Africa pushed the Arabian Shelf against the continental landmass of Asia, in this case the territory of Iran. As the pressure mounted, elements of Kuwait's sedimentary substrata buckled, thus forming the anticlines and deep underground pockets or massive natural storage tanks for that most valuable natural resource: oil.

One does not need to be a geologist to recognise that north and south Kuwait differ in their coastal structures. The northern region (studied by a number of workers in recent years ,notably: Al-Asfour, 1982; Al-Zamel, 1983; Reda, 1986; with Al-Zamel taking a close look at Bubiyan island) has experienced considerable sedimentary deposition of materials carried down by the Tigris—Euphrates—Karun multiple delta system and draining into the northern Gulf. An additional factor at play here has been the anti-clockwise tidal current pattern dominating water movements in this region, reworking sediments and transporting them into Kuwait Bay. In the southern region however the influence of terrigenous materials is much less apparent. Studies carried out by several workers (Saleh, 175, 1979; Picha and Saleh 1977) indicate that sediments are derived from marine organisms forming what

amounts to a "subtidal carbonate factory" (Ananda Gunatilaka, 1986). Despite Picha's claim (1978) that the coastal oolitic limestone ridges are of Pleistocene origin and Quaternary tectonic events have influenced the pattern of sedimentation; more recent work by geologists from the University of Kuwait tends to draw a different conclusion. They suggest that southern Kuwait's coastal zone is a classic carbonate platform or even-sloped (homoclinal) ramp.

Prior to the cataclysmic crack appearing in the Earth's crust, dividing Africa from Arabia, and eventually flooding to form the Red Sea, there were no physical barriers for the free movements of land animals from Africa to Arabia. It is therefore to be expected that Kuwait's wildlife shows signs of this African ancestry, while also displaying many aspects of its own uniquely Arabian evolution. After the last of the Pleistocene Ice Ages gradually receded in response to a slight warming of the earth, causing ice sheets to melt and sea-level to once more rise, Kuwait's savannah grasslands also diminished. As recently as five or six thousand years ago this area was once roamed by huge-herds of gazelle, together with ostriches, wild oxen and even lions, but the drying-out continued until the deserts we know today were created and where only specially adapted species are able to survive.

Sea-level changes along the north coast of Kuwait have formed the subject of an intensive study by Al-Asfour (1982) who examined the six coastal terraces along the coastline and utilised carbon 14 dating of shells found there. These indicate two periods of tidal flooding across today's landscape; ie between 42,850 and 23,300 years ago (give or take 600 years either way) and a second more recent period from 4,570 to 3,250 years ago (give or take 80 years). It is worth noting that as recently as 18,000 years ago, ie towards the end of the last glacial period, the climate was cooler, and sea level in the Gulf was about a hundred metres lower than it is today. This meant that virtually all the Gulf was above sea-level. As the climate warmed in subsequent years, sea level gradually rose until it reached today's level around six thousand years ago, since when it has shown relatively minor fluctuations, including a number of transgressions above today's level (see fig. 23). These latest sea level changes are of course of considerable interest to archaeologists in search of evidence of early occupation of the area by Man. Much of Kuwait's coastal province is so low-lying that it did not require a great rise in sea-level for the desert to become flooded. A recent study from southern Kuwait, based upon forty-five carbon-14 dated samples, suggests that the sea's transgression over the desert sands of Al-Khiran commenced around eight and a half thousand years ago and reached its peak four thousand years later, by which time the high tide mark was five kilometres inland from today's shoreline!

The Land

What of the vast desertic land which comprises the Kuwait of today? Khalaf and colleagues (1984) have summarised the surface deposits of Kuwait, producing what they describe as a "sedimentomorphic" map of Kuwait. Their study drew the conclusion that Quaternary deposits (ie those laid down during and since the last ice-age) may be classified into six major categories which are briefly reviewed below:– ie aeolian (wind-borne), residual, playa, desert plain, alluvial fan and coastal in origin. Wind-blown sand covers more than half of Kuwait's land area, primarily as sand-sheets, sand-dunes, sand-drifts and wadi fill sand. It is this enormous body of loose, transportable sand which fuels Kuwait's frequent sand and dust storms. The second category of sediment, ie residual deposits, occur mainly as a mixture of gravel, sand, silt and clay covering

Jal Az-Zor (*D. Clayton*).

Jal Az-Zor (*D. Clayton*).

much of northern Kuwait where they were deposited during Kuwait's pluvial period. The coarseness of gravel deposits here result from a long process of wind generated winnowing which has removed the fine particles. 'Playa' is a general term used to describe the lowest zone of desert depressions where rain-water may occasionally collect and fine sediments are deposited. Known locally as 'khobrat' or 'thamilat', they are most abundant in the north-western desert, especially in association with wadi drainage systems. The fourth category of sediment referred to by Khalaf and colleagues is that of the desert plain, also referred to as rainwash sediments which, in Kuwait, cover about twenty percent of the land area, especially abundant in Umm Al-aish basin; Al-Much and in some scattered areas of the western region. Desert plain sediments comprise a mixture of sand, silt, gravel, and clay formed by initial deposition across the desert plain and in shallow depressions by sheet floods, subsequent reworking by wind, and partial accretion due to precipitation of carbonate and gypsum. Slope deposits are limited in Kuwait, simply due to the scarcity of elevated ground and steep slopes. At the edge of the Jal Az-Zor escarpment accumulated rocks, boulders and detritus provide one of the few examples under this category. Similarly, alluvial fans require rainfall and they are therefore not particularly well represented in Kuwait. Some may be seen however along the Jal Az-Zor coastal plain, inter-layered with sabkha deposits.

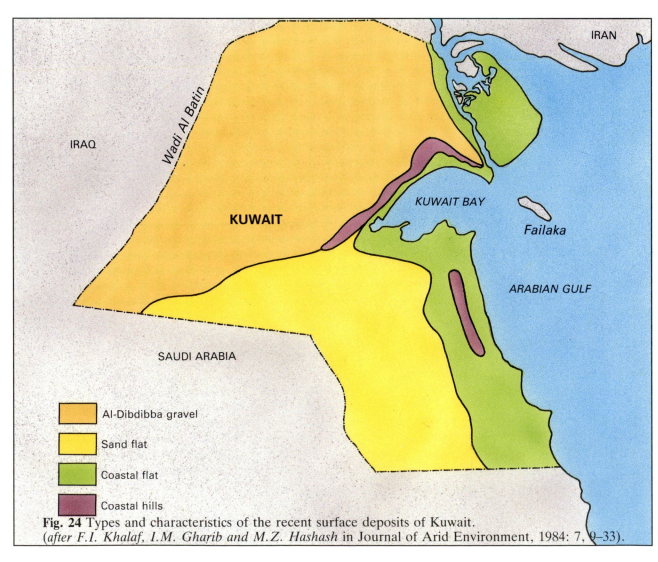

Fig. 24 Types and characteristics of the recent surface deposits of Kuwait.
(*after F.I. Khalaf, I.M. Gharib and M.Z. Hashash* in Journal of Arid Environment, 1984: 7, 9–33).

Finally, the last category of Kuwait's surface sediments recognised by Khalaf and his co-workers was that of coastal deposits. These fall under a number of categories, depending on local environmental conditions. Four main types occur; ie coastal plain deposits (known locally as 'gatch'), coastal dunes, sabkha deposits and beach/tidal flat deposits. Of these, special mention must be made of sabkhas which are low salt-flats bordering most of Kuwait's coastline, and may be categorised as of northern or southern variety.

One important aspect affecting this surface distribution of sediments is the fact that between 11,000 and 60,000 years ago the territory of Kuwait experienced a much wetter and more humid climate than that of today. Heavy rainfall, creating streams and rivers, washed gravel and other sediments across the landscape of northern Arabia. A measure of the powerful flow-rates which must have occurred in Wadi Al-Batin (towards Kuwait's western boundary with Iraq) is evidenced by the fact that this wadi is densely covered by Tertiary and Quaternary gravels formed from igneous and metamorphic rocks transported from a considerable distance away, into central Arabia. The gravels, whose origin is thus identified, and whose transportation depended upon heavy rainfall, were washed across the desert towards the coast, and eventually into the sea. As we have seen however, at this time sea-level was much lower than it is today and much of the northern Gulf was above tide level. Thus the gravels were washed into the basin which is today flooded by sea-water, and their existence on the present day sea-bed is further evidence of Kuwait's pluvial past.

Sedimentary in nature, but not entirely lacking in relief, Kuwait's landscape invites exploration, whether one is fascinated by desert scenery, cavernous limestone cliffs, or tracing the course of ancient waterways or wadis, there is much here to challenge the enquiring mind. The map on page 86 indicates the country's main topographical features, highlighting Wadi Al Batin which runs along the western border with Iraq draining into the fertile oases of Rawdatain. Other wadis are much less dramatic, generally consisting of a shallow, poorly defined, meandering depression, marking the course of an occasional flash-flood or of a much older river.

A recent study carried out by Kuwait's Institute for Scientific Research, has taken a close look at Kuwait's natural water resources. It was estimated that the total groundwater production

Coastal intertidal sand-flats along the southern coast of Kuwait (P.Vine).

A rocky outcrop in southern Kuwait (*P.Vine*).

capacity from existing well fields and from future potential areas is around 1.575 billion litres per day. Of this however, 99.6% is brackish. About half of pumped groundwater is used for cash crops while the rest is used for irrigating gardens. Unlike Bahrain, where the vast fossil water resources of the Eocene aquifer system underlying Arabia, arrive at the surface in naturally occuring springs, bringing relatively large quantities of freshwater to form fertile oases, Kuwait's aquifers remain deep underground and wildlife is dependent for the most part upon seasonal rainfall. It is interesting to note that isotope dating techniques have been employed recently to study paleowater or fossil-water resources trapped in

Arabia's rock strata. While most underground water held in the Arabian Shelf ranges from 8,000 to 32,000 years old, those held in the Damman formation, extending into southern Kuwait, have a maximum age of 40,000 years. These dates correspond closely with Arabia's moist pluvial period (ie 60,000 BP to 11,000 BP).

There are no such things as mountains in Kuwait, but the precipitous ridge of Jal Az Zor, extending for about eighty kilometres along the northern shore of Kuwait Bay, provides an impressive view of raised sandstone cliffs up to 145m in height, themselves the remnants of marine sediments. It is here, along the eroded edge of the Zor escarpment, that some of Kuwait's most impressive scenery is to be found. Beyond the crest of the ridge the escarpment slopes gradually towards the north until it forms a broad depression. To the south of Kuwait city there is another ridge running parallel with the shoreline, about eight kilometres inland. This Ahmadi ridge, rising to 137m. forms a natural dividing line between the Burgan plain and its attendent oil fields to the west and the coastal plain. Other less conspicuous ridges include Kura Al Maru and Al-Liyah which are aligned in a south-west to north-easterly line and whose low gravelly crests are hardly discernable above the surrounding countryside.

Other topographical features include depressions where rain-water may gather, and where the ground tends to be rich in clay and gypsum; low sand-dunes especially south of Kuwait city, between Ras Al-Ard and Al-Dbaiyyah, salt marshes or sabkhas such as those along the southwestern and northern shores of Kuwait Bay and along Khor Al-Sabiyah as well as at Bubiyan and Warba islands; together with a variety of marine habitats from mud-flats to coral-reefs.

Climate

Kuwait's climate is characterised by very hot, dry summers followed by cooler milder and unpredictably precipitate winters. Although the country is well known for its high summer temperatures, many visitors in winter time are surprised to find temperatures often falling below 10°C with a January mean of only 13°C (minimum recorded = minus 4.0°C), compared with a searing 37°C mean in July and August (max. around 45°C). Rain may start falling from late October and continues irregularly right through to May with inconsistent and erratic annual precipitation, from 28.1mm to 260.2.mm. (mean

Flash floods (*D. Clayton*).

annual = 115mm). On occasions a single thunderstorm may bring torrential hail and rain which falls so heavily that it damages crops.

Winds are primarily north-westerly and, to a lesser extent, south-easterly. They may be associated with sand and dust storms, known locally as "toze", which are of considerable interest to Kuwait since they can cause serious transport and communication difficulties. Khalaf et al (1984) summarised the situation as follows:–

"*In winter and spring, dust storms and rising sand are mostly associated with the strong south-easterly winds which are commonly developed during the passage of the Mediterranean depressions. In April (the season of Sarryat) thunder clouds usually develop in the afternoon and during the night and are occasionally accompanied by severe dust-storms, during which visibility may drop to zero. Spring dust-storms, which are generally generated by the south-easterly wind, are commonly of short period, severe and followed by rain.*

"*The dry and hot north-westerly winds ('Simoom') that prevail in the early summer, due to the effect of the monsoonal low pressure system, are mostly associated with dust-storms. During this season dust-storms are more frequent particularly in June and July.*"

Native Plants

Kuwait's wild plant-life is one of the country's unique natural heritages. Plants which are adapted to survive in the harsh conditions and extreme temperatures of Kuwait's desert deserve our highest respect. Unfortunately they have suffered under intense pressures caused by heavy grazing, collection for fuel, building development and through increased use of four-wheel drive vehicles criss-crossing the desert, destroying many plant habitats. These were primary conclusions of KISR's researcher, S.A.S.Omar, author of a report published by the prestigious research institute in 1985, entitled:– Baseline Information on Native Plants of Kuwait.

A sad by-product of Kuwait's rapid growth and socio-economic development, has been a deterioration in its natural ecosystems. Prior to the discovery of oil there were natural checks and balances in place helping to protect the environment, but now many of these have been removed. At the time of writing it must be added that the Kuwait Government has shown itself to be acutely aware of this problem. It is hoped that their efforts will bear real fruit in helping to protect some of what remains of the country's wild-plants.

Kuwait's flora have been studied by a number of amateur and professional botanists, leading to a series of publications including the report mentioned above and a more recent two-part book by Hazim Daoud (revised by Ali Al-Rawi) entitled 'Flora of Kuwait'. Earlier works are reviewed in these two publications and the interested reader is directed to these for relevant bibliographies. The ecological approach, typical of many recent botanical studies within the region, has led to the identification of a number of plant communities; ie. 1. *Salicornia herbacea*; 2. *Juncus arabicus*; 3. *Halocnemon strobilaceum*; 4. *Seidlitzia rosmarinus*; 5. *Nitraria retusa*; 6. *Tamarix passerionoides*; 7. *Zygophyllum coccineum*; 8. *Phragmites australis*; 9. *Aeluropes lagopoides*, 10. *Aeluripes littoralis*; 11. *Cressa cretica*; 12. *Halocnemon strobilaceum and Seidlitzia rosmarinus*; 13 *Seidlitzia rosmarinus, Zygophyllum coccineum, Traganum nudatum and Nitraria retuosa*. Omar's study also included a proposed vegetation map of Kuwait in which she classified four broad zones within the country, ie 1. *Haloxylon salicornicum*; 2. *Rhanterium epapposum*; 3. *Cyperus conglomeratus* and 4. Coastal sand dunes and salt marsh communities.

Four major plant ecosystems, reflecting the sedimentary pattern discussed above, may be recognised in Kuwait; ie those of:– (a) sand dunes, (b) salt- marshes and saline depressions, (c) the desert plain and (d) the desert plateau. Each of these are briefly described below.

Sand-dune ecosystem

Sand-dunes fringe the coast, south of Al-Dbaiyyah and there is also a system of dunes in the extreme north-east of Kuwait, at Umm Negga. The loose, poorly consolidated sand of such dunes is characteristically dominated by the

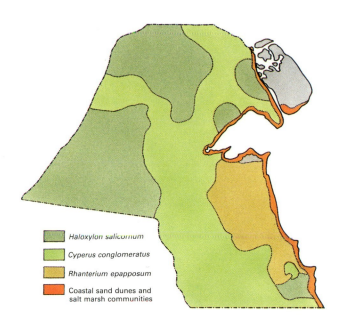

Fig. 25 Vegetation map of Kuwait (*after S.A.S. Omar* – KISR Technical Report AG–6)

Haloxylon salicornum

Cyperus conglomeratus

Rhanterium epapposum

Coastal sand dunes and salt marsh communities

perennial shrub 'Haram' or *Zygophyllum coccineum* together with 'Shinan' or *Seidlitzia rosmarinus* which is used as a medicine, together with *Atriplex leucoclada*; *Aellenia glauca*; *Nitraria retusa*; *Lycium shawii* and *Pennisetum divisum*. The root parasite *Cistanche tubulosa*, or desert hyacinth, may occur in association with either of the first two species listed above. In addition to the above dominant forms many other plants occur on sand dunes including the annual grass *Schismus barbatus*, the annual herb *Emex spinosus* whose red flowers may be seen in March-April; *Rumex vesicarius, Silene arabica, Astragalus annularis, Erodium laciniatum, Fagonia sp., Helianthemum lippii, Arnebia decumbens*; *Plantago sp.*, and *Senecio desfontainei*, and several others.

Salt-marshes and saline depressions

Salt-marshes are common along the shores of Kuwait, dominating much of the low coastal regions of Kuwait Bay and Khor Al-Sabiyah, but also occuring around Bubiyan and Warba islands. Plant-life here must be more than just salt-tolerant since this is very much a marine dominated environment affected by high tides and by the underlying sea-water table. Daoud describes a clearly defined zonation of plants associated with salt-marshes, dominated on the landward edge by *Halocnemum strobilaceum* and often by stands of the shrub *Tamarix aucherana*. Other plants found in salt marshes include *Juncus arabicus, Aeluropus lagopoides, Cressa*

Tamarix aucherana (*D. Clayton*).

Bassia eriophora (*D. Clayton*).

Salicornia herbacea (*D. Clayton*).

Erodiium laciniatum (*D. Clayton*).

cretica, Cornulaca leucacantha, Launaea mucronata, Cistanche tubulosa, Salsola baryosma, Seidlitzia rosmarinus, Aeluropus littoralis, Schismus barbatus, Asphodelus tenuifolius, Bassia eriophora, Salicornia herbacea, Salsola jordanicola, Schanginia aegyptiaca, Bienertia cycloptera, Mesembryanthemum nodiflorum, Paronychia arabica and *Spergularia diandra*. Saline depressions are basically similar with the centre frequently occupied by *Halocnemum strobilaceum*.

Kuwaiti Desert

The vast majority of Kuwait is occupied by desert and depending upon the type of soil, plant communities vary somewhat. Daoud, in his books on the flora of Kuwait, divides the desert firstly into the lower lying 'desert plain', and secondly into the more elevated 'desert plateau'. He further subdivides the former region into three vegetational zones which are briefly summarised below.

Desert plain: Cyperus steppe:
South and south-west of Kuwait city, where the substrate is formed by moderately deep coarse sand, the perennial pale green herb *Cyperus conglomeratus* is dominant over wide areas of the desert, together with scattered bushy clumps of the perennial desert grass, *Panicum turgidum*. In areas where the soil tends to be more gravelly, either naturally or as a result of disturbance, the annual bushy and succulent herb *Cornulaca leucacantha* may take over. Where the ground is harder, such as on the flanks of the Burgan hills, *Asthenerum forsskalli* and *Stipagrostis plumosa* may replace *Cyperus conglomeratus*. This *Cyperus* steppe plant community is also inhabited by many other plants among the most characteristic of which are *Panicum turgidum, Rostraria pumila, Cutandia memphitica, Schismus barbatus, Asphodelus tenuifolius, Dipcadi erythraeum, Silene villosa, Astragalus annularis, Erodium laciniatum, Fagonia bruguieri, Arnebia decumbens, Plantago spp.*, and *Launaea mucronata*. A full listing of other plants associated with this habitat is given by Daoud.

Desert plain: Rhanterium steppe:
This ecosystem is named after the small aromatic shrub known locally as 'Arfaj' the national plant of Kuwait, favoured by past populations of Rhim gazelle and today valued by camel and sheep herders as a nutritious forage species and a source of water in times of drought. The habitat

is found in the centre and north-east of Kuwait and is characterised by a soil layer of moderate depth associated with a calcareous or gypsiferous hard pan which may outcrop in places. *Rhanterium epapposum*, the dominant species, is found here in association with a variety of other species, notably *Convolvulus oxyphyllus*, *Moltkiopsis ciliata*, *Asthenatherum forsskalii*, *Stipagrostis plumosa*, *Cutandia memphitica* and *Schismus barbatus*. A more complete listing is provided by Daoud.

The term 'playa' refers to a low depression in the desert and a number of these exist on the desert plain. This habitat, generally a place where occasional rainfall gathers and where soil is very firmly compacted, is often occupied by dense stands of the attractive purple or blue flowered, iris-like plant, *Gynandriris sisyrinchium* together with *Plantago ovata*, *Plantago ciliata*, *Launaea capitata*, *Cynodon dactylon* and *Schismus barbatus*.

Ifloga spicata (D. Clayton).

Eruca sativa (D. Clayton).

Lycium shawii (D. Clayton).

Citrillus colocynthis (D. Clayton).

Desert plain: Haloxylon steppe:
Haloxylon salicornicum is a small shrub with woody stems, known locally as 'Remeth' and used by the bedu as both fuel and for its medical properties. *Haloxylon* steppe lands, where soil is generally very thin with regular outcrops of hardpan, are in the north, north-west and southern parts of Kuwait. In addition to stands of *Haloxylon*, there may be almost pure stands of the greyish, hairy herb *Chrozophora verbascifolia*. A full listing of plants occurring in this habitat is provided by Daoud.

Desert plateau:
In the extreme west of Kuwait the desert has a hard gravelly surface with very little vegetation. Here and there, pockets of sand accumulate and are colonised by *Haloxylon salicornicum*, thus providing a habitat for the associated root parasite and desert hyacinth, *Cistanche tubulosa*. Other plants occuring in soil pockets in these remote desert areas are listed by Daoud. In the far west of Kuwait, along the borders with Iraq, the Wadi Al-Batin is of interest to plant specialists for here one may encounter a variety of more water dependent species, including *Zilla spinosa*, *Stipa capensis*, and many others.

Native Fauna

In the introduction to a KISR report on the status of Kuwait's wildlife, Fozia Al-Sdirawi wrote, in 1986, "*. . . no efforts have been directed towards a comprehensive review of literature on the subject*". Her own report went some way towards putting together available data on Kuwait's wildlife and several other recent surveys have made important contributions towards our knowledge of the country's natural heritage. Included in the KISR report is a bibliography on the wildlife of Kuwait together with a more general one on Arabia. Those references which are of a general ecological or taxonomic interest are included within the bibliography to this chapter. A general review of Kuwait's natural history is provided by David Clayton and Keith Wells' book: Discovering Kuwait's Wildlife (Al-Marzouk Press, Kuwait, 1988) and the book published in 1983 by Kuwait Oil Company, entitled Kuwait's Natural History: An Introduction, edited by David Clayton and Charles Pilcher. Unfortunately the latter is not on general sale to the public while the more recent publication is only available within Kuwait.

Some of the many arachnids found in Kuwait, including (top right) a camel spider; (centre right) a scorpion; and (bottom right) a red velvet mite (*D. Clayton*).

Arachnids

Among the arachnids are many forms which are particularly well adapted for living in the desert environment. Scorpions, camel spiders, ticks, mites and the familiar spider all belong to this group. Several scorpions occur in Kuwait, including the black scorpion, *Androctonus crassicauda* and the less abundant yellow scorpion *Compsobuthus arabicus*. Camel spiders are nocturnal, remaining in their burrows during daytime but are attracted to a light source during darkness and are thus easily collected. Other forms found in Kuwait include wolf spiders (Lycosidae); harvest spiders; jumping spiders (Salticidae); crab spiders (Thomisidae); cobweb (Agelenidae) and orbweb (Argiopidae) spiders. A more comprehensive account is given by David Clayton in the KOC book on Kuwait's natural history.

Insects

Among Kuwait's diverse and interesting insect fauna, there is space here to mention only a few of the more prominent representatives. One of the most attractive groups is of course the butterflies which depend for their food upon flowers of native and cultivated plants. Several species undergo quite distinct migrations. For example, the painted lady (*Cynthia cardui*), the red admiral (*Vanessa atalanta*) and the clouded yellow (*Colias crocea*) each migrate north during spring and return southwards in autumn. Others, such as the long-tailed blue (*Lampides boeticus*) are irregular migrants. The best time to see butterflies in Kuwait is probably early spring, when many flowers are in bloom and migratory species have not yet departed. Apart from the species mentioned above, one may encounter a variety of forms, such as the Indian milkweed butterfly (*Dabaus chrysippus*), the elegant swallowtail (*Papilio demoleus*), the desert small blue (*Chilades galba*), the small blue (*Cupido minimus*), the Persian skipper (*Spialia phlomidis*), the desert white (*Pontia glauconome*), the green striped white (*Euchloe belemia*) and the small white (*Pieris rapae*). Damage to gardens and crops by caterpillars of moths and butterflies is a regular occurrence in Kuwait with the turnip moth (*Agrotis segetum*) and silvery moth (*Plusia gamma*) larvae frequently implicated. The real villain of the piece however with regard to crop damage is the desert locust (*Scistocerca gregaria*). Fortunately Kuwait is outside of the usual swarming range of this species, although it may be blown into the area from time to time. Within

Painted lady, *Vanessa cardui* (D. Clayton).

Mediterranean Pierrot, *Tarucus rosaceus* (D. Clayton).

the same order as locusts; crickets and grasshoppers are seasonally abundant in Kuwait, particularly in association with spring vegetation.

One of the most impressive insects to emerge in spring are the preying mantids (eg *Blepharopsis medica* and *Eremiaphila sp.*) of which at least two species occur in Kuwait. Dragonflies (eg *Selysiothemis nigra* and *Lindenia tetraphyla*), like butterflies, are migratory insects but they differ markedly in their feeding behaviour. Whilst butterflies extract nectar from flowers, dragonflies are predators capturing their insect prey in flight. Indeed, it is a feature of desert insects that they have adapted a wide range of strategies for food capture. Among the most fascinating of these is that of the ant-lion. The larvae of this species builds cone-shaped pits in the sand, remaining buried at the base, ready to pounce upon any

Arabian lobetail, *Lindenia tetraphylla* (*D. Clayton*).

prey which venture close enough for a strike. Observation of ant-lion larvae has shown that they have an uncanny ability to flick fragments of sand at the lip of their cone-shaped trap, causing more sand to dislodge, and any precariously balanced insect to fall into its waiting jaws.

This all too brief synopsis of Kuwait's insect fauna would be incomplete without mention of the Coleoptera or beetles which include such magnificently adapted forms as the legendary scarab beetles, including ancient Egypt's sacred beetle (*Scarabaeus sacer*) which lives on the dung of camels and goats and is present Kuwait. The beetle first turns the dung into a perfect ball, then rolls it along the ground to its underground chamber where it seals itself in until it has consumed the spherical food capsule. Other beetles commonly seen in Kuwait include the blister beetle (*Mylabris sp*); ground beetles (eg. *Graphipterus minutus*, *Calosoma imbricatum* and *Thermophilum duodecimguttatum*); darkling beetles (eg. *Erodius octocostatus*, *Paraplatyope arabica*, *Pimelia arabica*, *Ocnera philistina*, *Ocnera hispida* and *Ademsia cancellata*); tiger beetles (eg. *Cicindela nemoralis*); and ladybirds (eg. *Coccinella septempunctata*). Readers wishing to learn more about the behaviour and ecology of Kuwait's insect fauna are referred to David Clayton's excellent chapter in the KOC book on Kuwait's natural history and to his more recent publication 'Discovering Kuwait's Wildlife'.

Fig. 26 Dung Beetle, *Scarabeus sacer* (*U. Klinger*).

Darkling beetle, *Adesmia cancellata* (*D. Clayton*).

94

Jewel beetle (*D. Clayton*).

Scolud wasp (*D. Clayton*).

Red potto wasp (*D. Clayton*).

Mesosteria puncticollis (*D. Clayton*).

Termites (*D. Clayton*).

Desert cockroaches (*D. Clayton*).

Earwig (*D. Clayton*).

Reptiles

Kuwait is quite richly endowed with reptilian species, many of which are perfectly adapted to live in the desert environment. Largely as a result of the difficulties associated with making studies of them in the wild, our knowledge of the status of different species is extremely poor. It is to be hoped that this situation will improve as more and more attention is focussed upon the country's wildlife. At present our main knowledge centres upon which species are found in Kuwait and this information is based upon scientific collections and preserved specimens stored in various museums around the world. Table I lists the thirty-eight recorded reptiles.

The Reptilian fauna of Kuwait is similar to that of Northern Arabia in general, comprising a variety of snakes together with skinks, geckos and other lizards, including the large spiny-tailed lizard or dhubb, and the even larger monitor lizard together with marine turtles. Whilst many types of wildlife find survival in these hot arid conditions difficult or impossible, reptiles may actually flourish in desert environments where almost the only commodities which are not in short supply are the sun's burning heat and sand. Since reptiles (unlike mammals) do not use food derived energy for maintenance of their body temperature, but instead bask in the sun to warm-up or hide in the shade to cool down, they require relatively little food and are able to survive for long periods without eating.

Lizards are seen wherever one goes, around the house, in the garden, in cultivated areas, in wadis, or across the desert, often scurrying for cover among small clumps of vegetation. The largest of these, the grey monitor (*Varanus griseus* or 'warrel') reaching up to 140 cms in length is a voracious predator of smaller lizards and rodents. A more frequently sighted large lizard is the dhubb (*Uromastyx microlepis*), primarily a herbivore. These agile agamids have a prehistoric appearance and an impressive ability to alter their colour; something they may do

Desert monitor (*D. Clayton*).

when alarmed, or more naturally over the course of the day when their light-sensitive skin can change from a dark grey to brilliant yellow. Apart from the dhubb, there are several other agama lizards including the Arabian toad-headed agama (*Phrynocephalus maculatus*) which lives on soft sand, and the Egyptian agama. The blue-throated agamid (*Agama blandfordi*) is easily recognised by its bright blue gular pouch which is displayed during courtship and as a defensive signal. Sand skinks such as the Arabian sand skink are also found here, displaying numerous adaptations to their desert environment, including fringed scales on toes which prevent them from sinking into soft sand when they run. Among the true desert lizards, Lacertids are well represented with five species present, each occupying a separate ecological niche (eg. short-nosed desert lizard, *Eremias brevirostris*; Bosc's sand lizard, *Acanthodactylus boskianus*; the fringe-toed sand lizard *Acanthodactylus schmidti*; *Acanthodactylus scutellatus* and *A. opheodurus*.

In contrast to most of the above species which are active during daytime, geckos, as their large eyes and soft skin suggest, are nocturnal creatures. House geckos, belonging to the genus *Hemidactylus* (eg. *Hemidactylus flaviviridis*) are extremely appealing and fascinating lizards, welcome in many homes throughout Kuwait.

Blue-throated agamid (*D. Clayton*).

Skink (*D. Clayton*).

Snakes are not seen often in the wild in Kuwait, partly because of the relatively sparse population and partly due to their cryptic behaviour. Most of the venomous species are vipers, with two species present; ie Burton's carpet viper (*Echis coloratus*) and the sand viper (*Cerastes cerastes*). Burton's carpet viper tends to inhabit moist wadis, irrigated plantations and natural drainage depressions such as Jahra pool, Umm Al Aish and among the reed beds of Abdali where it feeds on toads (*Bufo viridis*). The sand viper on the other hand lives in dry sandy areas,

Table I: Reptilian fauna of Kuwait
(after Al-Sdirawi, KISR report, 1986

Common name	Scientific name	Status
Persian gecko	*Hemidactylus persicus*	?
Yellow-bellied house gecko	*Hemidactylus flaviviridis*	?
Keeled rock gecko	*Gymnodactylus scaber*	?
–	*Stenodactylus doriae*	?
Sleven's gecko	*Stenodactylus sleveni*	?
Stone gecko	*Bunopus tuberculatus*	?
Blandford's gecko	*Bunopus blandfordii*	?
Blue-throated agamid	*Agama blandfordi*	?
Persian agamid	*Agama persica*	?
Toad-headed agama	*Phrynocephalus maculatus*	?
–	*Uromastix aegyptius*	?
Spiny tailed lizard (Dhubb)	*Uromastix microlepis*	?
Desert monitor (Warrel)	*Varanus griseus*	?
Arabian worm lizard	*Diplometopon zarudnyi*	?
Fringe-toed sand lizard	*Acanthodactylus schmidti*	?
Lacertid lizard	*Acanthodactylus opheodurus*	?
Bosc's sand lizard	*Acanthodactylus bosktanus*	?
–	*Acanthodactylus scutellatus*	?
Short-nosed lizard	*Eremias brevirostris*	?
–	*Ablepharus pannonicus*	?
–	*Scincus mitranus*	?
Skink	*Scincus scincus*	?
Flowerpot blind snake	*Typhlos braminus*	?
–	*Leptotyphlops macrorhynchus*	?
Sand boa	*Eryx jayakari*	?
Horned viper	*Cerastes cerastes*	?
Burton's carpet viper	*Echis colorata*	?
Greyish green banded sea snake	*Hydrophis lapemoides*	?
Blue-banded sea snake	*Hydrophis cyanocinctus*	?
Black desert cobra	*Walterinnesia aegyptia*	rare
Arabian cobra	*Naja haje arabica*	?
Arabian rear-fanged snake	*Malpolon moilensis*	?
Hissing sand snake	*Psammophis schokari*	?
Rat snake	*Coluber ventromaculatus*	?
–	*Lytorhynchus gaddi*	?
Leaf-nosed snake	*Lytorhynchus diadema*	?
Green turtle	*Chelonia mydas*	breeds

Top and centre: dhubb, *Uromastyx microlepis*; bottom: juvenile dhubb impaled by shrike (*D. Clayton*).

Lizard, *Acanthodactylus schmidti* (*D. Clayton*).

Sand lizard, *Acanthodactylus ephoedurus* (*D. Clayton*).

Gecko, *Stenodactylus* sp. (*D. Clayton*).

disguising itself by lying under the sand, and feeding on rodents and lizards which it disables with a most efficient delivery of venom through what amount to hypodermic fangs. Jayakari's sand boa (*Eryx jayakari*) also lives in loose dry sand, and is a nocturnal species depending upon its ability to squeeze its prey rather than poison it. Mention should also be made of that strange creature, part snake, part lizard, an Amphisbaenian or Arabian worm lizard (*Diplometopon zarudnyi*): a limbless, cylindrically bodied reptile whose body is marked by concentric grooves. It spends most of its time underground, feeding on insects. The false cobra or Arabian rear-fanged snake, *Malpolon moilensis* lives in stony desert

country and has a habit of extending its neck when alarmed. The sand snake, *Psammophis schokari*, has a thin, striped body, pale ventrally and brown and yellow along its flanks. It feeds on birds and lizards, frequently climbing trees in pursuit of its prey.

Sea-snakes are also common in the Gulf waters bordering Kuwait, where the blue-banded *Hydrophis cyanocinctus* and Arabian Gulf sea-snake *H. lapemoides*, prowl the sea-bed in search of food, usually in the shape of an unwary fish. The pelagic yellow-bellied sea-snake *Pelamis platurus*, is also recorded but seems to be much less common than *Hydrophis* species. Despite their awesome reputation, sea-snakes are not generally aggressive.

The most deadly of Kuwait's snakes is the black desert cobra (*Walterinnesia aegyptia*) which, while being highly venomous and dangerous to Man is also exceedingly rare. It is a nocturnal hunting predator which partially explains the scarcity of recorded sightings of this species. As a general rule, any black snake found in Arabia is deadly poisonous and should be avoided.

The other marine reptiles present in coastal waters are turtles, including the green turtle (*Chelonia mydas*) which nests on the beaches of islands in the Gulf.

Sand boa and lizard (*D. Clayton*).

Legless lizard (*D. Clayton*).

Black desert cobra (*D. Clayton*).

Amphibians

Only one amphibian exists in Kuwait, ie the green toad: *Bufo viridis*. This may be seen wherever there is standing water of a fairly permanent nature, where tadpoles may hatch and grow. They hibernate in winter and are rarely observed during this period which lasts from September until April.

Mammals

The Arabian desert, despite its apparently inhospitable conditions for wildlife, is inhabited by a remarkable variety of mammals. In his excellent study on this subject David Harrison lists fifty species known to occur in the Gulf region and most of these have been recorded in Kuwait. These desert mammals are of particular interest to biologists since they show fascinating adaptations enabling them to survive on very little water and to contend with temperature extremes.

No review of our knowledge of Kuwait's mammals would be complete without reference to Dr Harrison's three volumes of a work entitled 'The Mammals of Arabia' (1964, 1968 and 1972; Publishers:– Earnest Benn Ltd., London). These have become standard references for scientists interested in Kuwait's mammals. Much of Harrison's work was based, as a matter of necessity, upon preserved material held in various museums. There was, and indeed still is, a relative dearth of knowledge concerning the ecology, distribution and behaviour of the country's natural mammalian population. Unfortunately, not all of the species listed by Harrison as being recorded in Kuwait are still to be found there. In some cases these animals are extremely difficult to observe and the absence of records on a particular species may not actually signify its complete disappearance from the landscape, but it does provide a measure of its relative scarcity. Examples of such apparently disappeared species include the sand cat (*Felix margarita*), live individuals of which are still known to occur in Saudi Arabia, although the last reported sighting in Kuwait seems to have been in 1967. The plight of the fennec fox (*Fennecus zerda*) may be even more disastrous since the last known sighting of this beautiful animal was as far back as 1925!

Kuwait's existing mammalian fauna is listed in table II on page 100 which is adapted from Al-Sdirawi's report to KISR. In terms of our knowledge of this delicate and sensitive wildlife, the column indicating status of each species makes particularly poignant reading since only three out of twenty-seven species are considered to be under no threat. Predictably these are the house rat, brown rat and house mouse! Local knowledge of Kuwait's mammalian fauna has been reviewed by David Clayton in 'Kuwait's Natural History: An Introduction' published by Kuwait Oil Company and in 'Discovering Kuwait's Wildlife' published by Fahad Al-Marzouk of Kuwait.

Among the order Insectivora, two families are present in Kuwait, shrews and hedgehogs. The Indian house shrew occurs in association with Man, frequently in port areas, and has been introduced by sea, originally from India. Despite its superficial rat-like appearance it can be recognised as a shrew by its long pointed snout and minute eyes. It is a nocturnal mammal which may sometimes be seen around rubbish tips. Hedgehogs are perhaps more endearing to the general public, and two species occur locally, i.e. the Ethiopian hedgehog (*Paraechinus aethiopicus*) which has a characteristic dark snout and smart white band on its forehead; and the smaller, black-snouted long-eared hedgehog (*Hemiechinus auritus*). Both species appear to be virtually water-independent, living in extremely arid areas of the desert or escarpments. More

Table II Mammals of Kuwait and their status
(after F.A.Al-Sidrawi, KISR 1986)

Common Name	Scientific Name	Status
Long-eared hedgehog	*Hemiechinus auritus*	?
Ethiopean hedgehog	*Paraechinus aethiopicus*	?
Naked-bellied tomb bat	*Tophozous nudiventris*	?
Trident leaf-nosed bat	*Asellia tridens*	?
Rhul's pipistrelle bat	*Pipistrellus kuhli*	?
Wolf	*Canis lupus*	endangered
Common red fox	*Vulpes vuples*	endangered
Fennec fox	*Fennecus zerda*	rare
Honey badger	*Mellivora capensis*	endangered
Indian grey mongoose	*Herpestes edwardsi*	endangered
Wild cat	*Felis silvestris*	endangered
Caracal lynx	*Caracal caracal*	locally extinct
Arabian oryx	*Oryx leucoryx*	extinct in wild
Dorcas gazella, afri	*Gazella dorcas*	endangered
Goitered gazella, rhim	*Gazella subgutturosa*	endangered
Cape hare	*Lepus capensis*	endangered
Euphrates jerboa	*Allaclaga euphratica*	?
Lesser jerboa	*Jaculus jaculus*	?
House rat	*Rattus rattus*	too many
Brown rat	*Rattus norvegicus*	too many
House mouse	*Mus musculus*	too many
Baluchistan gerbil	*Gerbillus nanus*	surviving
Wagner's gerbil	*Gerbillus dasyurus*	surviving
Cheeseman's gerbil	*Gerbillus cheesmani*	surviving
Indian gerbil	*Tatera indica*	?
Libyan jird	*Meriones libycus*	surviving
Sundevall's jird	*Meriones crassus*	surviving

Fennec foxes and jerboas (*old engraving*).

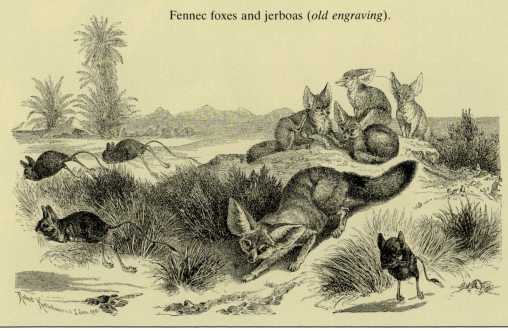

recently, they have appeared in increasing numbers in local gardens and parks, often hiding under rocks or in hollows. Their heat control mechanisms are quite unusual in that the Ethiopian hedgehog's long legs are regarded as important contributors towards cooling, permitting cold night air to ventilate the underside of its body as it pursues its nocturnal activities. Large ears are used in several mammals as a cooling device and this is true of the long-eared hedgehog which is a strictly nocturnal species. Hedgehogs are unfortunately often collected from the wild and kept as pets, usually in the mistaken belief that they will be "better off". Such pets not infrequently give birth to young and these have soft spines, feeding from their mothers for a few weeks before the spines harden and they are able fend for themselves.

There are three species of bats found in Kuwait, the naked-bellied tomb bat (*Taphozous nudiventris*), the trident leaf-nosed bat (*Asellia tridens*) and Khul's pipistrelle (*Pipistrellus kuhli*). The naked bellied tomb bat is a well-built species easily recognisable by its tail which protrudes from the membrane between the two back legs. As its name suggests, it lives in colonies in darkened rock crevices or among old buildings, especially along the banks of the Tigris and

Fig. 28 Head of leaf-nosed bat (*U. Klinger*).

Euphrates rivers. They migrate seasonally and some stray into Kuwait. The trident leaf-nosed bat (*Asellia tridens*) is probably one of the most widespread bats in Kuwait and has relatively long ears, together with a characteristic nose-flap over the muzzle. It is a colonial species occurring in underground tunnels or caverns, and in ruins of old buildings. Harrison aptly describes their flight as "butterfly-like". Like the naked bellied tomb bat, it is primarily a stray migrant, frequently arriving in Kuwait (presumably from Iraq) in association with weather disturbances such as dust storms. Kuhl's pipistrelle (*Pipistrellus kuhli*), on the other hand is more akin to a resident species and the smallest of the locally occurring bats. It is especially common around house gardens and in parks, roosting in cracks and crevices of buildings and is a frequent sight in the evening.

Among the order Carnivora, thirteen species occur in the Gulf region as a whole, with the majority having been recorded albeit in small numbers, from Kuwait. The desert wolf (*Canis lupus*) was once the scourge of bedu herdsmen but is now believed to be on the edge of local extinction. H.R.P. Dickson describes in his classic work: 'The Arab of the Desert' how two wolves would attack his friend's flock. One distracting the guard dog whilst the other moved in for the kill. After a successful attack the wolves switched roles so that each of them could kill its own prey. The last definite sightings of wolves in Kuwait seems to have been about thirty years ago when they were seen along the northern shores of Kuwait Bay. By far the most widespread carnivore in the region is the Arabian form of the common red fox (*Vulpes vulpes*). Hiding in holes and burrows during daytime, it emerges at night to feed on a very wide variety of food items ranging from small birds, lizards or mammals to fruit and even insects. The smallest of the desert foxes is the dainty fennec fox (*Fennecus*

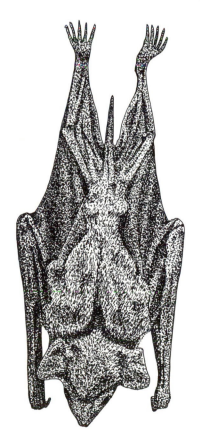

Fig. 27 Naked-bellied tomb bat (*U. Klinger*).

zerda) which has pale coloured fur, large ears and a bushy tail with a prominent black tip. As we have mentioned above, this is a rare species in Kuwait, last recorded in 1925, and perhaps now locally extinct. Wild cats, belonging to a distinct species, *Felis silvestris*, occur locally with the subspecies: *Felis sylvestris iraki* reported from the Kuwait desert, but now very rarely seen. They are nocturnal predators, hunting small birds, rodents and reptiles.

Unfortunately all wild-cats in Kuwait have suffered from hunting and disappearance of natural habitats and may now be approaching local extinction. In addition to the species mentioned above, this applies also to the caracal lynx (*Caracal caracal*), a medium sized cat recognisable from its reddish/sandy colour and the absence of any body pattern. It lives around the base of mountains and on dry steppe lands where it is well camouflaged, a fact which, together with its reclusive behaviour, renders it very difficult to see in the wild. It is a powerful and impressive hunter, able to bring down a bird in flight, and unfortunately implicated in attacks on domestic livestock, inevitably leading to it being hunted and virtually wiped out from the region. A young female caracal lynx was caught in Kuwait in 1939, but none have been reported since then.

Gazelle (*D. Clayton*).

Kuwait's wild ungulates include (or included) the, Arabian oryx (*Oryx leucoryx*), goitered gazelle or rhim (*Gazella subgutturosa*), and Dorcas gazelle (*Gazella dorcas*). One has only to read Dickson's accounts of pre-oil Kuwait to realise how abundant the country's gazelle population once was. Not surprisingly his stories are of hunting parties, stalking gazelle on camels, and then sending salukis after them. "*It is a curious fact*", he writes, "*that well-trained salukis will rarely lose a gazelle once it is sighted. They gallop after it for miles until their quarry, either from terror or exhaustion, collapses and lies down. The rest is then easy, for the hounds seize and hold it till the hunter comes up on his speeding camel, dismounts and cuts its throat. On most occasions, however, the gazelle gives its pursuers a run for their money before it is caught and killed.*" In the light of our knowledge today of what has happened to the country's gazelle population such accounts have a goriness and sadness which its author or his described huntsmen could hardly have predicted. It was not such traditional hunting, however cruel it may seem, which sounded the death knell for wild gazelle, but the advent of four wheel drive vehicles and machine gun toting huntsmen who brought about the almost total demise of these magnificent animals.

The Arabian oryx was once abundant in the wild in the Kuwait but today it can only be seen in captivity. Captive herds in the Gulf region are producing sufficient animals to permit cautious re-introduction of them into the wild. This has already taken place in Oman where results are extremely promising. The rhim or goitered gazelle is the typical sand desert gazelle of Arabia, where it is found feeding on desert succulents, its pale colour blending perfectly with the surroundings. The present century has brought the local population down to extinction and the only specimens one may now find in Kuwait are in the zoo.

The cape hare, *Lepus capensis*, is an adaptable small mammal occurring in many of the Gulf countries, and showing a fair degree of local variation. It often hides in shallow scooped holes built in the sides of sand-hills, and is very difficult to see. A desert adapted species, it can survive without the supply of free drinking water, maintaining its water balance by eating green vegetation. Unfortunately it is considered an endangered species in Kuwait.

An especially appealing small mammal, widely distributed in Kuwait, and probably the commo-

Gerbil, *Gerbillus cheesmani* (D. Clayton).

nest of the desert's rodents, is the lesser jerboa (*Jaculus jaculus*) which carries a distinctive black and white tipped tail. It is extremely well adapted for living in desert conditions, hibernating during intense heat, remaining in their burrows and surviving on stored food reserves. Captive jerboas do not require fresh water, but obtain their moisture from vegetable food. A study carried out by the Zoology Department of Kuwait University in desert south of Burgan oilfield indicated that the jerboa population went through quite large fluctuations, apparently more abundant in spring and early summer than in winter; a fact possibly explained by the degree of predation and vulnerability of jerboas to attack (a phenomenon which David Clayton refers to as "meals on heels"!). The Euphrates jerboa (*Allactaga euphratica*), a somewhat larger species, is also present in Kuwait although it is not as common as the lesser jerboa.

Sundevall's jird (*Meriones crassus*) is another small, nocturnal rodent, well adapted to desert life and not uncommon in Kuwait, mainly in sandy terrain and frequently in small colonies burrowing under thorn bushes. Its relative, the Libyan jird (*Meriones libycus*) is, as its name suggests, a north African species whose distribution extends as far as Kuwait and to most of the Gulf countries. Look out for it in association with stands of the donkey melon or 'Eshsherry' (*Citrullus colocynthis*) whose bitter fruit it eats.

There are three species of gerbil found in Kuwait, the Baluchistan gerbil (*Gerbillus nanus*) living in saline flat sandy areas, Wagner's gerbil (*Gerbillus dasyurus*) which prefers rocky habitats and the hairy-foot gerbil (*Gerbillus cheesmani*) which lives in loose sandy areas. Jirds and gerbils tend to occupy complimentary niches, with the former consuming leaves, stems and roots of wild- plants while the latter tend to concentrate on seeds of the same plants.

Birds

Over 280 species of bird have been recorded in Kuwait with the majority of species occurring as migratory visitors. The country's avian fauna has been studied, over the years, by numerous ornithologists either operating alone or else under the aegis of a local study group such as the Ahmadi Natural History and Field Studies Group. This group, which was particularly active in the 1970's, computerised records from a variety of sources dating back to as long ago as 1922. A brief synopsis of this accumulated knowledge is provided in the bird chapter written by Bill Stuart and Charles Pilcher in 'Kuwait's Natural

One of the best bird watching sites in Kuwait is at Jahra pool, surrounded by reeds, a regular wintering site for many migratory species. The site is in need of complete protection as a wildlife reserve (*P. Vine*).

History: An Introduction' (Kuwait Oil Company, 1983). In addition, Michael Jennings, whose work on a bird atlas of Arabia is well known to many naturalists interested in this region, has reviewed information on Kuwait's birds, in a book entitled: 'Birds of the Arabian Gulf' (George Allen & Unwin, 1981). Kuwait offers a wide range of interesting bird-life to those who take the trouble to bird-watch. The annual migrations of raptors such as steppe eagles and buzzard are impressive sights and Kuwait is on a flight path for numerous birds heading south from Europe and Asia during winter, or moving north again in springtime. Indeed, many of the temperate western palaearctic species rest here for the winter months. Sea birds are also present in large numbers with Bubiyan island reported as a breeding location for a number of species including white pelican, spoonbill, grey heron, purple heron, greater flamingo and crab plover.

Kuwait's bird watching site par-excellence is probably Jahra pools and the surrounding tamarisk plantation area. Here the constant supply of ground water creates a focal point for many birds

and at least a hundred and fifty species have been recorded. In the far west of Kuwait, alongside the border with Iraq, the Wadi Al-Batin forms a habitat for several interesting species including the thick-billed lark; eagle owl; cream-coloured courser and several larks.

Bird watching in Kuwait need not be a particularly arduous pursuit. In winter for example, some of the best bird locations are along the inter-tidal shoreline of Kuwait Bay. Here one may see quite large numbers of greater flamingoes (*Phoenicopterus ruber*), redshank (*Tringa totanus*), dunlin (*Calidris alpina*), curlew (*Numenius arquata*), bar-tailed godwit (*Limosa limosa*), greater sandplovers (*Charadrius leschenaultii*), lesser sand plovers (*Charadrius mongolus*) and ring plovers (*Charadrius hiaticula*). The unmistakably avocet (*Recurvirostrata avosetta*), with its characteristically upturned beak and black and white plumage, may also be seen here, and one may also be fortunate enough to catch sight of crab plovers (*Dromas ardeola*) and perhaps a few spoonbills (*Platalea leucorodia*). At freshwater pools such as Jahra one may observe snipe (*Gallinago gallinago*), jack snipe (*Lymnocryptes minimus*), little stint (*Calidris minuta*) together with ring and kentish plovers. Also found along the shore are several species of gulls including the black-headed (*Larus ridibundus*), herring (*Larus argentatus*), lesser black-backed

Table III. List of Breeding Birds of Kuwait

(after F.Al-Sdirawi, KISR, 1986 with additional data incorporated from:- Stuart and Pilcher in Clayton and Pilcher 1983).)

Common Name	Scientific name	Status
White pelican	*Pelecanus crispus*	FRM*
Dalmattian pelican	*Pelecanus onocrotatus*	FRI*
Grey heron	*Ardea cinerea*	FRI*
Purple heron	*Ardea purpurea*	FRI*
Reef heron	*Egretta gularis*	FRI*
Spoonbill	*Platalea leucorodia*	FRI*
Greater flamingo+	*Phoenicopterus ruber*	FRI***
Crab plover	*Dromas ardeola*	PB
Kentish plover	*Charadrius alexandrinus*	PB
Houbara bustard	*Chlamydotis undulata*	FRI***
Slender billed gull	*Larus genei*	FRI*
Gull billed tern	*Gelochelidon nilotica*	FRI*
Caspian tern	*Sterna caspia*	FRI*
Lesser crested tern	*Sterna bengalensis*	FRI*
White-cheeked tern++	*Sterna repressa*	FRI*
Bridled tern	*Sterna anaethetus*	FRI*
Moorhen	*Gallinula chloropus*	PB
Crested lark	*Galerida cristata*	PB
Desert lark	*Ammomanes deserti*	PB
Hoopoe lark	*Alaemon alaudipes*	PB
Bimaculated lark	*Melanocorypha bimaculata*	PB
Black-crowned finch lark	*Eremopoterix nigriceps*	PB
Temminck's horned lark	*Eremophila bilopha*	PB
House sparrow	*Passer domesticus*	PB
Eagle owl	*Bubo bubo*	PB
Little owl	*Athene noctua*	?PB
Brown-necked raven	*Corvus ruficollis*	PB
Cream coloured courser	*Cursorius cursor*	PB
Collared dove	*Streptopelia decaocto*	PB

Moorhen

Crab plover

Little owl
(*Illustration by U. Klinger*)

Note on status codes:- FRM = Past records of this species breeding on Kuwait mainland.
FRI = Past records of this species breeding on islands off coast of Kuwait.
PB = Current records exist of this species breeding in Kuwait.
* = present breeding status of this species is not known and until new corroborative evidence is presented it would be safer to assume that no breeding by this species occurs in Kuwait at present.
*** = it is extremely unlikely that this species is still breeding in Kuwait.
+ = Greater flamingo eggs were first collected from Bubiyan island in May 1878 and most recently at Khor Milah, Bubiyan island, in April 1982. In all, the British Museum of Natural History in London has seven egg records of this species from Kuwait.
++ = The most recent breeding record of the white-cheeked tern, *Sterna repressa* is in 1983, when an egg of this species was collected at Khor Abdullah.

(*Larus fuscus*), slender billed (*Larus genei*) and the occasional great black-headed (*Larus ichthyaetus*). Two species of cormorants may be observed in Kuwait, with the familiar form of the common cormorant (*Phalacrocorax carbo*) gracing many of the hadra fish-traps in winter while it flies north in spring to be replaced, along the Kuwait's southern coastline, by a few socotra cormorants flying in from the southern Gulf where large breeding colonies exist. A visit to Kuwait's shoreline in winter can be a very rewarding experience in terms of observing birdlife, and two elegant species which the ornithologist is almost certain to come across are the reef heron (*Egretta gularis schistacea*) and grey heron (*Ardea cinerea*) which stalk the shallows in search of small fish.

Bee eater (*D. Clayton*).

Among the water-birds, moorhen (*Gallinula chloropus*), coot (*Fulica atra*), little crake (*Porzana porzana*), water rail (*Rallus aquaticus*), great crested grebe (*Podiceps cristatus*), black-necked grebe (*Podiceps nigricollis*) and the little grebe (*Tachybaptus ruficollis*) may occur. Around the edge of such pools visited during winter months, one is likely to observe the white wagtail (*Motacilla alba alba*) and the water pipit (*Anthus spinoletta spinoletta*).

During winter months Kuwait's desert and semi-desert areas are home for a variety of larks such as the lesser short-toed (*Calendrella cinerea*), crested (*Galerida cristata*), desert (*Ammomanes deserti*), temminck's horned (*Eremophila bilopha*) and the hoopoe lark (*Alaemon alaudipes*). Among that other group of arid country small birds, the wheatears, one may encounter the mourning wheatear (*Oenanthe lugens*), pied wheatear (*Oenanthe pleschanka*) and the isabelline wheatear (*Oenanthe isabellina*).

Lesser kestrel (*D. Clayton*).

Kuwait's vigorous programme of "greening" the city and urban areas has created many new habitats which are capable of supporting birds which would otherwise not occur here. The gardens of Al Ahmadi have long been a haven for such familiar species as the song-thrush (*Turdus philomelos*), robin (*Erithacus rubecula*), blackbirds (*Turdus merula*) and the stonechat (*Saxicola torquata*). Less common visitors include the attractive blue-throat (*Luscinia svecica*), chaffinch (*Fringilla coelebs*), brambling (*Fringilla montifringilla*) and predatory shrikes : great grey (*Lanius excubitor*) and isabelline (*Lanius isabellinus*). Sadly, the houbara bustard (*Chlamydotis undulata*) is very much depleted in numbers now but there is some cause for hope since considerable efforts are being applied regionally to protecting the habitat of this species and also to investigate the possibility of re-stocking from captive reared birds.

Major bird migrations occur in spring and autumn. Kuwait is on the northwards route of many birds returning to Europe and northern

Unfortunately birds in Kuwait remain in need of more effective protection against hunting. This Kite has been shot for no other reason than as an object for target practice. It is a sad end to a noble bird, and one which affects all too many of Kuwait's avian visitors (*P. Vine*).

Asia after over-wintering nearer the equator. Activity begins towards the end of February when the passage of swallows (*Hirundo rustica*), sand martins (*Riparia riparia*), house martins (*Delichon urbica*) and red-rumped swallows (*Hirundo daurica*) heralds the arrival of spring. Many of the birds which over-winter in Kuwait leave in spring time to fly north, escaping from the oppressive heat of an Arabian summer, towards more temperate climes. In this category are the white wagtails which are a regular feature of the winter bird scene but have disappeared by mid to late April. The major event of Kuwait's spring migration is however the arrival of a variety of birds of prey . Steppe eagles (*Aquila rapax orientalis*), booted eagles (*Hieraaetus pennatus*), Bonnelli's eagle (*Hieraaetus fasciatus*), spotted eagles (*Aquila clanga*) and imperial eagles (*Aquila heliaca*) all transit Kuwait in March and April with steppe eagles being most common. These soaring birds depend upon thermal air currents to gain height before covering distance with their long gliding flight paths. The raptors return through Kuwait in autumn, along with many other migratory birds, on their passage southwards.

In table III we have reproduced a list of those birds which breed in Kuwait. It is likely that as irrigation and agriculture develop the number of breeding species will increase. Readers seeking a more comprehensive account of Kuwait's avifauna are referred to the two natural history books mentioned above together with Michael Jennings' book entitled 'Birds of the Arabian Gulf' (George Allen and Unwin, 1981).

Marine Life

Kuwait lies at the north-western extremity of the Arabian Gulf, a relatively shallow marine basin which is connected to the vast Indian Ocean via the Straits of Hormuz. The shallowness of the Gulf, whose maximum depth is only around one hundred metres, with an average depth of only thirty-five metres, has an important bearing on its biota. It means that the water column is generally well mixed, from the surface to the seabed, and that the opposing influences of intense solar heating on the one hand and powerful evaporative cooling on the other, play vital roles in creating the wide differences between summer and winter sea temperatures. Nowhere is this more apparent than in waters of the northern Gulf, off Kuwait for example, where summer sea temperatures reach a tepid 31°C (or even higher

Shells and corals washed-up on a Kuwaiti beach provide evidence of a rich and interesting marinelife offshore (*P.Vine*).

close inshore), contrasting with winter levels which drop to as low as 16°C offshore and as low as 10°C in the shallows. Despite the inflow of fresh-water from the Shatt al Arab and its connected rivers, loss of water from evaporation exceeds input from rivers, run-off from surrounding land or direct rainfall. The salt balance is thus maintained primarily through exchange of sea-water with the Indian Ocean, via the Straits of Hormuz. Were it not for this connection with the world's oceans, the Gulf would simply become more and more saline until virtually all marine-life was unable to survive. The salinity of Kuwait waters, and Gulf waters in general, is nevertheless higher than that of the Indian Ocean, fluctuating from 37 to 43 ppt.

Physical oceanography of the Arabian Gulf has recently been reviewed by J.R.Hunter in Marine Environment and Pollution (Proceedings of the First Arabian Gulf Conference on Environment and Pollution, edited by R.Halwagy et al, published by Kuwait University, Faculty of Science, 1986). Scientists agree that the Arabian Gulf is an area where evaporation exceeds run-off and precipitation, giving rise to dense saline water. Circulatory currents have been studied and an overall turn-over time for water in the Gulf is estimated as 2.4 years with a flushing time of 3 to 5.5 years. A number of oceanographic surveys have been concentrated in Kuwait waters, among the most recent of which is one undertaken in 1984 by KISR (Fisheries Management Project MB-56) which drew a number of conclusions from an intensive year of study. Their findings are briefly summarised in table IV.

Table IV.
Summary of Oceanographic Characteristics of Kuwait waters.
(after KISR report no. 1964)
Note:– Readings relate to 1984

Atmospheric pressure:–
Max......1,023.8 mb...November.
Min......1,000 mb.......June.

Wind speed & direction
Monthly mean max. = 5.93ml/1 March
Monthly mean min. = 4.37ml/l June.

pH
Mean pH from Feb-August > 8.02.
Mean pH from Sept-Dec < 7.92.
Mean max pH = 8.51 April.
Mean min pH = 7.88 Sept.

The effects of these factors on marine-life are that many species are stressed at one or other of the seasons, either through high summer temperatures, locally high salinities, or through rapid and severe falls in sea temperatures, below the tolerance levels for some species. From the viewpoint of marine-life this constitutes the negative side. On the positive side however, one may point to the very large area of seabed within the light wave-band range for photosynthesis to occur. Also, the shallowness of the sea and the consequent mixing of the water column ensures that nutrients are not lost into deep water. Tidal currents in Kuwait waters (mathematically modelled by J.R.Hunter in Kuwait Bulletin of Marine Science, 1984(5):11–35.) can also be quite strong with semi-diurnal and diurnal fluctuations creating well defined intertidals. The net result of these various factors is that the Gulf is a remarkably productive body of water, supporting a flourishing and diverse marine biota, including economically important finfish and shellfish stocks.

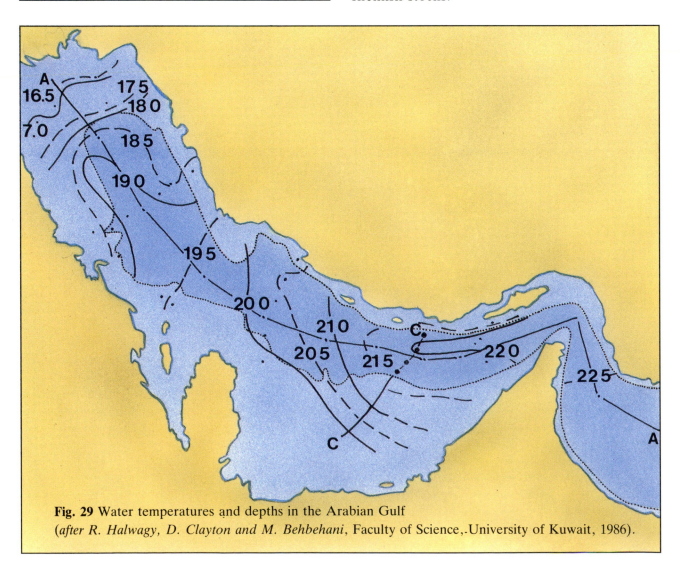

Fig. 29 Water temperatures and depths in the Arabian Gulf
(*after R. Halwagy, D. Clayton and M. Behbehani*, Faculty of Science, University of Kuwait, 1986).

Plankton are of course at the base of Kuwait's marine food-chain and several workers have concentrated on this important area of local marine biology. Marine scientists at KISR carry out regular planktonic surveys in the Gulf and results of one such intensive investigation, conducted between September 1979 and August 1980, are presented by H.B.Michel and co-workers in Marine Environment and Pollution (Kuwait University, 1986). This led to identification of over 95 species in 14 phyla with dominant forms comprising copepods such as *Paracalanus crassirostris* and several others. As these authors conclude, "Kuwaiti waters can be compared to an estuarine backwater or embayment in which the zooplanktonic community is dominated by a few very abundant and widely distributed species which are tolerant to the extremes in temperature and salinity as well as other conditions created by such strong coastal influences as industrial and domestic pollution, concentrated shipping activities, and poor water circulation." It does not sound like a perfect formula for high productivity and yet: ". . . the area has been biologically so rich that its fisheries resources have been exploited for many years. There is evidence that the water column is thoroughly mixed through most or all of the year, so that nutrients appear to be available at all times, even during the annual minimum of plankton production in March".

Kuwait and Kuwaitis have long maintained an especially close relationship with the sea. Their traditional role in pearl-diving predates historical records. Their sea-faring and boat building prowess were also key elements in their success. As we have seen in the historical chapter of this book, the island of Ikaros (Failaka) was already used by local people when Alexander the Great commanded a base there. Despite the fact that the Gulf's pearl beds are concentrated a good distance south of Kuwait, especially around Bahrain and off Qatar, Kuwaitis nevertheless played an active role in harvesting pearls and marketing them. The importance of the lowly bivalve shell, *Pinctada margaritifera*, otherwise known as the pearl oyster, can hardly be over-emphasised in the context of Kuwait's early development for it was largely on the wealth created from pearl diving that the people inhabiting the land of Kuwait depended.

While pearls fuelled the pre-oil economy of Kuwait the Gulf's rich resources of sea-food sustained its population. Fish and shellfish form a staple and vitally important part of the Kuwaiti

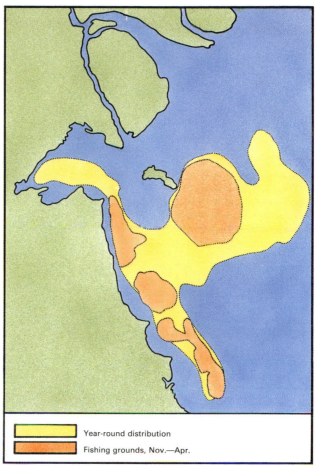

Year-round distribution

Fishing grounds, Nov.—Apr.

Fig. 30 Year-round distribution and fishing grounds, November to April, for the shrimp *Penaeus sulcatus* in Kuwait Waters (*after A.S.D. Farmer and M. Ukawa*, Kuwait Bulletin for Marine Science, 1986[7]: 23–44).

diet, even today, when oil revenues have lifted the country far above a direct dependence upon local food resources, Kuwaitis remain highly enthusiastic about their local sea-foods.

Kuwait's fisheries may be divided into two key segments; ie the shrimp fishery and the finfish fishery. In terms of its commercial exploitation, the shrimp fishery is a very recent phenomenon with organised shrimp trawling only commencing around 1964. In a recent review of Kuwait's fisheries (Hopkins, Mathews and Samuel: Kuwait Bulletin of Marine Science [5] 37–59, 1984) the shrimp fishery was classified under two headings, ie one sector orientated towards export and a second sector supplying domestic requirements. The commercial fishery started with a bang and then experienced a period of retrenchment as the effects of intensive over-fishing became apparent. Two species form the backbone of this fishery, ie the 'white shrimp' or 'soft shrimp' *Penaeus semisulcatus* and the 'hard shrimp' *Metapenaeus affinis*. In order to protect stocks of these species a closed season has been introduced, from 1st February to 30th June.

Shrimps form one of Kuwait's most valuable marine resources with two species forming the backbone of the industry; i.e. 'soft shrimp' *Penaeus semisulcatus* and the 'hard shrimp' *Metapenaeus affinis* (*P. Vine*).

Kuwait's fin fishery is based upon a variety of catching methods, from hook and line, through fixed hadra traps, to mobile gargoor traps and to modern trawling and drift gill netting. A visit to the fishing harbours along Kuwait's coast will almost certainly reveal graceful wooden dhows with large wire gargoor fish-traps strapped to their upper decks. These are carried to offshore fishing grounds where they are set on the sea-bed at twenty to fifty metres depth, and baited to catch hamoor (*Epinephelus tauvina*), hamra (*Lutjanus coccineus*), and nakroor (*Pomadasys argenteus*) during spring and early summer (March to June) and primarily sheim (*Acanthopagrus latus*) in winter. Drift gill-netting is employed to harvest zobaidy (*Pampus argenteus*) and suboor (*Hilsa ilisha*) in larger mesh nets or maid (*Valamugil seheli*) and Beyah (*Liza macrolepis*) in small mesh nets.

Hadras, whose closely tied bamboo poles form a prominent feature of the coastline, are owned by fishermen or local residents who may then rent them to other fishermen to work them. In actual fact, Kuwait has reached such a peak of affluence in recent years that many Hadras are fished as much for pleasure as for any financial reward. Based upon a design which has probably remained unchanged for over a thousand years, the hadras evoke images of Kuwait's maritime past and of its proud seafaring heritage. The hadras depend upon the existence of regular tides since fish arrive into the shallows or across the intertidal as the tide floods, and seek to depart with the ebb. Hadras work on the principle that fish are guided by a long straight fence of bamboo poles, set at right angles to the beach, towards deeper water. Close to low-water mark the straight fence leads fish into a large trap where many of them remain until they are picked out by the fisherman at low-tide. A refinement in the design is that there is also a smaller, inner trap into which caught fish are led since the entrance appears to offer an escape route. Once inside however the fish are held within a smaller area and are thus more easily caught later. The prime fish caught in the hadras are blue-spotted mullet or maid (*Valamugil seheli*), large scaled mullet or beyah (*Liza macrolepis*) and various small carangids. Each hadra trap is licensed with local authorities and the Ministry of Public Works reported that in 1981 there were 129 such traps in use in Kuwait. Table V provides a list of Arabic, English and scientific names of commercially valuable fish caught in Kuwait waters.

A comprehensive scientific review of Gulf fish has recently been published by Kuwait Institute

Kuwait's fin-fishery is based on a variety of catching techniques, many of which result in mixed catches including carangids, groupers and other species (*top photo P. Vine; bottom photo by D. Clayton*).

Table V. Arabic, English and scientific names of various fish species in Kuwait.

Kuwaiti name	English name	Scientific name
Zobaidy	Silver pomfret	*Pampus argenteus*
Suboor	River shad	*Hilsa ilisha*
Nakroor	Silver grunt	*Pomadasys argenteus*
Hamoor	Brown-spotted grouper	*Epinephelus tauvina*
Maid	Blue-spotted mullet	*Valamugil seheli*
Newaiby	Silver croaker	*Otilithes argenteus*
Chanad	Barred spanish mackerel	*Scomberomorus commersoni*
Hamra	Crimson snapper	*Lutjanus coccineus*
Beyah	Large-scaled mullet	*Liza macrolepis*
Hamam	Trevally, Jack	Carangidae species
Sheim	Yellow-finned black porgy	*Acanthopagrus latus*
Firsh	Three-banded grunt	*Plectorhynchus cinctus*
Kassoor	Lizard fish	*Saurida tumbil*
Sherry	Emperor	*Lethrinus nebulosus*
Khabbat	Spotted spanish mackerel	*Scomberomorus guttatus*

for Scientific Research; ie Fishes of the Arabian Gulf by Katsuzo Kuronuma and Yoshitaka Abe KISR, 1986. The book represents one of many scientific contributions which KISR has made towards our knowledge of Kuwait's marine resources. Much of the work of KISR's marine scientists has been directed towards understanding the biology of local fish and shrimps in order that natural stocks may be correctly managed, and that efforts to farm locally occurring species may be advanced. Results of the work carried out in this field are published in periodic volumes of the Kuwait Bulletin of Marine Science in which certain editions contain proceedings of important regional conferences such as the shrimp and fin fisheries management workshop. Indeed, it is in the area of mariculture that the Kuwait Institute for Scientific Research has made some of its most significant contributions. Despite the success of their shrimp rearing programme (stimulated by a dramatic fall in Kuwait shrimp landings from a peak of 3,150 tonnes in 1966 to around 1,000 tonnes in the 1970's) leading to the release of literally millions of young shrimp to shallow nursery grounds in the Gulf, it was decided that the only effective way to protect the Gulf's shrimp fishery is to control the fishing effort and preserve natural nursery grounds. The technological achievements of KISR's shrimp rearing are in no way diminished by this pragmatic change in direction and the

Institute is responsible for considerably advancing our knowledge of the Gulf's commercially important penaeid shrimps. It is in the area of rearing marine fin-fish however that KISR has demonstrated a determination to establish the technology for commercial fish-farming in Kuwait. The impetus for mariculture research and development comes, not from a decline in local fisheries, but from a desire to produce more of certain fish species and a realisation that fishing effort cannot increase indefinitely without Kuwait's rich fish stocks suffering. The findings of a KISR survey of Kuwait's fin fisheries, carried out under a carefully planned Fishery Management Project, (KISR 2177, December 1986) makes interesting reading, stating that the country's fin-fish landings increased steadily from 3,500 metric tonnes in 1980 to 7,500 tons in 1984. The report concluded that there was no need to limit effort on any of Kuwait's commercial fin-fisheries; there was no evidence of damage caused to the fin-fisheries by trawling and there was no need to limit trawling for fin-fish in Kuwait waters since there was no evidence of excessive exploitation of any fish species. Catch analysis revealed that the main bulk of the seven and half thousand tonnes catch of 1984 comprised a few key species; ie 1,800 tonnes of hamoor (*Epinephelus sueli* also referred to as *E.tauvina*) and 1,300 tonnes of hamrah or crimson snapper, *Lutjanus coccineus*. Between them these two species comprised over 40% of total landings and 65% of gargoor (wire fish-trap) landings. Despite its dominance on the market, hamoor also commanded a high price, varying at that time between KD1 and KD2 per kilogram at the main fish-market. It was therefore a prime species to focus more biological attention upon, both from the viewpoint of understanding its natural ecology and in order to determine its suitability for mariculture. One of the first findings was that Hamoor is a 'protogynous' species, i.e. it starts life as a female and later changes to become a male. As a result, only 1.5% of hamoor caught in Kuwait are males. At about nine to ten years old, and a total length of 70 to 90 cms long, the females change sex to become males. Such findings have an immediate and obvious bearing upon fisheries management or mariculture planning. Study of fish ear-bones or otiliths provide a means of ageing individuals and research has indicated that most groupers caught in Kuwait are less than ten years old, with the odd crusty grand-daddy of a Hamoor reaching 25 or so years old. As we have seen above, the vast majority of hamoor are caught in gargoor traps and a recent paper by Samuel, Mathews and Bader (Kuwait Bulletin of Marine Science, Vol. 9, 1987) suggests that this fishery should be carefully monitored with a freeze upon effort.

Farming fish in Kuwait waters presents a number of major biological challenges. First of all one must master the reproductive biology of the species so that captive fish can be induced to spawn and fertilised eggs can be reared through the delicate larval stages to become tiny fry. Many marine fish simply refuse to spawn in captive tanks and even among those which will do so, the difficulty of feeding their larvae on the correct live diets has proved in some cases insurmountable. KISR's success with hamoor and sobaity (*Acanthopagrus latus*) is therefore all the more remarkable. KISR began its finfish research programme in 1977 by testing the suitability of six species; ie maid or mullet (*Liza macrolepis*), hamoor or grouper (*Epinephelus sueli*), sheim or porgy (*Acanthopagrus latus*), sobaity (*Acanthopagrus cuvieri*), bolti or tilapia (*Oreochromis aureus*) and safi or rabbitfish (*Siganus oramin*). From 1980 onwards research was concentrated on hamoor, sobaity and bolti and success has been achieved with each of these. Captive spawning of sobaity was first achieved in 1979 and is now a routine procedure with pilotscale farming in operation and commercial plans already underway. Sobaity are sold

at around 600 to 800 grams, about a year and a half from the fry stage. Reared in coastal ponds and floating cages results have been extremely good, with stocking ratios of 700gram fish reaching 42 kg/cubic metre in floating cages. Work on tilapias led to selection of *Oreochromis spilurus* for rearing in sea-water (incidentally reflecting similar conclusions made by the author who worked on rearing tilapias in the Red Sea in 1978). While both the above species are excellent eating and could provide a useful cultivated food source, neither species commands the high market price of hamoor. KISR's work on *Epinephelus sueli* (also referred to as *E.tauvina*) has broken new ground in tropical mariculture. Captive breeding and larval rearing over a number of years has now led to a complete closing of the reproductive cycle with eggs and larvae now raised from captive bred adults. It is expected that this work will lead to full-scale hamoor farming becoming established in the Gulf during the next few years. At the time of writing plans for this are already well advanced, and pilot scale sea-cage farming of grouper in Kuwait has already produced fish of 850 grams within 18 months from stocking fry. KISR's research in this field will be of benefit, not just to Kuwait, but to all Gulf countries and to areas further afield.

Visitors to Kuwait may gain first-hand experience of Kuwait's rich marine-life by visiting its shores. These may be broadly classified into rocky, sandy and muddy with each harbouring a characteristic range of species. On rocky shores the effects of tides can be clearly discerned in the

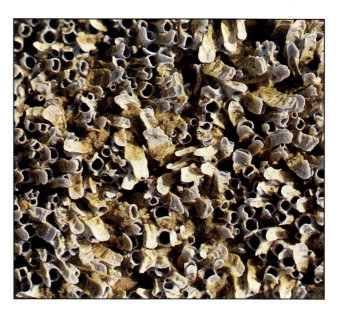

Colonial serpulid tube-worms colonise intertidal rocks along the southern shores of Kuwait (*P.Vine*).

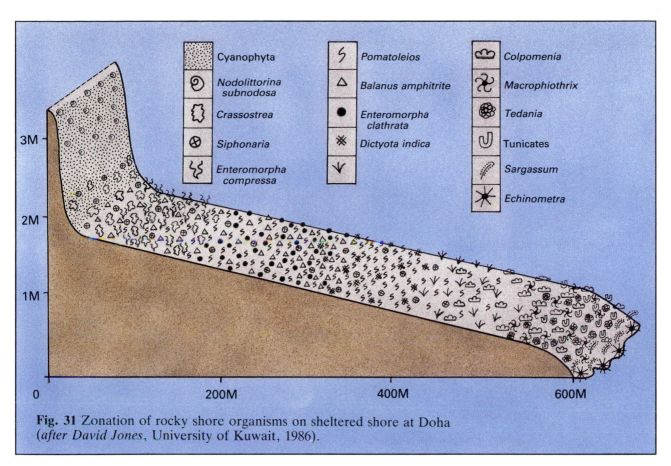

Fig. 31 Zonation of rocky shore organisms on sheltered shore at Doha (*after David Jones*, University of Kuwait, 1986).

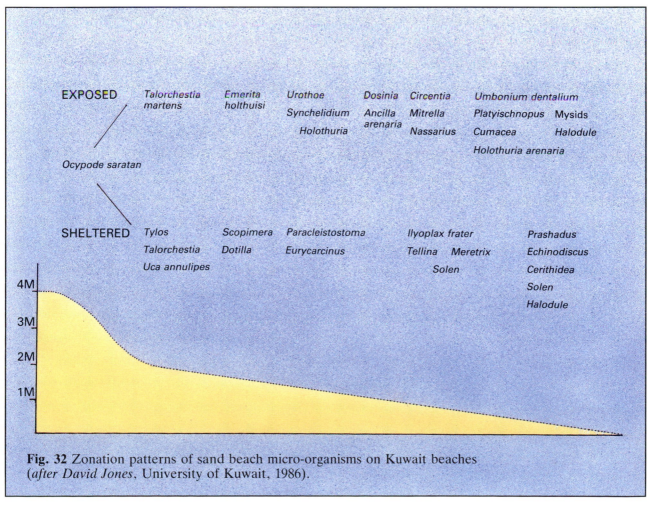

Fig. 32 Zonation patterns of sand beach micro-organisms on Kuwait beaches (*after David Jones*, University of Kuwait, 1986).

zonation of several abundant species such as the periwinckle or littorinid, *Nodolittorina subnodosa*, which grazes on blue-green algae at the top of the shore, in the splash zone; the barnacle *Balanus amphitrite* and the oyster *Crassostrea cf. margaritacea* dominating the upper intertidal with the serpulid tubeworm *Pomatoleios kraussi* confined to the lower shore. An excellent guide to Kuwait's intertidal has been written by Dr David Jones ('A Field Guide to the Seashores of Kuwait and the Arabian Gulf', published by the University of Kuwait and distributed by Blandford Press, 1986). Dr Jones also recently contributed a review article on Kuwait's rocky and sandy shores which was published in Marine Environment and Pollution (Kuwait University, 1986). Our knowledge of Kuwait's intertidal is in fact very recent, and remarkably enough, Jones' paper represents the first general account of the ecology of rocky and sandy shores of Kuwait. The zonation of species on rocky and sandy shores is summarised in figures 31–2 which are derived from David Jones' paper on the subject. He draws close parallels between Kuwait's assemblage of intertidal species and those found on warm temperate shores of South Africa and east Australia, commenting: *"Further parallels are present with the faunas of these shores demonstrating that the eulittoral in Kuwait is characterised by warm temperate elements similar to those present at the southern end of the Indian Ocean"*. He goes on to draw a similar comparison between Kuwait's sublittoral fauna and that of warm temperate South African shores. This picture is clouded somewhat however by the presence of a few tropical species which appear to be at the limits of their range in the northern Gulf, but increase dramatically further south.

The third element in Kuwait's fascinating intertidal is its extensive mud- flats which have been investigated and described by Dr David Clayton from the Zoology Department at Kuwait University (Ecology of mudflats with particular reference to those of the northern Arabian Gulf in Marine Evironment and Pollution, Kuwait University, 1986). As David Clayton points out, mudflats are often considered by developers as of no environmental merit other than as a

Tidal flats are the habitat of many waders which feed on small crustaceans, worms and molluscs living in the sand or mud (*P. Vine*).

Mudskippers on the mud-flats of Sulaibikhat bay (*P. Vine*).

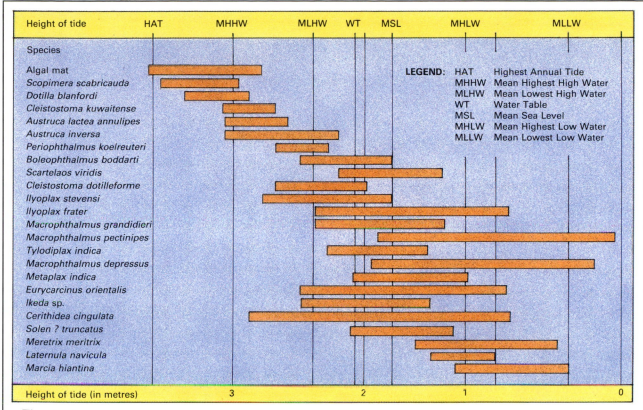

Height of tide	HAT	MHHW	MLHW	WT	MSL	MHLW	MLLW

Species

Algal mat
Scopimera scabricauda
Dotilla blanfordi
Cleistostoma kuwaitense
Austruca lactea annulipes
Austruca inversa
Periophthalmus koelreuteri
Boleophthalmus boddarti
Scartelaos viridis
Cleistostoma dotilleforme
Ilyoplax stevensi
Ilyoplax frater
Macrophthalmus grandidieri
Macrophthalmus pectinipes
Tylodiplax indica
Macrophthalmus depressus
Metaplax indica
Eurycarcinus orientalis
Ikeda sp.
Cerithidea cingulata
Solen ? truncatus
Meretrix meritrix
Laternula navicula
Marcia hiantina

LEGEND:
HAT — Highest Annual Tide
MHHW — Mean Highest High Water
MLHW — Mean Lowest High Water
WT — Water Table
MSL — Mean Sea Level
MHLW — Mean Highest Low Water
MLLW — Mean Lowest Low Water

Height of tide (in metres)	3	2	1	0

Fig. 33 Zonation of the fauna of intertidal mudflats of Kuwait.
(*after R. Halwagy, D. Clayton and M. Behbehani*, Faculty of Science, University of Kuwait, 1986).

large flat area of coastline inviting reclamation. Sadly, this has happened at many localities around the shores of the Arabian Gulf. Kuwait's mudflats are however still in existence and support a varied and interesting assemblage of plants and animals. Dr Clayton argues quite convincingly that interference with these by Man will probably have a deleterious effect on the whole marine environment. Mud predominates as the sediment of the northern Arabian Gulf and is therefore of great importance to shallow-water marine-life. Along the shores of Kuwait,

tidal sand of coarse grain size and rock flats are confined to small stretches at Al Jadailiat and Al Doha with the rest of Kuwait Bay, including Sulaibikhat Bay, consisting of mud-flats. The most productive mud-flats in Kuwait are at Sulaibikhat Bay and at Kadthma near the western extremity of Kuwait Bay.

Faunal distribution on these mudflats is summarised in table 33 which is derived from an earlier paper on crustacean fauna of the mudflats (Jones and Clayton, 1983). Just below high-water, in the upper intertidal, is a zone occupied by burrowing fiddler crabs (*Austruca lactea annulipes*, *A.inversa*, and *Cleistostoma kuwaitense*). Capable of surviving in burrows where water salinities have been recorded to reach 130 parts per thousand and temperatures as high as 40°C, these fiddler crabs are impressive creatures. Slightly overlapping this zone and extending down beyond it is the mudskipper zone whose unusual inhabitants provide a most interesting spectacle as they 'skip' around the mud, slithering across its surface in search of food. There are three mudskipping gobies found locally, ie. the carnivorous *Periophthalmus koelreuteri*, the herbivorous *Boleophthalmus boddarti*, and the omnivorous *Scartelaos viridis*.

Modern Kuwait
Prior to August 1990

It would be quite wrong to measure Kuwait's modern success by evaluating its urban architecture, its extensive and impressive motorway system or its other infrastructural developments, all of which are worthy of praise but do not in themselves constitute the nation's fundamental achievement. To the casual observer Kuwait of today is a very different country from that of 50-odd years ago when the sheikhdom's economy, like that of several other Gulf states, was supported by the long-established traditional exploitation of marine resources, especially pearls. There is no denying that great developments have taken place and the nation has experienced something akin to a whirlwind of change, challenging the very foundations of its existence. One only has to meet Kuwaitis, however, to realise that these charming, hospitable and gentle people have retained the unique qualities of their forebears. One should not be fooled by the sleek Mercedes, Rolls Royces, BMWs and other luxurious automobiles; nor by the palatial villas packaged within verdant gardens; nor by the elegant yachts and motor-cruisers tethered at the numerous marinas which are so conveniently distributed along the corniche; nor indeed by any of the other trappings of universal wealth. Kuwait's real success story is that of its people who despite their oil-fired economic boom remain firmly guided by the tenets of Islam and by their abiding love of God, their fellow man, and of the beneficent land of their birth.

Kuwaitis are justifiably proud of their nationality, at ease with their birthright and, in the down to earth manner of the nomadic Bedu, pleased to share their good fortune with their brothers. Here lies the real achievement of Kuwait, for Kuwaitis have retained a great deal of their traditional grace, kindness, good humour and unerring hospitality. As we review the physical changes which have occurred since the early part of this century and focus upon the sheer magnitude of Kuwait's strides, we should not lose touch with this one abidingly important fact. The shape of its development, priorities of its planners and the foresight of its administrators are truly Kuwaiti. As we shall see, it is this which has enabled the State of Kuwait to maintain its distinct and commendable individuality among the roll-call of nations.

Kuwait's modern era may be said to have begun around 1125 AH corresponding to 1714 AD when members of the Utub, together with their families, were forced by drought to leave the Aflaj region of Najd (now part of Saudi Arabia) in order to seek new areas suitable for settlement. The Utub, also known as the Bani Utbi, comprised several large family groups from major tribes of the area, including the Al-Sabah, Al-Khalifa, Al-Zayed, Al-Jalahima and Al-Muawida. The area of present day Kuwait was already occupied by a fragmented section of the Bani Khalid and arrival of the newcomers was welcomed by all inhabitants who unanimously elected Sabah bin Jaber (Sabah I) as their overall leader. Gaining its name from the fort or 'Al Kout' which was reputedly built by the leader of the Bani Khalid and presented to Sabah I upon

Table VI
Significant Dates in Kuwait Oil Company's History

1934 February 2nd: Kuwait Oil Company registered in London with a capital of 50,000 one pound shares, divided equally into A and B units with the Anglo-Persian Oil Company (now BP) and the Eastern Gulf Oil Company having equal shares. December 23rd: Shaikh Ahmad signed agreement granting KOC exclusive right to explore, search and win natural gas and crude oil as well as the rights to refine, transport and sell those products within and without the state.

1935-36 Geophysical exploration carried out. First exploration well drilled at Bahrah.

1938 February—oil discovered at Burgan.

1938-42 Eight more wells drilled at Burgan, confirming the earlier and extensive production from the field; further development suspended until the end of the war.

1945 Operations resumed.

1946 The first sub-sea pipelines laid for the loading of tankers. June: the first cargo of crude oil exported.

1946–49 The South Pier and a 25,000 barrels a day refinery (later raised to 30,000 barrels a day), with a power station and seawater distillation plant, constructed at Mina Al-Ahmadi. A complete township, including administrative headquarters, workshops, residential quarters and amenities built at Ahmadi.

1951 Drilling extended to Magwa.

1953 Drilling extended to Ahmadi ridge. Production started from the Magwa/Ahmadi Field, an extension of the Burgan Field.

1955 Oil discovered at Raudhatain in North Kuwait

1958 Refinery expansion raised input to 190,000 barrels a day.

1959 Oil discovered at Minagish, 21 miles west of Burgan.

1959 June—the North Pier commissioned, raising export capacity of Mina Al-Ahmadi to over two million barrels a day.

1959 July—platformer commissioned at Mina Al Ahmadi refinery to upgrade the octane rating of motor spirit produced.

1960 April—production from the North Kuwait fields (Raudhatain, Sabiriyah and Bahrah) began. July: production began from the Minagish Field.

1961 June: plant commissioned at Burgan for injecting up to 100 million standard cubic feet a day back into the oil formations.

1962 March: regular bulk exports of propane and butane LPG began. July: production began from Umm Gudair Field.

1963 May: processing capacity of the refinery expanded to 250,000 barrels a day, and subsequently by stages to 292,000.

1965 June—the 1,000 millionth ton of oil produced. September: plant commissioned at Raudhatain for injecting up to 50 million standard cubic feet of natural gas a day.

1967 July: plant commissioned at Minagish for injecting up to 168 million standard cubic feet of natural gas a day. 35 miles of pipeline was laid for the transmission of crude oil from Umm Gudair to the Kuwait National Petroleum Company refinery at Shuaiba.

1968 Expansion of Mina Al-Ahmadi loading facilities was completed. World's largest submarine crude oil pipeline (48ins) laid to Sea Island terminal 10 miles offshore. The first two mammoth tankers of 326,000 tons dwt. loaded.

The central control room at Mina Abdulla Refinery modernization project (*Kuwait National Petroleum Co.*).

1969 February: His Highness Shaikh Sabah Al Salim Al Sabah, the Amir of Kuwait, inaugurated the Sea Island terminal and associated facilities.

1970 October: billionth barrel of oil refined at KOC refinery. Four new gathering centres were commissioned together with a new pipeline between North Kuwait and Ahmadi, bringing the total number of gathering centres to 25. New third generation computer installed.

1972 February: the largest tanker ever to visit Kuwait—the Nisseki Maru (372,000 tons dwt) loaded at Mina Al-Ahmadi

1974 A participation agreement was ratified by the Kuwait National Assembly giving 60% control of the operations of KOC to the State of Kuwait, the remaining 40% being divided between BP and Gulf.

1975 March: Kuwait Government took over the remaining 40% shares thus assuming full control of the company.

1976 November: the Gas Project foundations laying ceremony took place under the auspices of H.H. the Amir of Kuwait, Shaikh Sabah Al Salim Al Sabah.

1977 February: the world's largest oil tanker "Bellamya" (553,662 dwt), berthed at Sea Island terminal.

1978 May: KOC entrusted with oil-producing operations formerly carried out by the Americal Independent Oil Company, before latter's concession expired. October: new bitumen plant inaugurated.

1979 A single point mooring near Sea Island was commissioned, facilitating the loading of giant 500,000 dwt tankers. Drilling of a deep well commenced at Burgan.

1980 Kuwait Petroleum Company, established by Amiri Decree, unified the activities and orientation of the oil sector. Kuwait International Petroleum Investments Company was also established to undertake investments in petroleum activities outside Kuwait.

1981 Kuwait External Exploration Company was founded.

1982 Crude oil exports amounted to 134,601,000 barrels.

1983 September: "Al Baz" drilling rig commenced offshore drilling.

1984 Refined oil products reached 176,447,000 barrels.

1986 Al Ahmadi Refinery was operating at an August production level of 275,000 barrels per day.

LPG plant (*Kuwait National Petroleum Co.*).

his arrival, this territory offered these desert people a new source of fresh-water and some seasonal pastures for their camels. It also soldered a relationship between its new inhabitants and the Arabian Gulf. While winter was a time for fattening animals and hunting with falcons or salukis, summer offered the chance to take to the water, sail down towards Bahrain, and participate in the pearl-diving. As we have seen in earlier chapters, this was a lifestyle which suited the Al-Sabah's broad talents, and provided the basis for a stable and viable local economy.

Among the direct descendents of Kuwait's first ruler, Sheikh Saber bin Jaber, few have experienced greater changes than Sheikh Ahmad Al Jaber Al Sabah whose thirty years of leadership spanned the pre-oil pearling era, from 1921, when the third city wall was completed and when eight hundred pearling boats, manned by 10,000 sailors were working out of Kuwait; through the years of increasing frugality marked by soaring prices of essential commodities, a general collapse of pearling, and the destruction by torrential rain on 7th December, 1934, of many local houses; to the exploration for oil commencing in 1935 and its discovery at Burgan in 1938; to the start of oil exporting in 1946 and through the next four years of improving circumstances. In those three decades of Sheikh Ahmad's leadership Kuwait lost its economic dependence upon the fickle international market for natural pearls, exchanging one vital natural resource for another even more lucrative one: oil.

A study of Kuwait's development since then is inextricably linked to the growth of Kuwait Oil Company which provided the vehicle for oil exploration, drilling, international marketing and the fuel for Kuwait's dramatic economic growth and structural metaphormosis. The key events in this meteoric industrial calendar are summarised in table 6 on page 144.

In her excellent co-authored book entitled

Kuwait: Prospect and Reality, Zahra Freeth, daughter of the political resident of Kuwait in those crucial years, Colonel Dickson, gives a fascinating blow by blow account of the negotiations which led to granting of the first oil concession. The importance of oil to the future economy of Kuwait had been foreseen to some extent by the various protaganists, but none could have imagined the incredibly rich hydrocarbon resources which were to be discovered, or the wealth which would be created in this seemingly barren desert. Indeed, as Zahra Freeth and Victor Winstone comment, comparisons between the economics of pre- and post-oil Kuwait are virtually meaningless since: "*The two periods are of totally different dimensions*". While there is no doubt that this is true, geographers have not shifted the land of Kuwait to another continent or planet! Kuwait of the mid 1920's, however different from that of today, is indeed the same country, occupied by the same families as today. In 1926 the fortified city of Kuwait held around 50,000 inhabitants, a more heterogenous group than the pure Arabs who still roamed the desert region, for here lived, apart from settled Arabs, approximately: "*10,000 Persians, 4,000 Negroes, a few Jews, and two or three Chaldean Christians from Iraq*" (Colonel J.C.More's trade return, 1926). Kuwait's recorded exports, consisting of hides, pearls and trans-shipped sugar and tea, amounted to £495,972 in the year 1925–26 and, while this figure is suspect, particularly with regard to pearling, it provides an interesting contrast with the position six decades later, in 1986, when the recorded national income was 6,756,600,000 Kuwaiti Dinars or roughly thirteen billion pounds!

What were the early priorities of post-oil Kuwait? Among the very first was the provision of adequate health care in the form of modern hospitals and clinics. Since its establishment in Kuwait in 1911, the Arabian Mission of the Dutch Reformed Church in America, under the directorship of Dr C.S.G.Mylrea, had provided the only organised medical facilities in Kuwait. The shock of a devastating smallpox epidemic in 1932 combined with the persistent ravages of tuberculosis, led to Sheikh Ahmad setting up a health ministry in 1936, together with a free clinic which was to relieve some of the pressure from Dr Mylrea's pioneering American Mission Hospital. The Emiri Hospital, completed in 1949, marked the first major step in the establishment of a unique national social services programme whose scale is unparalleled anywhere in the world!

Oil had provided the means for Kuwait's leaders to ease the lives of their people, firstly by the introduction of comprehensive medical facili-

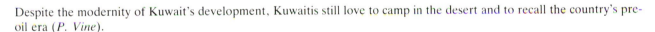

Despite the modernity of Kuwait's development, Kuwaitis still love to camp in the desert and to recall the country's pre-oil era (*P. Vine*).

Kuwait University campus (*D. Clayton*).

ties, and secondly through development of a universal education programme. The 1950's saw frenetic activity in various fields of social development, particularly health services, with schemes to eradicate TB supported by construction of new sanitoria and by more hospitals. Expenditure on hospitals and medical facilities continued to grow dramatically with Al Sabah hospital opening its doors in June 1962 , at a cost of over four million KD. Today the Ministry of Public Health provides one of the world's finest state medical systems. Virtually free health care is offered at each of Kuwait's major hospitals and at the numerous medical clinics conveniently distributed throughout the country. In addition to the general hospitals, specialist units include the maternity, chest and cancer hospitals. 1986 figures on health services record a total of 24 hospitals and sanitoria, with 945 clinics and other health centres. There were 5,521 beds in public hospitals, 2,802 doctors (ie one for every 572 residents), 327 dentists and 805 pharmacists. Measured on a world scale, these ratios of services to population figures are almost unbeatable but the Kuwait Government is continuing to improve on its record and is constantly planning new facilities for its growing population. One recent addition to Kuwait's impressive record in the medical field is that of the Islamic Medical Centre which is dedicated to reviving the Islamic medical heritage based upon natural treatment of illnesses such as allergic rhinitis; chronic bronchitis, diabetes, migraine, hyperacidity and rheumatism through use of medicinal plants. In addition to providing treatment to increasing numbers of patients, the centre, which is headquarters of the Islamic Organization of Medical Sciences (founded in 1984), also has a large library devoted to the Islamic sciences, a conference centre and a mosque.

While health care was an early priority it has been flanked throughout Kuwait's post-oil period by education. In the early years of modern and technological progress Kuwait depended heavily upon expatriates to provide the trained professionals they required, but at the same time they set about educating their own people so that in the course of time Kuwaiti doctors would run the hospitals, Kuwaiti pilots fly the planes and Kuwaiti engineers operate the oil-fields. Education in Kuwait began with the establishment of "kuttabs" where children were taught how to recite the Holy Koran . Then, in 1911, the first boys school, the Mubarakeyah, was opened in the boom period of Kuwait's pearling industry, but it bore little resemblence to the educational facilities available today. In the absence of suitable texts, the school's headmaster produced his own, and teaching staff were so limited that only a small proportion of children were able to

Art is encouraged in Kuwait from infant school right through the education system (*P. Vine*).

attend the institution. Eventually the decline in pearling led to the school's demise in 1931, at a time when prospects for Kuwait and Kuwaitis had never seemed bleaker.

For five years Kuwait was without any formal educational centre, until a special Education Council, the 'Majlis Al-Ma'aref' was set-up in 1936 leading to the introduction of an education tax levied on local merchants who thus provided the funds for a cautious re-birth of formal education. By 1937 there were 600 boys and 140 girls registered at local schools. Then oil provided the means to make a nationwide attack on education and by 1954 Kuwait had forty-one schools. At the same time a new integrated free education programme was established, covering all levels of education from primary, through secondary general and special education to university level. Kuwait University was founded in 1966 and in 1982 the Public Authority for Applied Education and Training was set up for the supervision of four polytechnics and one training centre. Formal religious education is provided through the Holy Koran Recitation Centres, the Religious

Institute which operates a number of schools, and the Faculty of Sharia at Kuwait University. The rise in Kuwait's education budget rose even more dramatically than its expenditure on health facilities with a 1946 figure of KD 83,000 multiplying by a factor of six in four years to reach 500,000 KD in 1950; and then it grew by twice that rate in the next five years, reaching KD6 million in 1955.

This stupendous growth continued, reaching KD 14 million in 1958, KD 24 million in 1967 and a staggering budgetted figure of KD 374.5 million in fiscal year 1986/87! In terms of facilities provided, this impressive flow of cash had created, by the 86/87 review period, 606 schools with 11,259 classrooms serviced by 26,756 teachers and attended by 364,412 students. Kuwait University had more than 17,000 students attending courses during the 86/87 academic year while more than 6,000 were gaining further training at applied educational institutes. While considerable success has been achieved in the process of educating Kuwaitis to fulfil managerial and professional roles, more emphasis will be

Currency market alongside old souk area of Kuwait city
(*P.Vine*).

placed in the years ahead on equipping them to carry out other technical tasks. While there is no suggestion that foreigners will be less welcome in Kuwait it is entirely natural and healthy that Kuwait should equip its own people to run their country and to be considerably less reliant in future upon expatriate workers.

A visit to any of Kuwait's schools may leave expatriate observers such as the present author in something akin to culture-shock! Kuwait is preparing its young people to meet the challenges of the twenty-first century square on. Every Kuwaiti student is trained to become computer literate at primary and early secondary school. Teachers are properly trained to communicate the technological advances of our age and sharp-witted, bright-eyed and intelligent pupils are eager to snap up the unique opportunities they are being offered. Kuwait's educationists are not only seeking to match their system against that of western European countries such as Britain, but are determined to surpass others in their striving for excellence. One suspects that complacent western educationalists may be surprised to discover the high levels of early computer fluency already achieved in Kuwait. This is

however only one of many fields in which Kuwait's education system is proving its worth. Another is in the field of art and artistic expression. Each year the Department of Education sets up special centres for children to paint outside of normal school hours. The results have been quite remarkable with all the centres packed to capacity and with thousands of children totally engrossed in their creative activities.

From the above brief accounts of Kuwait's transition from pearling to petroleum based economies, and the impressive story of exponential growth in the country's social-services sector, together with the continuous lineage of the Al-Sabah as rulers of Kuwait, the reader may conclude that Kuwait has experienced a period of total political stability for all this time. To some extent this is true. Unlike some other territories in the region, Kuwait has not suffered under an occupying force. It was not however until 1961 that a "Treaty of Independence" was signed under which Kuwait became an internationally recognised separate country. This so called treaty basically disentangled the loose matrix of formal and informal agreements linking Britain and Kuwait, substituting contractual obligations. Britain would still be responsible for military protection of Kuwait but her special position régarding such economically vital areas as oil exploration and her influence on Kuwait's external politics were ended. Britain, through its resident Political Agent which it maintained in Kuwait since 1904, had played a role in Kuwait's foreign affairs but despite these technicalities, Kuwait has, since the original declaration of Shaikh Sabah as ruler in 1756, enjoyed a continual period of effective self government. This point is well made by Zahra Freeth and Victor Winstone who write:– "*None of this is inconsistent with the fact that Kuwait remained for the best part of two hundred years a free Arab state, able in the last resort to make up its own mind on issues of domestic policy. If evidence of this was ever lacking, it was surely made good by the insistence of the British during the negotiations for the original oil concession. The Indian government, the Colonial Office and the Foreign Office all maintained explicitly that the Shaikh of Kuwait was an independent ruler who could be guided by Britain but no more. Thus, when foreign writers and Kuwaitis themselves talk of independence they employ an inexact term*".

Kuwait's present system of government owes much to its traditions, evolving over the years into a practical means of dealing with the changing circumstances of this modern Arab nation and hereditary Amirate. Principles have been laid down in a formal Constitution, including 183 articles, which states that: "*The system of government in Kuwait shall be democratic, under which sovereignty resides in the people, the source of all powers*". The Constitution combines the best elements of presidential and parliamentary systems and is a blueprint for pragmatic and effective government. Legislative authority is vested with the Amir and Head of State who also appoints the Crown Prince and Prime Minister, following approval of the National Assembly. The Cabinet is then appointed by the Prime Minister and executive power is exercised by the Amir and his Council of Ministers in accordance with the Constitution. The title of 'Amir' may only be inherited by descendants of the late Mubarak Al-Sabah. The present Amir, His Highness Sheikh Jaber Al Ahmad Al Jabar Al-Sabah, thirteenth Amir from the Al-Sabah family, has held office since December 1977. Kuwait's desert origins and maritime traditions are embodied in its national emblem which depicts a falcon whose wings are furled around an old sailing boom and which rests on a shield decorated by the national flag's colours: black, red, white and green.

While maintaining its own clear and concise foreign policy, with a primary objective of securing and consolidating peace throughout the world, Kuwait is an active and steadfast member of all major international organisations with a role in the region. Kuwait's historic links with neighbouring Arab nations are at the root of her unshakable belief in a common Arab destiny and the desirability of Arab solidarity. They have been long standing supporters of the Palestinians' cause and have played an active role in providing support to displaced Palestinian families. Kuwait's determination to work towards international harmony is illustrated by her active role in the Islamic Conference Organisation and the Non-Aligned Movement. Her willingness to maintain and strengthen relations with all countries irrespective of their social systems has earned international respect and many friends and allies. Among Gulf States, Kuwait has played an enthusiastic role as a member of the Gulf Co-operation Council which plays a significant role in coordinating development efforts within the region. Internationally, Kuwait is represented by fifty-five embassies, ten consulates and two permanent offices at the United Nations, one in New York and one in Geneva.

Kuwaitis love their cars almost as much as their forbears revered the camel. Four-wheel drive has enabled automobiles to traverse even the roughest terrain in Kuwait, and the country's superb system of roads and motorways ensures that most places are accessible on smooth, tarmacadam surfaces (*P. Vine*).

In the days before oil, Kuwait was generally approached by sea, and by the 'ship of the desert':– camel caravans. Roads were at best confined to urban areas, and generally more suitable for the adaptable camel than the unforgiving suspension of the automobile. Today Kuwait is blessed by one of the most up to date and sophisticated arterial road systems in the world. Designed and built with future development needs in mind, it has played a major role in assisting in the country's economic and social growth. One has only to drive out of Kuwait city,

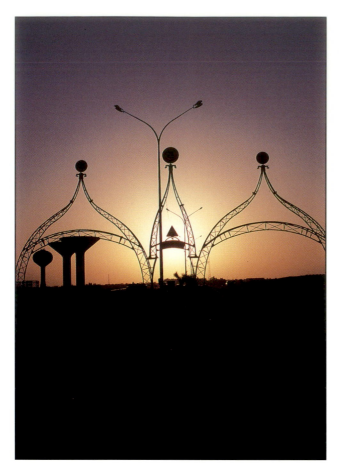

in any direction, to realise the enormous scope of this gigantic road construction effort. While the old city of Kuwait, once encircled by a high wall and entered through large gates, is now surrounded by the first ring road, a radiating network of major highways emanate from the heart of the city leading parallel to the coastlines or directly into the desert. 'Greening' of the city begins here with many of the highways divided by verdant central islands and flanked by grassy banks. While other cities may be satisfied with just one or two ring-roads, Kuwait has seven broad ring-roads encircling the city, served by flyovers which ease traffic flow at main intersections, and in many cases add a welcome and artistic splash of colour to the scene. One may drive comfortably from Kuwait to Saudi Arabia or Iraq along three dual carriageway international motorways and almost any town in Kuwait is easily accessible by smooth surfaced roads.

Much of the organisation and planning for Kuwait city's development falls under the responsibility of Kuwait Municipality which celebrated its golden jubilee in 1980. To mark the occasion a Municipality Exhibition was established at which the city's history and development is displayed through photographs, relief maps and models distributed in five halls. The first two of these show Kuwait in its pre-oil era and document its development with a series of photographs, starting in 1952.

As we have stated already, Kuwait's major source of wealth is of course oil. Unlike many oil producing countries, Kuwait's oil does not require pumping to the surface, but flows spontaneously to gathering centres where gas is separated from it before it is sent to one of the crude oil storage tanks situated in two groups, or tank farms, on the 120m. high Al Ahmadi ridge. Oil flows from these by gravity to the tanker loading berths at Mina Al Ahmadi. Loading rates with this efficient gravity feed system are as much as 12,500 tons per hour or even 19,400 tons per hour with the crude oil pumping units in operation. Between the gravity lines and the tank farms is a complex system of manifolds which virtually allows the use of any tank on any gravity line. The entire system is controlled from a central control room at Al Ahmadi and tanker loading at Kuwait's modern oil terminal is one of the most efficient operations one can see anywhere with very rapid turn-around times and no time wasted.

Apart from exporting crude oil, Kuwait has three oil refineries, at Al Ahmadi, Shuaiba and Mina Abdullah which between them possess a

126

refining capacity of 614,000 barrels per day. The refineries are all operated by Kuwait National Petroleum Company, a subsidiary of Kuwait Petroleum Corporation, which is able to coordinate them into a comprehensive refining unit, maximising the overall capacity. During 1986–87 total thoughput of the refineries was about 212.6 million barrels at an average of 582.4 thousand barrels per day with production of around 28.5 million metric tons of petroleum products. Coordination of the three refineries can lead to crosslinking of facilities at the different plants with, for example, one refinery providing storage for product from another unit. Ahmadi refinery, which was originally built in 1949 and is the country's oldest refinery, has recently been modernised and upgraded so that it can produce low sulphur fuel oil and improve quality of certain other products. The Mina Abdulla refinery was established in 1958 in order to refine heavy crude oil produced from the Wafra region. It has been expanded and upgraded since then to reach a daily capacity of high quality petroleum products in excess of 200,000 barrels. The third refinery to come on stream in Kuwait was the innovative plant at Shuaiba, believed to be the only refinery in the world completely powered by hydrogen. It is a highly adaptable plant, producing more than thirty different products and capable of switching from refining heavy oil to light oil at the press of a button.

Kuwait has not only demonstrated an adeptness at producing and refining petroleum products, but it has also played an active role in marketing. The launching of Kuwait Petroleum International's new marketing brand, 'Q8', was an important event for the European petroleum industry which had not seen the launch of a major new brand for fifteen years. The international call for unleaded petrol has also been met by KPI with its brand '2085' now a leader in this field. Another exciting innovation is a new odourless diesel fuel which is cleaner burning than ordinary diesel. In addition to the basic fuel oils, Kuwait Petroleum Company is actively engaged in other manufacturing. Urea production in 1986–87 actually exceeded design capacity by two percent, reaching 804.3 thousand metric tons while 683,000 metric tons of ammonia were produced. Salt and chlorine plants, including new units at Shuaiba, are another success story. Total net production of salt, chlorine and caustic soda in 1986–87 was approximately 43 thousand metric tons, a significant increase over previous years.

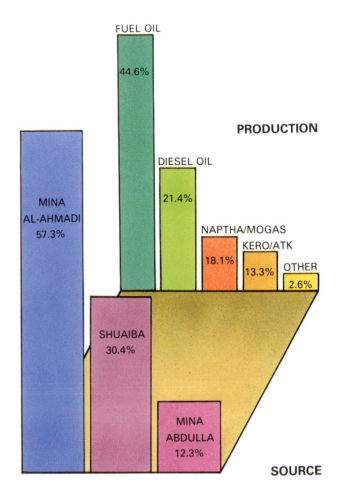

Fig. 34 Refined products profile from Kuwait refineries

Concern over the gradual depletion of light-crude oil has led to research work in maximising the gains from heavy residues. Whilst the 'H- Oil Process', as it is known, has been in operation at the Shuaiba refinery since 1968, there remains room for improvement and further development in this area. One of Kuwait's foremost research institutes, Kuwait Institute for Scientific Research, has recently teamed up with K.N.P.C. to investigate this field. The process of converting residues like asphalt to light products such as gasoline and kerosene uses a special ebullated reactor in which the residues remain very well mixed with hydrogen and the catalyst. Despite considerable success in Kuwait with this system, problems have arisen such as coking and excessive utilisation of expensive catalyst. A joint K.N.P.C. and K.I.S.R. team is, at the time of writing, investigating how to improve the system and they only require a one percent increase in productivity in order to pay back all research expenses in two years.

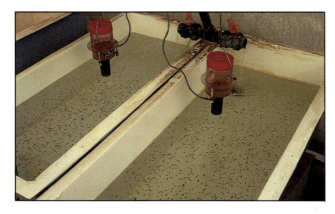

Shrimp trader at Kuwait's main fish market (*P.Vine*).

Mariculture research in Kuwait is carried out by Kuwait Institute for Scientific Research which has made impressive progress with raising several species including shrimps, sea-bream and groupers. At the time of writing (early 1989) their work was in the process of being translated into the commercial reality of Kuwaiti sea-farms (*P.Vine*).

As we have seen already, considerably importance in Kuwait is attached to scientific research which is regarded as the corner-stone for growth of the modern State. Several organisations play key roles in this field; eg. Kuwait Foundation for the Advancement of Sciences, Kuwait Institute for Scientific Research and Kuwait University. The first of these, KFAS, was established in 1976 upon the initiative of Sheikh Jaber Al-Ahmad Al-Jaber Al-Sabah, the present Amir of Kuwait, when he was Crown Prince. Various forms of support are provided to KFAS by both the Kuwait Chamber of Commerce and Industry and by Kuwait shareholding companies which contribute five percent of their profits each year to KFAS. The Foundation funds research work being carried out at the University, KISR, or at other research centres. Important support has been given to projects in basic and applied sciences as well as the arts and letters.

The Kuwait Institute of Scientific Research, commonly referred to as KISR, has already been mentioned in connection with some of the work carried out in the natural sciences field. Originally established in 1967, the Institute moved to new premises in February 1986, and is one of the most impressive research institutes in the world. Among the Institute's major objectives is undertaking applied scientific research related to food resources, fish cultivation, earth sciences, petrochemicals, engineering, techno-economics, and development of water resources particularly reverse osmosis of sea-water. A measure of the State's deep interest in KISR's work is provided by its 1986 budget of 56 million US dollars (KD 20 million) while a measure of Kuwait's success in the field of higher education is given by the fact that the institute's executive management and scientific staff are at least fifty percent Kuwaiti. KISR's pioneering work in warm water

RECREATION

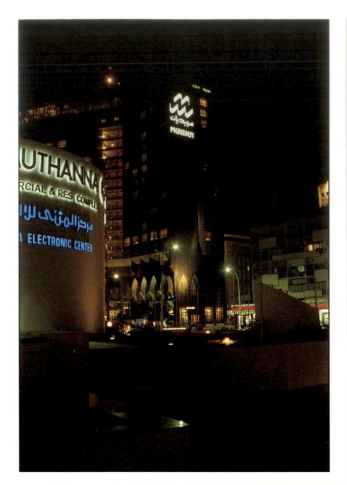

mariculture and fisheries science has already been described. Its work in other fields is equally fascinating and important in terms of providing support and guidance to Kuwait's agricultural and industrial sectors.

Given the financial resources of Kuwait, and its enthusiastic development of social facilities for its people, it is not surprising that the area of sport, leisure and recreation has also been given serious attention. Many coastal areas have been provided with comfortable facilities making visits to the beach considerably more enjoyable. Public recreation beaches have been established at Messilah, Aqila and Mangaf where a wide range of facilities are on offer such as swimming pools,

gardens, restaurants, amusement rides, and sea-fishing vantage points. Domestic tourism is promoted in Kuwait by the Touristic Enterprises Company which does an excellent job of managing various facilities as well as spreading information regarding what functions are scheduled. The company manages facilities with a total value in excess of a billion US dollars and estimates for visitors in 1987 were in excess of four million. The Khiran Resort, south of Kuwait city, is an attractive Arabian Gulf tourist complex where families can relax and enjoy a host of facilities. There are five sea-clubs along the shores of Kuwait which, in addition to providing convenient marina-style moorings for a host of boats, also have beaches, play-grounds, gymnasiums, saunas, swimming pools and other indoor attractions. Other major attractions for the citizens of Kuwait are the Entertainment City, a major ice-skating rink, Kuwait Towers and a host of world-class restaurants and hotels. Those in search of cultural interest have only to visit Failaka island where the excavations of various experts trace the island's past to the Bronze Age; or to enter one of the country's

magnificent museums such as Kuwait National Museum; Dar al-Athar al-Islamiya; or the Tareq Museum. Fascinating exhibits are also on view at Failaka Museum, Jahra's Red Palace, Beit al-Bader, and al Sadu House.

Whether one is travelling to Kuwait on business or pleasure, there is a strong chance that one will fly into the country on board a Kuwait Airlines aeroplane. KAC traces its origins back to March 1954 when the Kuwait National Airways Company was formed, providing a three times a week service to Basrah from an airport with a corrugated shed which doubled up as passenger terminal and maintenance hanger! Today Kuwait Airlines operates one of the most

modern and comprehensively equipped airline fleets in the world including Boeing's 747's, 767's, 727's and the Airbus A-300 and A-310 passenger aircraft together with several other kinds for special services. KAC places the highest possible priority on servicing, maintenance and safety and has its own fully equipped workshops and expert ground-crews. Despite difficulties experienced as a result of shrinkage of travel within the Gulf region during the recent Iraq-Iran war, KAC managed to improve its operating efficiency and maintain profitability. It is expected that the new improved situation in the region will bring many advantages and even greater success for KAC in the coming years.

A ruined market-place with telecommunications tower still standing in the background *(Peter Vine)*.

Invasion and Occupation

August 2nd 1990 to January 15th 1991

Colonel Salem Masaoud Saad Al-Sorour rose before the sun after less than two hours sleep. First he washed his face, hands and feet with water from a container strapped to the back of his command vehicle, then he knelt down to face the Holy City of Mecca which lay just over a thousand kilometres to the southwest. He began to pray. A quarter of an hour later he stood up. Still wearing yesterday's battle fatigues, he pulled on his boots and set out quietly to check on his men. He was deeply proud of what they had accomplished but confused and angered by the events of the previous 24 hours. Amidst the fray of battle, with men dying before his eyes, not knowing whether he and his comrades in the 35th Armoured Brigade would survive the fierce onslaught by Iraq's Republican Guard, there had been little time for emotion. Now however, as he walked among the tanks and other military vehicles of his exhausted brigade, he began to reflect upon the events of the previous 24 hours. Most of his soldiers still slept, many slumped at the wheels of their vehicles, their faces unusually pale, lips cracked and dry, uniforms dishevelled and covered in dust. Every slumbering soldier hugged his personal weapon as dearly as if it were a loved one. Colonel Salem savoured the moment. Deeply saddened by the loss of four of his men he nevertheless felt great pride in his battalion's performance.

Admittedly they had been unprepared for such a battle. For many days, as they had watched Iraq's forces gather across the border, they had been expecting instructions to arm their tanks, artillery vehicles and rocket launchers in order to prepare to defend against an attack. But the Kuwaiti government, deeply concerned about the enormous size of Iraq's army and the apparent impossibility of defending such a small country against a determined onslaught from their neighbour, had been engaged in urgent negotiations to find a peaceful solution to the mounting crisis. Whilst denying the litany of claims which Iraq had brought against Kuwait, faced by the threat of an invasion and the potential destruction of their country, the government had not given up hope that these talks would succeed. Anyone who has bartered for goods in an Arabian market will understand that facial expressions and body language are almost as vital as the spoken word in communicating one's message. Iraq had been trying to force Kuwait to 'buy peace' at an extortionate price. Kuwait was in the process of trying to talk the Iraqis into behaving responsibly. In such a delicate and sensitive situation they had been anxious not to send any signals to Baghdad which might be interpreted as indicating a willingness to participate in a military showdown. For the Kuwaiti government the best chance to solve their differences with Iraq was at the negotiating table rather than on the battlefield.

With the wisdom of hindsight things might have been different but at the time not one person in Kuwait, not even Colonel Salem and his military colleagues, suspected that Saddam Hussein would send his forces all the way to Kuwait City, occupying the entire country. First of all he had promised that he would not do so. Secondly, the extent of his recent territorial claims seemed to be restricted to the Kuwaiti section of the Rumaillah oilfield and Bubiyan island. At worst the country's political and military strategists believed that his forces might cross the border in an attempt to occupy these areas and there would be an early ceasefire and military standoff whilst peace negotiations under the additional duress of Iraq's temporary and partial occupation of Kuwaiti lands would take place. The secret of Saddam's plan to invade the whole country was well kept; not even revealed in full to many of the troops whom he sent in to do battle. Colonel Salem recalls how, when on the afternoon of August 2nd they captured officers of the elite Republican Guard, young men in civilian clothes with pockets full of money, the Iraqi soldiers had enquired from him why his forces had blocked their way. Astonished by such a question he asked them what they thought they were doing marching into Kuwait with battalions of armoured vehicles. "We are on an exercise," they replied, "it's part of our training". Unimpressed by the disingenuousness of their reply, and unable to take them with him, he tied them up, and left them in the desert.

Defence at Dawn

It was not until late on the night of August 1st, after the Iraqi force had entered Kuwaiti territory, that the armoured brigades of Kuwait's army were given the order to arm their tanks and other weapons in preparation for a military response. But it takes time to prepare a full brigade for war. Six hours or more are needed to load all the necessary ordnance and munitions to enable the military columns to leave their barracks as an effective fighting force. Colonel Salem did not have six hours and his men laboured all night, without rest, to prepare their tanks and other vehicles. The Iraqi army were advancing so fast that information was very difficult to analyse or verify. The Sixth Brigade to the north had not even been able to get out of their barracks, they had been so rapidly surrounded.

At 2am on the morning of August 2nd Colonel Salem received orders from army headquarters for their first mission. They were to take up positions outside of the camp, 70 kilometres to the north, and to spread out in an attempt to stop the enemy's advance. But there were reports that sections of the Iraqi army had already entered Kuwait City and it was becoming increasingly difficult to obtain clear information. Colonel Salem called in his company commanders and asked them how soon they would be ready for action. His tank and artillery commanders told him that the earliest they could leave the barracks would be in another four hours, at 6am. By 4am all he could muster was a TOW column of armoured vehicles together with his command vehicle and a jeep. He ordered that these be lined up at the main gate and went back to his communications centre to clarify the situation. His officers there informed him that they expected an order to be "moving soon". Fearing that they too would be overrun before they were able to get

Above: destroyed tank in front of a ransacked building.
Right: Al Seif Palace in ruins. *(Ministry of Information)*.

away from the barracks, he once again called the military headquarters in Kuwait city. It was now after 4am and the HQ once again told him that they were awaiting more information.

As the first light of dawn was beginning to show on the horizon, Colonel Salem went to pray at the small mosque within the barracks. On his return, there was still no clear information regarding the position of the advancing Iraqi forces and Colonel Salem decided that he must leave with those forces which he had ready. "I'll be in touch with you on my way north", he told his communications officer as he led his force out from the barracks at 4.30am.

Twenty minutes later, as they were speeding northwards, his base informed him that the main headquarters had been abandoned, that everything had been destroyed, but that the commanders were operating from a secret fall-back position and his force had been issued with three missions. Firstly they were to secure the Ali Salem Air Base; secondly they should secure the Atraf junction, east of the air-base and thirdly they were to block the main north-south road at Mutlaa, close to Jahra.

Instructing his TOW Company commander to use his forces to attempt to secure both the airbase and the junction, Colonel Salem continued towards Mutlaa with just his command vehicle and jeep. On arriving close to the camel market at Jahra he stopped. "To tell you the truth", he told me, "I knew the Iraqis must be in Jahra since I could hear the noise of hundreds of their vehicles." Waiting there for a moment, unsure of what he could do, a Kuwaiti soldier came running up to his vehicle. "The Iraqis are there in the school. They told us that unless we all strip off our uniforms they will kill us. How did they get there?" he asked, totally bewildered by what had happened.

Deeply angered by this news and incensed by the belligerence of the Iraqi army, Colonel Salem picked up the microphone of his radio and called his camp. "Send me anything that you have ready", he

commanded. Fortunately, Seven Company commander was there at the time. "Yes sir, I'm coming. Where are you?" he replied. Within minutes 25 Chieftain tanks were on the road north, racing against time to support their Brigade Commander and to challenge the Iraqi army. Colonel Salem awaited their arrival with mounting anxiety.

As soon as they reached Colonel Salem's position, at around 6.30am, he discussed their task with the company commander. "Our mission is to block the Abdali road, in front of the Iraqis. Let's go. Let's do what we have been instructed to do. Let us accomplish our mission", he ordered. Moving to take up position on the opposite side of the road, close to the Jahra Cemetery, a line of military vehicles appeared in front of them. "Who are those vehicles, Sir?" the company commander asked Colonel Salem. "Those are the enemy!" the brigade commander replied, "So Fire!" It was the first time the Seven Company commander and his men had ever been ordered to fire in a real battle and the order took a split second to fully register. "Should I fire?" the commander asked again. "Yes, fire!" ordered Colonel Salem and so began the longest and bloodiest battle of the day. It was a quarter to seven in the morning.

The advancing Iraqi force had clearly not expected this opposition. As the tanks of Kuwait's 35th Brigade began hitting and destroying the enemy vehicles, hundreds of soldiers dismounted. Within minutes the road was blocked by damaged vehicles and soldiers, halting the progress of a long line of tanks, armoured personnel carriers, trucks and unmarked civilian cars. The Kuwaiti force kept up a relentless and highly effective barrage of fire against the invading army. It was not until later in the day that they discovered they had been fighting against the crack forces of the Republican Guard and that the men in unmarked cars were their commanding officers. After a while they were joined by 16 tanks from 8th Company whose commander was told to take the right flank. Instinctively understanding what was required of him the Kuwaiti officer ordered his tanks to spread out and they began firing immediately, hitting and destroying the first advancing vehicle in a new wave of the Iraqi attack.

Again the Iraqis dismounted from their burning vehicles, gathering on the road and along each side of it. As each tank or armoured personnel carrier approached within range of the Kuwaiti brigade it was hit. "We learned later that this new advancing force belonged to the Mugharabhi Republican Guard", Colonel Salem explained. "By late afternoon we could see that despite our success against this particular force the battle to save Kuwait had moved against us. We watched flights of 30 Iraqi helicopters flying towards Kuwait City and then returning before flying south again." It was clear that Kuwait's armed forces had been outnumbered and now the 35th Brigade was also at risk from an advancing mass of soldiers, this time on foot. "I told my Artillery Company commander to stop shooting at the tanks so that my infantry force could deal with the Iraqi infantry. We could not capture them since we knew their tactics. They were moving to surround us before using anti-tank weapons against us". Iraq's army officers were using their soldiers on what amounted to suicide missions since the Kuwaitis were left with no option but to halt their advance, killing large numbers of them.

By two in the afternoon, following about eight hours of fighting by the Al-Shahid 35th Brigade, under command of Colonel Salem, the mission begun earlier in the day had been well accomplished with the north-south road blocked, Ali Salem airbase defended and the area from the junction to their northern position secured, but in the absence of a large back-up force there was no chance of holding such a position.

At what seemed to be the eleventh hour it looked as if help was on its way. The observation officer of the force which had been seconded to secure the Atraf junction radioed to Colonel Salem that a brigade of tanks had passed along the road, coming towards his position from the south-west. Both men initially thought that these tanks were coming from a special force stationed in Saudi Arabia. "Make sure that they are friendly forces", Colonel Salem told his fellow officer. He had reason to be cautious and immediately spoke on the radio to an officer at the new temporary HQ in Kuwait City. "Nobody informed us about such a special defensive force from Saudi Arabia," they told the colonel.

A complete brigade of this unidentified force managed to reach about two kilometres from where Colonel Salem had his troops deployed. "They look different, Sir. Their vehicles are different and we can hear them on the radio, they are speaking differently", his observation officer told him. By this stage Colonel Salem was used to the tactics being employed by the Iraqis and without a moment's hesitation he replied, "This is the enemy. Fire! Destroy the enemy!". It was an intense and close fought battle in which every type of available weapon was employed, from small arms to tank guns. The Kuwaiti force destroyed a complete brigade of what they later discovered was the Al Madina Republican Guard.

The Withdrawal South

By now the 35th Brigade knew that they had enemy forces advancing from the north and from the south-west. Repeated requests for air and artillery support to come to their aid were met by no response. "At that time it seemed that nothing was available", Colonel Salem explained. "We were running short of ammunition. By three o'clock all the commanders notified me that their ammunition would be finished if we were going to continue fighting and we had no means of replenishing our supplies. By this stage we had already finished our third supply of ammunition. The situation was such that I felt obliged to ask HQ for assistance in the form of air and artillery. I asked four times for assistance. Then the Iraqis began to realise what situation we were in and I could see that they were gathering, moving in on us from both the left and the right. They began to shell us with mortars. I lost four in my command and ten were injured. We tried to stay but the situation began to turn on us. It was no longer in our favour. I could see that the Republican Guard were stopped way behind the junction and they started to spread from the west to the east. I knew that they were going to flank us from all directions and they would then ask for the Iraqi air force to destroy us. I told the HQ about the situation. 'I am certain you should send me some help', I told them. They said 'You are the man in this situation. You have to decide what to do. To tell you the truth, it is impossible to offer you support from the air force or artillery'. Within our area of the conflict one Kuwaiti aircraft had been active, striking forces from the junction to the south-west. I took the decision and informed my commanders that we would retreat to the south. It was

Devastation at Al Seif Palace (*Ministry of Information*).

the only way. We had to break through the Iraqi forces to the south."

"I am very proud of my officers. They appreciated the situation we were in and the 8th Company moved with their artillery and missiles, covering our retreat and defending a new base. We retreated to an area called Al Haya, to be away from enemy fire and we managed to break through and go there. But the enemy managed to damage two tanks. When we arrived at Al Haya we found that the area was good for the track vehicles but too soft for the wheeled vehicles which sank in the sand. In addition there was no cover, we were in the open. Also, to tell you the truth, the Iraqis were on the same channel. I could hear them and they could hear me! They thought that we were going to go to the broadcasting station and they said: 'OK… let's have them going there and we will encircle them and destroy them with artillery'. They didn't know that I was going south and we went further, to get away from their mortar shells and then we waited and regrouped. I called on my commanders to make sure that everyone was there and to check on their situation. Whilst we were regrouping six Iraqi fighter planes flew over us. We realised that if we stayed in the area the enemy would follow us. It was going to be very difficult at night and we had no logistical support. We had only the water, ammunition, food, fuel etc, that we carried with us. We had 31 tanks… two had broken down. We had 17 APCs to our BMB2s and we had 18 with our 113s. So I decided to move further south to the last point, before the Saudi border.

"We moved in formation, with the commander of the Second Company in the front tank as a guide. Then the artillery was behind, followed by the rest of the logistics. Whoever could manage. It was very difficult with vehicles getting bogged down in the sand but we had to keep going. I was concerned to protect my soldiers. We reached our destination close to the Saudi border and, after we re-formed, I sent my last message of that day to our HQ, explaining where we were. Next we discussed our situation with the Saudi border guards and they were very understanding. I told them that we were expecting the enemy at any time so I might be forced to cross into Saudi Arabia. I said that if this caused any inconvenience to them they should let me talk with their senior officers. They sent a message to their command HQ and after two hours, at 8pm, the commanding officer came and told us that he had orders to request us to move inside Saudi Arabia since if we stayed on the border the enemy would come to us."

"These preparations to move took a long time. At two in the morning we began to enter Saudi Arabia. I am very grateful to the Saudis for their efforts. They supplied everything, water, fuel, rations, tents, everything we needed except ammunition. We went south until we reached a new defensive location about 20 kilometres inside the border. We took up a defensive position and immediately I told everyone, except those assigned to guard the place, to go and rest. We had been going for a long time. We had struck the enemy at a quarter to seven the previous morning and we fought until four o'clock. Just over nine hours, fighting non-stop. Then we drove from four o'clock, reaching the Saudi border at six o'clock. We regrouped and it took us a long time to gather our vehicles and forces. Some people went back to gather the broken-down vehicles. When they had become stuck the soldiers had stayed with them so we went back to bring them with us. Some even went back to our main base camp to bring rations and vehicles. The enemy did not actually find and enter our 35th Brigade barracks until Sunday so we were able to save some equipment.

"At seven o'clock on the morning of August 3rd, I heard loud explosions. A bit later in the morning some intelligence officers arrived, sent to me from the Saudi Arabian government. They told me that the Iraqi forces had been searching for our brigade and had crossed into Saudi Arabia, dropping four bombs. They had violated Saudi air and land space.

"I told the Saudi officers that our country had been invaded, that we had not finished our battle and that we were ready to fight to defend our land, if necessary until the last one of us was killed. For us the battle was not over and we said that we wanted to re-arm our weapons and return to fight. They understood our position but we were told to await further instructions. After a week I managed to get in touch with the Ministry of Defence in Saudi Arabia and I was asked to meet with them in Dharan. I went there and so began our cooperation with the coalition forces in the eventual liberation of Kuwait".

Saddam's Propaganda Offensive

In order to find out more about how the situation had appeared from the viewpoint of Kuwait's military command, we spoke with Major-General Jaber Khaled Al-Sabah, Deputy Head of the Armed Forces. "Before you talk of August 2nd", he told us, "You have to consider what happened on July 15th. The memorandum which was sent to the Arab League and United Nations shocked us completely with the unbelievable stories and completely unjustified accusations which it contained. We believed that there must be some hidden reason behind Iraq's sudden raising of the temperature. Although these were political events they affected military thinking. It is like the carriage and the horse, we are the carriage and the political arm

Iraqi vehicles destroyed near the 6th Ring Road/Motorway *(Ministry of Information)*.

of government is the horse. You cannot divide the political side from the military because we represent the muscle which the political arm of government uses when it is necessary to do so.

"During the 'Seventeen Days Period', as we call it, before the 2nd August, there was very high political activity. It did not need any great intelligence to confirm that the Iraqis had their forces on the border all the time, as they had done since day one. We had a bad feeling among the military and we expressed that feeling. But the political answer for us was to be patient, to not raise any tension, that it was mainly a show of force which we were witnessing. To me it exceeded a show of force. Our observations of their manoeuvres on the border seemed to indicate that Saddam Hussein was definitely planning something. But I do not blame the politicians. Virtually all analysts, including the Americans and the British, believed that it was a show of force.

"There is one very sensitive question which we must consider. Supposing that we, as the military, had dispersed our forces: there is a strategic theory known as 'one to three'. For each man in defence you need three in attack. But if you are one in defence against 22 in attack you are in a very critical situation".

This point had been made to us by others and it was

quite clear that many people's opinions of what happened or should have happened during the 'Seventeen Days' period and on August 2nd itself, depended upon their own particular perspective of the situation and their insight into the issues at stake. We found it hard to disagree with the view that, had the Kuwaiti military shown themselves to be ready to do battle against the vastly superior Iraqi force, that many more military personnel and civilians would have lost their lives and much greater destruction would have been wrought to Kuwait. It might also have been more difficult to develop a clear picture to the world of who had been the aggressor in the conflict since there is little doubt that Saddam Hussein would have added one more spurious claim to his list of accusations: i.e. that Kuwait had fired the first shot. Whilst many observers have found it difficult to understand the insistence by Kuwait's leaders, right up to the moment of the invasion, on a political solution, we believe that when all the facts are considered, the strategy employed was probably in the best interests of the country and its people.

Hindsight is a very accurate science and it is all too easy to be wise after the event. As Major-General Jaber Al-Sabah reiterated, "Nobody knew the mind of Saddam Hussein, even his forces did not know what

Iraqi tank in trench *(Ministry of Information)*.

he was planning to do. Nobody knew, except God. Even his soldiers whom we faced did not know why they were here. When they found a resistance against them they said, 'Why are you resisting? We are coming to assist you!' There was a propaganda inside the Iraqi army itself which camouflaged the truth. Thus nobody expected that Iraq was intending to invade and occupy the whole of Kuwait. To be honest with you our Military Command thought that the Iraqi forces might cross our border to occupy those areas which they had laid recent claims to: on the Rumaillah oilfield and at Bubiyan island. We expected that this border dispute would give us time to mount a response. But nobody, not even the superpowers with their high technology surveillance equipment, thought that Iraq would invade.

Kuwait's Military Response

"Up to that point the entire calculation had been political. The military started to switch on on Wednesday night, August 1st. At two o'clock on Thursday morning we gave orders for our army to begin to disperse in order to face the Iraqi army. At that time the Sixth Brigade in Raudithain area began to try to move but they could not even get outside their gate. Many of the Iraqi column had already passed their gate on the road heading south. The 35th Brigade on the west side was in a kind of readiness. They got the order to defend Al Jahra. We knew at this stage that the Iraqis were advancing with three ground columns, one from the west, the major one straight down the middle of Kuwait, from the north, and the third from the east. We instructed the 35th Brigade to hold and defend Al Jahra Ridge. This is the only brigade which got the chance from among the ground forces to fight. They fought very bravely".

We asked Major-General Jaber to summarise what happened to his other forces. "The air force also fought very bravely. Between themselves and our ground air defences we put about 53 enemy helicopters out of action. In addition the 15th Brigade which was stationed to the south started to push one battalion towards the headquarters in order to support the HQ. We also had a platoon in the other headquarters. The 80th Brigade, which is a reserve brigade, started to gather its force but by that time the Iraqis surrounded them so they could not move or get out of their camp. The two major battles which took place were with the 15th Brigade led by Colonel Mohammed and the 35th Brigade led by Colonel Salem. The 15th Brigade had great difficulty getting away from their barracks but they used a rear gate and nearly got a full battalion out, including some TOWs, some BMB2s and some tanks. So far as the air force was concerned, they fought very bravely but when our ground forces were no longer able to secure the airfields it became impossible to land and operate from there so they took their aircraft south and into the safety of Saudi Arabia."

The battle continued after August 2nd. Major-General Jaber explained to us that he had been in touch with the 80th Brigade on Friday August 3rd at 3pm. They were more or less trapped within their camp. He gave them an order to try to break through, but the Iraqi force was far too strong for them. They were surrounded by forces on the 7th Ring Road and the Al Jahra road. Following orders to do so, many of their officers escaped during the night, and secretly made their way back into Kuwait city in order to help establish the Resistance. "A large percentage of the Kuwait Resistance were from the military. They moved and re-organised themselves, saving some of their equipment so they could start to resist."

Although Kuwaiti records confirm that 120 military personnel were killed by Iraqis during the invasion and occupation, at the time of writing there remain over a thousand who are unaccounted for. Among those who died on August 2nd was Sheikh Fahd al-Ahmad al-Sabah, half brother of the Emir of Kuwait. Sheikh Fahd was well known and well liked in Kuwait since he was a committed supporter of all forms of sport. As a member of the International Olympics Committee and president of the Olympic Council of Asia, he was one of the most influential people in the world of sport. His personal love of football had led him to become president of the Kuwait Football Association and vice-president of the international governing body of football, FIFA. He died from injuries sustained in fierce fighting at the Dasman royal palace. It is said that the Iraqi soldiers were unaware of whom they had killed butwwhen it was later discovered, the Iraqi government sent officers on a vain mission to locate Sheikh Fahd's body. No Kuwaiti would ever have cooperated with them on such a foul mission and the Iraqis gave up. Meanwhile he was secretly buried in an unmarked grave in the main cemetery on the outskirts of Kuwait city.

Roots of Iraqi Aggression

Many analysts believe that the Iraqi invasion was planned and prepared for long before Saddam Hussein launched his propaganda campaign against Kuwait. Military build-up for an attack on Kuwait appears to have begun in 1989, not long after the Iran-Iraq War ceasefire. Having failed in the political and military objectives of his aggression against Iran, the Iraqi leader apparently turned his attention to how best to use the awesomely powerful war machine which he had acquired. Peace did not appear to be on the Iraqi dictator's agenda for peace brought the opportunity for his long suffering populace to direct their thoughts towards the political arrangements which were at the root cause of their suffering. Peace threatened to cause internal instability for Saddam Hussein and his compliant Baath government. War kept his armed forces fully occupied and justified a continuing state of high security in the country. Not only did it take people's minds off the daily hardships they faced through massive over-spending on weaponry and armed forces, but it brought the promise of a quick profit for all echelons of Iraqi society, from the ruling elite to the poorly paid foot-soldier.

Iraq's small but wealthy neighbour offered a suitable target for a renewed military campaign. On a purely cost-benefit accounting basis Iraq stood to gain a great deal if it could conquer and hold Kuwait. By July 1990 the military forces were ready. A hundred and twenty officers who cautioned against such aggression, refusing to support the invasion, were reported to have been summarily executed. (This was later confirmed by a number of Arab diplomats who arrived in Syria, from Kuwait, in late August.)

In order to provide some basis for an attack on Kuwait Saddam turned to his propaganda advisors. What could they throw at Kuwait? How could they justify such aggression? How could they invade an Arab neighbour and yet still maintain the support of other Arab nations? In short, how could Iraq walk into Kuwait, take over the country, steal its wealth and remain with the moral high ground? A difficult game to play. Most would have said impossible but that would not have been a wise response to make to a president who was reported to murder those who disagreed with him. Propaganda is a powerful weapon since it can convince people to risk their lives for a tissue of lies. The main objective of the Iraqi leadership was that the message which went out to the world, and to the people of Iraq, should cloud the truth. The great danger, or perhaps one might describe it as a strength, of such propaganda is that the instigators (in this case the Iraqi government led by Saddam Hussein) come to believe in their own side's distortion of the truth. Such "feed-back" is a constant hazard of covert disinformation activities, generally feared by security forces engaged in these activities. In the case of Iraq however the security personnel involved in propaganda probably felt rewarded if their efforts to create the much needed justification for war happened to convince their paymaster as well as a large number of their own countrymen and fellow Arabs.

Wanton destruction – the evidence which remained in Kuwait photographed after the liberation

Top: sunken vessels in a wrecked dhow harbour

Right: computer room with smashed terminals

Bottom left: the gutted interior of Kuwait National Museum

Bottom right: the blown-up historic monument, remnants of the old city wall and gate of Kuwait City

(Photographs: Ministry of Information)

A large partoof Iraq's problems were financial. Despite the fact that it was one of the world's largest oil producers with ten percent of the planet's proven reserves within its territory, Iraq had paid a heavy price for the hostilities against Iran and it was seeking means to write off its debts to the Arabian Gulf States. A weak price for oil in the world market was used as a basis for criticising Kuwait despite the fact that the Jedda Meeting of July 10-11 reached an agreement by all participants (including Kuwait) to curb production until the reference price of $18 per barrel was restored. But it appeared that Iraq was not really seeking a genuine negotiated resolution of its declared differences with Kuwait. Six days after the accord in Jedda, Saddam Hussein, in a revolution day speech, stated "if words fail to protect Iraqis, something effective must be done to return things to their natural course and return usurped rights to their owners". In a subsequent letter addressed to the Secretary General of the Arab League, Chedli Klibi, the Iraqi Foreign Minister, Tariq Aziz, developed his leader's case against Kuwait, claiming that Kuwait had been mounting a long-standing policy aimed at weakening Iraq, a claim which the Kuwaiti Government were quick to deny, stating that it had "no factual basis". Given that Kuwait had been making generous loans to Iraq throughout the Iran-Iraq War it was also an accusation which many felt hard to sustain. Aziz's claim that Kuwait had been using the cover of the Iran-Iraq conflict to occupy Iraqi territory was also firmly rebutted as "a falsification of reality and a resumé of inverted truths". The Kuwaiti rebuttal further stated that, far from having designs upon Iraqi territory, the boot was on the other foot with Iraq having a "full history of violations of Kuwaiti territories".

The Search for Peace

Kuwait had no designs on Iraqi territory and sought only peaceful relations with her much larger and heavily militarised neighbour. On the diplomatic front Kuwait sought to defuse the effects of Iraq's propaganda, stressing that her main interest was in peaceful and friendly relations. But Iraq kept up the verbal attack on Kuwait, focussing its efforts at garnering support from other Arab countries. So far as control of the oil price was concerned, Iraq's earlier arguments against Kuwait had been neutralised by a rise in the oil price and by the oil ministers' OPEC meeting in Geneva on July 26-27 when it was agreed to raise the reference price to $21 per barrel. It was clear however that Iraq intended to keep up the tension. The decision to invade Kuwait was already made. It was essential that the attack appeared to come as a result of a peak of tension over apparently insurmountable disagreements.

During the build-up to Iraq's aggression against Kuwait there had been fierce diplomatic activity. The Iraqi leader and his emissaries were trying to consolidate whatever promises of support they had been able to extract from fellow Arab states. We have no direct knowledge of what offers, if any, were made to the handful of countries which sided with Iraq. Of course it is hard to be certain precisely what was said or what secret agreements were reached, but it is clear that the Iraqis were actively engaged in some form of power brokering. To be fair to the other participants in this dangerous international intrigue, nobody has accused them of actively encouraging Iraq in its aggression. It was the Iraqis who made the running and who proposed various arrangements to different heads of government. Their arguments were persuasive, supported by propaganda which they had generated against Kuwait, and were backed by one of the largest military machines in the world. In each case, one can be sure that Iraqi negotiators picked upon the most effective arguments, tailored to each nation's own needs. For their own part the leaders of these client-nations listened to what was said, took note of what was offered, most likely cautioned against the dangers of failure, were influenced by the sheer might of Iraq's military forces, and presumably agreed to at least sit on the fence for a while, if not to publicly support the venture. This was as much as the Iraqis could expect. They were bargaining on a nucleus of Arab support which would help to influence other nations and prevent their complete isolation.

President Mubarak of Egypt was aware that Iraq had designs upon Kuwait and that Saddam Hussein was seeking support for military action from some other Arab countries. The Iraqis would have been delighted to draw him into their plan but President Mubarak had made it clear that he was not interested in supporting any such moves against a fellow Arab nation and that he believed in peaceful settlements to international disputes. On July 24th, he made flying visits to Kuwait, Saudi Arabia and Iraq, listening to each leader's viewpoint and stressing the need for a negotiated settlement. On his return to Cairo he announced that a special meeting would be held between Iraqi and Kuwaiti delegates in Jeddah at the end of July. He also stated that the Iraqi president had assured him that Iraq had no intention of attacking Kuwait or of moving his forces along the Kuwaiti border.

At the same time however, Iraqi forces were being moved into position for an attack against Kuwait. Satellite surveillance indicated that two Iraqi armoured divisions numbering around 30,000 soldiers were approaching the Kuwaiti border at the very time when Saddam denied all such intentions to President Mubarak. Military strategists in Kuwait and elsewhere believed that this build-up of forces against Kuwait was aimed at creating undue pressure for fellow Arab countries to toe the Iraqi line on oil prices at the forthcoming OPEC conference in Geneva (on July 26-27). Whilst fearing Iraq's intentions, few believed that it would really invade Kuwait. In the event, the Geneva meeting did result in rapid agreement on an oil price hike to $21 per barrel, albeit not as high as the $25 figure which Iraq and Libya had requested. Iraq's military threat in the Middle East had no influence on the South American nation of Venezuela which was the most outspoken in its opposition to Iraq's position, arguing that the $18 price should be maintained.

The promised talks between Iraq and Kuwait were eventually held late on July 31st in Jeddah. They were led on the Iraqi side by Izzat Ibrahim, vice-chairman of the Revolutionary Command Council, and on the Kuwaiti side by Prime Minister and Crown Prince Sheikh Saad al Abdullah as Salim as Sabah. During the two-hour meeting the Iraqis presented a series of demands to Kuwait including a requirement that all debts by Iraq should be written off by Kuwait and that Kuwait should cede to Iraq certain areas of Kuwaiti territory. In all, the Iraqis were reported to have demanded 10 billion US dollars in aid; debt write-offs of a further 10 billion dollars; relinquishing of Kuwait's section of the Rumaillah oil field which straggles the border between the two countries; 2.4 billion US dollars in payment for oil which Kuwait had legitimately extracted from its section of this field; and finally a long-term lease (effectively a total gift) of the islands of Bubiyan and Warba.

Kuwait rejected the demands as unjustified, unreasonable and threatening in their nature. The talks broke down and the Iraqi delegation left abruptly for Baghdad. It is quite clear that a decision had already been made to attack Kuwait and that these 'talks' were part of the sham aimed at creating some form of *casus belli* for the imminent invasion. Had the Kuwaitis been intimidated into appeasement of her belligerent neighbour, conceding these unjustified demands, Iraq would have been in a position to maintain its blackmail against Kuwait, always threatening military action and continuing to threaten other Arab countries with similar action. In short, Iraq's belligerence destabilised the whole region, risking new wars, causing widespread oppression, bloodshed and suffering. Somebody had to call a halt to the madness which was gripping the region and Kuwait was about to bear the brunt of the punishment for its brave stand against the bellicose Iraqi leader's ruthless and self-aggrandising pursuit of power. Less than two days after the Jeddah conference Iraq's deceit was revealed to the whole world.

Iraq Invades

Shortly before 2am local time on August 2nd 100,000 Iraqi troops, including 30,000 Republican Guards already massed at the Kuwaiti border invaded Kuwait. Despite the efforts of Kuwait's armed forces to stem the tide of the invasion, the Iraqis were inside Kuwait City by 7am local time. They were supported by the Iraqi air force which attacked the airport and other key installations. For most of that day fierce battles raged between Kuwaiti forces and the Iraqis with some considerable acts of bravery by the vastly outnumbered Kuwaitis. By mid-afternoon most of the city was under Iraqi control although fierce fighting continued to the north of the city.

As part of its propaganda programme the Iraqis decided to put some clothes on their naked aggression. They made several attempts at this. First of all they declared that this was not an invasion at all. What it was, they announced, was a visit by Iraqi forces in response to an urgent invitation by internal 'revolutionaries' who were mounting a popular coup against the Kuwaiti government. Having taken control of the broadcasting station a 'Provisional Free Kuwait Government' began broadcasting. The only problem with this 'government' was that it was not 'free', nor did it contain a single Kuwaiti! It was a very crude attempt to make Iraq's outright rejection of the norms of international law and moral decency gain some level of legitimacy. Needless to say the attempt completely failed and was seen by the international community for exactly what it was: an inept attempt at disguising the true situation with regard to Iraq's unprovoked attack.

Whilst declaring that its efforts in Kuwait had some form of local support, Iraq simultaneously closed the Kuwaiti border and imposed an indefinite curfew. Having completed the first phase of aggression the Revolutionary Command Council in Iraq broadcast warnings against "foreign intervention" in Iraq or Kuwait and one of these early broadcasts declared that Iraq would "turn Kuwait into a graveyard" if any country was "moved by the lust of invasion". It was quite clear however that it was Iraq which had been moved by the "lust of invasion" and her troops wasted little time in giving vent to that lust.

Two days after announcing the establishment of a 'Provisional Free Government of Kuwait', and in the midst of a military build-up and clamp-down, Iraq claimed to have commenced its withdrawal from Kuwait. In reality a number of Kuwait's tanks and other military hardware, together with commandeered trucks laden with the spoils of looting were being driven to Iraq. Simultaneously Saddam Hussein recalled elements of his Revolutionary Guard to control mounting unrest within Iraq and to take part

The United Nations votes to approve the use of force (©1990 Christopher Morris/Black Star – Colorific!).

in the massive military cordon around himself. The need to maintain essential services and to establish security control over the population of occupied Kuwait led the Iraqis to demand that key workers return to their jobs. Whilst many Palestinians responded to this demand, almost no Kuwaitis did so. (In fact the Kuwaitis who did return to work were hospital staff who had Kuwaiti patients under their care.) It is doubtful whether Iraq's claim to be "withdrawing" was believed by any of the international community since all the evidence pointed to the contrary. Indeed, having failed to prop up a puppet government, Saddam Hussein had little option but to reveal his true hand and to admit that Iraq intended to erase the existence of a free and independent Kuwait from the world map. On August 8th, after six days of belligerent rhetoric, prevarication and a barrage of lies, Iraq announced that it had annexed Kuwait.

The Iraqi propaganda machine, in overdrive by this time, presented this annexation as a direct result of a request by Colonel Hussain (an Iraqi army officer) who had been earlier appointed as premier of the puppet government. It was announced that the cabinet members of the 'Provisional Free Kuwait Government', all of whom were Iraqis, would join the cabinet of Iraq with Colonel Hussain becoming a Deputy Prime Minister in Iraq. Needless to say, this

incredibly naive deception fooled nobody, except perhaps the officers who had so suddenly lost their positions in the PFKG puppet regime. On August 28th Iraq declared that Kuwait was now the 19th governorate (*liwa*) of Iraq.

Whilst Iraq was trying to redraw the political map of the Middle East, the rest of the world was making its position clear. Sadly, Iraq's move against Kuwait, together with its bribery of other Arab governments, caused a split in Arab ranks. On the one hand the legitimate government of Kuwait, together with Egypt, Saudi Arabia, Syria, Bahrain, Morocco, Oman, Qatar and the UAE firmly supported the exiled Kuwaitis, whilst on the other hand Jordan, the PLO, Yemen, Sudan, Tunisia, Mauritania and Algeria failed to do so. It is still not clear precisely why these governments took the view they did for by giving even tacit support to Iraq they were in effect discarding the norms of international law and consequently placing themselves in a position to be harshly judged by the world community. Outside the Arab world, condemnation of the invasion was virtually unanimous. The United Nations Security Council (comprising China, France, USSR, UK and USA as permanent members and Canada, Colombia, Ivory Coast, Cuba, Ethiopia, Finland, Malaysia, Romania, Yemen and Zaire as non-permanent members) passed a series of resolutions condemning the invasion.

The United Nations Acts

On the day of the invasion, August 2nd 1990, Resolution 660 was unanimously passed, without the participation of Yemen. It condemned the Iraqi invasion, demanded an immediate and unconditional withdrawal of Iraqi forces and called for a negotiated settlement. On August 6th Resolution 661 was passed unanimously (with Yemen and Cuba abstaining). It imposed mandatory sanctions against Iraqi and Kuwaiti trade, effectively isolating Iraq and occupied Kuwait from sale or transshipment of oil or other commodities and products. The resolution further banned new investments and sale to Iraq or occupied Kuwait of any products except medical supplies and foodstuffs in "humanitarian circumstances". On August 9th Resolution 662 was passed unanimously and declared Iraq's "annexation" of Kuwait as null and void. The resolution demanded that Iraq rescind its declaration and called upon all states and institutions to give no signs of direct or indirect recognition to the annexation. On August 18th Resolution 664 also received unanimous support. It demanded that "Iraq permit and facilitate the departure from Kuwait and Iraq of the nationals of third countries" and that consular officials be given immediate and continuing access to such foreign nationals. The resolution also called for rescindment of orders closing down consular offices in Kuwait and for withdrawal of diplomatic immunity from their staff. On August 25th Resolution 665 was passed by 13-0 with Cuba and Yemen again abstaining. It authorised the use of maritime force to maintain an effective blockade against Iraq and called upon all states to cooperate by political and diplomatic means to ensure compliance with sanctions.

Four more UN resolutions were passed in September 1990. Resolution 666 was passed by a vote of 13-2 with Cuba and Yemen voting against. It allowed for an Indian ship to deliver food to its stranded nationals in Iraq. Cuba and Iraq had favoured an alternative resolution which would have removed all restrictions on food being sent to Iraq, effectively lifting a major part of the sanctions policy. Resolution 667, passed unanimously on September 16th, condemned the break-in by Iraqi soldiers into diplomatic premises in Kuwait. It also resolved to discuss measures to tighten the embargo on Iraq. Resolution 669, unanimously passed on September 24th, authorised the sanctions committee to review requests for assistance from countries experiencing economic difficulties caused by their observance of the embargo against Iraq. Resolution 670, passed by a 14-1 vote with only Cuba opposed, extended the trade embargo to provide for effective control of air-traffic into and out of Iraq, permitting interdiction of aircraft believed to be break-ing the sanctions policy. It also called on member states to enforce the sanctions policy as rigorously as possible, including detention of Iraqi ships and freezing of Iraqi assets. It also firmly condemned the "human shield" policy, describing it as a "grave breach" of the fourth Geneva convention on the rules of war.

Unfortunately however the determined international protest at Iraq's invasion and occupation of Kuwait did not seem to influence Iraq's dictator. Whilst the world community was intent on making its abhorrence known, Iraqi forces in Kuwait were engaged in dismantling the physical and social structure of the country. Within a week of the invasion, by August 9th, explosive charges had been placed on all of Kuwait's oil installations together with its vital desalination and electricity generating plants. Whilst preparing for a long occupation, Iraq was also determined, if forced to withdraw, to execute its threatened scorched-earth policy which had been earlier announced by the Revolutionary Command Council.

Refugees, Hostages and Torture

Shortly after the invasion, on August 9th, Iraq closed the borders of Iraq and Kuwait to foreigners who were trying to flee the country. Whilst Kuwaiti resistance fighters and Bedouin people who knew the desert area intimately showed great courage in escorting many groups of people out of Kuwait and into Saudi Arabia, there were considerable risks involved. On August 12th Iraqi soldiers at the Saudi-Kuwait border shot and killed Donald Croskery, a British businessman, who had been trapped in Kuwait and was trying to escape. On August 16th the Iraqis demanded that all American and British citizens in Kuwait should surrender themselves to the Iraqis or face unspecified "difficulties". After several debacles most but not all of these people complied with the threatening instructions. Iraq then used many of these hostages as "human-shields" transferring them to strategic sites such as air fields, weapons plants, nuclear facilities and oil installations in Iraq. It was felt that the deposition of these foreign civilians would deter attacks from the rapidly mounting coalition of forces arrayed against Iraq.

Iraq of course denied that these people were prisoners, hostages or 'human shields". They chose to describe them as "guests". Western governments were anxious to avoid any suggestion that what President Bush described as this "ruthless assault on the very essence of international order and civilised ideals" would influence their firm opposition to Iraq's aggression. After weeks of this mistreatment wives and children of the male hostages were permitted to leave Iraq but men were retained, suffering terribly under the conditions of their detention and in constant fear of their lives.

During the first month after the invasion there was a massive exodus of refugees into Saudi Arabia, Jordan and Turkey. Well over half a million people left Kuwait at this time. The exodus of Western women and child hostages began on September 1st but around 5,000 Western men were detained in the two countries with at least 500 of these deployed as "human shields". Iraq was also anxious to force all diplomats out of Kuwait. Having ordered the embassies closed and diplomats to transfer to Baghdad, the Iraqi army sought to enforce expulsions of those diplomats who had refused to be intimidated. Thus the troops entered many of the embassies, including among others those of the Netherlands, Canada, Belgium and France. A great deal of looting took place, including the residence of the French Ambassador. These acts merely served to strengthen the resolve of governments to oppose Saddam Hussein's aggression.

Whilst the world's politicians and the media focussed upon the tragic fate of the Western hostages, little information was published concerning the oppression, torture and murder of Kuwaiti people. There were several reasons for this muted response to the horrendous situation within Kuwait. First of all the Iraqi security forces operated in an atmosphere of great fear and secrecy. In public they often appeared to be firm and polite. Once their victims were arrested and taken into their hastily established torture cells it was another story.

Virtually everyone who remained in Kuwait during all or part of the occupation has a story to tell. These range from harrowing arbitrary arrests, beatings and subsequent terrorisation to methodical torture, rape and accounts of murdered friends and relatives. It was clear policy of the Iraqi military and security forces to intimidate Kuwaitis into submission. On many occasions they used their powers to enrich themselves. Whilst we do not have space to deal at great length with this issue some examples will help to highlight the brutality of the Iraqi occupation of Kuwait.

Jassim is in his mid-thirties and works as a liaison officer in the Ministry of Information. He helps journalists and other media people who are visiting Kuwait to meet the people with whom they wish to talk. He is keenly interested in journalism and the process of news gathering and has found his work in the Ministry very rewarding. Like many Kuwaitis, he was instructed to appear for work by the Iraqis but refused to do so. We asked him how he had got away with it. "Whenever soldiers stopped me and asked me why I was not at work I used to tell them that I had

been to the Ministry and had been told they would call me when they needed me", he explained. His main preoccupation had been to help his family survive. His father was ill in hospital and his mother was under great strain. He was sharing a flat with two other Kuwaiti men. One night at around three in the morning he was woken by an Iraqi security officer with a gun pressed against his head. The Iraqi shouted and swore at him, ordering him to get up. He and his two friends were then blindfolded and taken downstairs, whereupon the Iraqi used Jassim's car to drive the three of them to the nearby police station. Each of them were severely beaten. "The worst thing was hearing the screams of them torturing other people," Jassim told us. "We always felt we were going to be next but in fact they did not go too far with me, just punching me in the face and generally beating me up. They kept at us like this for two days. All the time they were asking questions. They wanted us to give names of military people and politicians. They used psychological methods, threatening time after time to kill us.

"When the beating began to get really bad I decided I had to do something to survive and so I pretended to be an idiot. When they asked me one thing I answered something else. I denied I knew anything about the Ministry of Information and said I was a very junior guy. After a while they found me amusing and did not hurt me so much. Then after two days they called me in and said I could go... but before I did I had to do something for them. They wanted me to bring them two video cassette players, some clean white dishdashes (*thobes*), and five thousand dinars. Then they set me free. I borrowed from friends and changed money on the black market in town so that I could give them what they had demanded. It was illegal to change Kuwaiti money for Iraqi money but I did it. When I had the things all ready the Iraqi officers came to my house. We sat and ate lunch as if nothing had happened. I had to behave as if they were friends! Then they took the money, the video recorders and the dish-dashes and said they did not need anything more from me except for one thing: I must sign a paper to say I would cooperate with them and inform them of anyone who was working against them. Of course I signed the paper but had no intention to cooperate. They left. After about two hours the telephone rang. It was an Iraqi officer who asked why I had broken the law and who had I changed money with, and they would have to arrest all the people who had cooperated with me in breaking the law, changing money and so on. He told me to return to the station to inform on those who had assisted in this misdemeanour! I told him I would come.

"I knew that their punishment would never end and that my only chance was to escape so I grabbed a few things and left the flat in a mad rush. I went to hide with friends on the far side of town. I stayed in hiding for the rest of the occupation. After about two months I managed to get a message to my mother. She was distraught, not knowing what had happened to me. She told me that my father had died in hospital three weeks previously. It was the first I knew of it and it really upset me. I told her I was safe but had to stay in hiding. I moved between houses until, two days before the liberation, Iraqi soldiers came to the house I was in. I was with my wife in the house of a friend. A soldier came inside whilst his officer stayed outside. They were going from house to house gathering up all the men. We did not know what they were doing and thought that we could be shot. We learned later that they were collecting hostages whom they would send in bus loads to Iraq. The soldier forced my friend out of the house and he saw me praying in an adjacent room. He waited until I had stopped and told me to get ready. I told him that my wife was expecting a baby and that I needed to be with her. He hesitated for a moment, took a quick look to check that he was the only soldier who had seen me, and whispered to me to hide. Then he went outside. His officer asked him if there was anyone else inside and he told him there was just the wife. Then my wife went running out, begging them to release my friend. She pretended to be his wife and she pleaded that she was pregnant and needed her husband. But it didn't work with the officer and they took him away with the others. The soldier told my wife that our friend would soon be back and then they put him in a coach with the other Kuwaiti men and they were driven to Iraq."

Jassim knows that he was lucky and that many others suffered a much worse fate than he did. Nevertheless many Kuwaitis will tell similar stories of how security forces picked people up at random.

Hani Ali Mohammed was not quite so lucky. He is a 30-year-old Kuwaiti whom we met when we visited Kuwait after the liberation. Still showing the psychological symptoms of deep trauma, he gave us this brief account: "At the beginning of October, at 2.30 in the morning, some Special Brigade Iraqis jumped the wall and pushed inside my house. They took my two uncles and myself. They tied us outside the house and then put us all into a car. The officers did not allow us to speak to each other. They took us to the Jabriya Police Station, then we were taken to the headquarters of the Special Guard at Adliya on the north side of the city. We were left standing against a wall, facing the wall for about an hour or an hour and a half. Next they took us to G1, the headquarters of the army. At ten o'clock the following morning they took us to an Iraqi general. He said that we should tell him everything or we would be punished. Then we were returned again

Above: a torture victim with a bullet hole in his head. Below: the corpse of a torture victim. *(Ministry of Information)*.

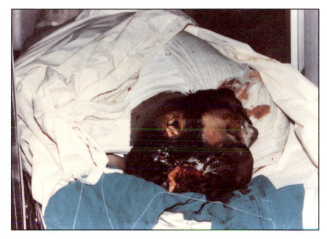

to Adliya. Then they blindfolded us and took us to a house which we knew was near the sea. I don't know exactly where it was but it was a very big house. We stayed in the car there for a while and then they took us to Jahra where there was a prison that they had made into a torture place. This was the main security headquarters. We were still blindfolded. They took us to the basement and left us there until about one o'clock in the afternoon when we met their officer.

"The officer in charge at the Jahra prison told us that we must tell the truth or we would be tortured. They kept threatening us like this until six o'clock in the evening. After six o'clock they split us up into separate rooms and they began to torture us and each of us listened to how the others were being tortured. First of all we were beaten by different kinds of sticks and tubes. Next they used cigarettes on our bodies. Then they gave us electric shocks. Then they tied us and started beating us again. By their standards these were weak tortures and they went on from 6pm to about 9pm, for around three hours. If we lost consciousness they put our heads in a bowl of water until we woke up and then they continued with the torture. Afterwards they made us stand on broken glass and tied against a door. All this torture they did to us when we had no information to give. If they found that we had something the torture would have become much much worse. What we suffered was the official torture, the torturer came with an officer and he supervised our torture, but during the whole period, when the officer was somewhere else, and when people were passing us, they kicked us and beat us, just as they were walking by us.

"After ten o'clock they took us down to the basement where there were three cells. They were full of Kuwaitis. There were only two ways out of these cells, either you were set free or you were executed. If you were called out of the cell after this they just asked you a question, you answered, and you were returned back, there was no more torture. Or else they asked you out, killed you, and took your body back to be thrown outside your house. They had one very severe Iraqi man who used to come to our cells. We called him Abu Dira. He came with his bodyguards and just watched us. He judged whether we would go to our death or go free. He just stood there and pointed, saying 'this death, this free, this death' and so on. He was a very intelligent person. If he saw you once he would never forget you.

"After four days they took nineteen of us to another prison in the north. We were staying there for a few days and suddenly this man, Abu Dira, came and said, 'All of you will be freed'. We walked out of the cell towards the prison gate but before we could all get away they took seven of our group and shot them. They were part of the same group that Abu Dira had said would be freed. We were so frightened, we were unable to ask anything. They just stood there and issued orders: 'Get out', you got out; 'Inside', you went inside. We were like animals. On the day they freed me, they took me to the police station and made me sign that I respect the revolution and the Baath Party, and that I would cooperate with the government and things like that. Then from time to time they would call and say, 'Give us information!'. Then, because we gave them no information they would say, 'OK bring us a television, bring us a video, bring money, bring your car', anything they wanted they just told us to bring and we brought it to them. In January we were having a family party and had a tent pitched next to the house. Suddenly we were surrounded by a large number of Iraqi soldiers who arrested us and took us back to the police station. Then, when we got there, the officer who we had been giving things to, videos, cars, anything, he saw us. He looked at us and then turned to the officers who had brought us and said, 'Ah, no, free these men'. This is how we were freed."

In the final round-up of Kuwaiti men, just before the liberation of Kuwait, Hani was once again picked up by the Iraqis and he was taken to a prison in Basra.

Instruments of torture: above left, an electric toaster and sandwich-maker used for torture. Above right, a table laid out with torture instruments. Below: a helmet wired for electrical torture. *(Peter Vine)*.

He was tortured very badly there and saw many fellow Kuwaitis suffering severely at the hands of the Iraqis, including some prominent people.

It was a crime in occupied Kuwait to be found with a pamphlet or leaflet which criticised Iraq, or spoke of freeing Kuwait. People found with such literature were liable to be tortured and killed. Men were given electric shock treatments and beaten until they died. Women were raped repeatedly and tortured until they begged to be killed. Corpses of people who had been killed in captivity were either secretly disposed of or were used as macabre "bait" to bring other family members to a place where they were also arrested.

Many have wondered why more information did not become available during the course of the war. As we have already stated, much of the torture and killing of civilians took place in secret locations. Relatives were afraid to speak out about their fears in case they were themselves arrested or in case their actions brought more suffering or death for their arrested relatives. There was such terrible fear inside Kuwait that people did not want to speak about what was happening. When many of these people escaped from Kuwait they may have had relatives or friends who were still held captive. They were aware that anything said to the media could cause much greater suffering for these people. Thus the terror and fear travelled with them, continuing to influence what they said. Finally, there were those who did speak up; people who put their own lives on the line and who risked the lives of others in order to communicate to the world the truth about their savaged nation. Having told the truth, having taken a calculated risk in favour of revealing Iraq's dreadful massacre of Kuwaiti people, they found that their accounts were not believed or were felt to be too risky to publish. It was not the first time that such widespread abuse of human rights took time for the world at large to comprehend. During the Second World War Hitler's holocaust against the Jews was not even known to the mass of Germans, let alone the international community, until after the war. The same happened with the Khmer Rouge's slaughter of Cambodians. The carnage in Kuwait was not on a scale comparable to either of these human tragedies but it was much greater than was believed by the world's media.

What the world's press did wish to cover was the story of foreign nationals trapped in Kuwait. Whilst the plight of Kuwaitis received very low news coverage, the plight of the hostages was a major international issue. Saddam Hussein, for his part, was using the hostages like a political football. Increasingly isolated by the gradual squeeze of sanctions and by the continued resolve of the international community, the Iraqi leader sought every chance he might have to break the cohesion of the allied forces. A visit to Baghdad by Austrian President Kurt Waldheim during August led to the release of 80 Austrians. On October 1st Iraq released nine French hostages and followed up on this with an approval towards the end of the month for the release of all remaining French nationals. Two hundred and sixty seven of these arrived in Paris on October 30th. The French government, whilst welcoming the release of their people, emphasised that there had been no deal accompanying this and that such actions could not divide the coalition. On October 21st former UK Prime Minister, Edward Heath, visited Iraq and had a long meeting with Saddam Hussein. This led to the release of 40 British nationals. Other similar representations led to various hostage releases until, on December 6th, with Christmas approaching, and pressure from within his own 'camp' for an end to the policy becoming overwhelming, the Iraqi President ordered that all the remaining "guests" be allowed to leave. In time honoured fashion the order was passed down to the Iraqi parliament which without fail rubber-stamped any decision of the President. This time he urged the Iraqi parliament "to adopt your just decision to lift the travel ban on all foreigners and to restore to all of them the freedom to travel, apologising to those who may have been harmed, and seeking forgiveness from God". He added that the decision had been made following consultations with representatives from "Jordan, Yemen, Palestine, Sudan and the Arab Maghreb".

To outsiders this seemed to mark the end of Iraq's imprisonment of civilians but this was of course far from the truth. Many Kuwaitis were imprisoned in Kuwait and Iraq and they were being subjected to methodical torture. A policy of complete terrorisation was in place in Kuwait but the world's press was focusing on other aspects of this terrible tragedy.

Further United Nations Security Council resolutions were passed in November. On the 29th, Resolution 677 categorically rejected Iraq's attempts to populate Kuwait with Iraqis, thus upsetting the demography of the country. It was passed unanimously. Resolution 678, passed on the same date, was carried by 12-2 with Cuba and Yemen voting against and China abstaining. It recalled and reaffirmed all the resolutions which had already been passed (i.e. 660, 661, 662, 664, 665, 666, 667, 669, 670, 674, and 667) and demanded that Iraq fully comply with these. It further stated that "while maintaining all its decisions, to allow Iraq one final opportunity, as a pause of goodwill, to do so;" and "Authorises member states cooperating with the government of Kuwait, unless Iraq on or before January 15th, 1991, fully implements, as set forth in paragraph 1 above, the foregoing resolutions, to use all necessary means to uphold and implement Security Council Resolution 660 and all subsequent relevant resolutions and to restore international peace and security in the area". The resolution also called upon states to provide the necessary support for actions taken "in pursuance of paragraph 2 of this resolution" and requested that the council be kept informed of what actions were being taken.

Iraq's response was, as usual, full of bluster and rhetoric. But the cards were now out on the table. Saddam Hussein had six weeks to take his forces out of Kuwait. He chose to leave them there and to make sure that, should he lose the military battle, his army would cause serious and lasting damage to Kuwait. These last six weeks were one of the worst periods for the civilian population remaining in Kuwait.

Kuwaitis celebrate their country's liberation (©1991 Peter Turnley, Black Star/Rapho – Colorific!).

Liberation
August 2nd 1990 to February 27th 1991

Birth of the Resistance Movement

The fight against Iraq's occupation of Kuwait began the moment Iraqi troops entered the country on August 2nd. Whilst Kuwait's formal military response contained many examples of heroism, it stood little chance of rebuffing the determined onslaught by Iraq's armed forces. Once the invasion and military occupation was completed many Kuwaitis set about resisting the aggression against their country in whatever manner they were able to do so. Many Kuwaiti soldiers played an important role in this process and weapons and ammunition were rescued from army stores before the Iraqis took complete control. Other arms were stolen from the Iraqis or smuggled into the country. One of the first examples of Kuwaiti citizens' total rejection of the Iraqi invasion was the campaign of non-cooperation which was immediately mounted. Kuwaitis refused to work, refused to open their shops and refused to provide services or any form of assistance to the Iraqis. As we have seen in the previous chapter many people suffered as a result of their courageous stance against the invaders. There were other Kuwaitis, and indeed other nationals, who took an active part in resisting the invasion. The Kuwaiti Secret Resistance undertook numerous missions aimed at undermining the confidence of the occupying army. These efforts were fraught with extreme danger. Suspected resistance fighters were arrested and tortured in order to gain information about others who may have been involved. The risks to people engaged in these secret activities were extremely high since it was very difficult to guard against infiltration by people who, for one reason or another, had been persuaded to act as informers; or to protect oneself against the risk of one's loyal comrades being arrested and persuaded to release information under torture.

In addition to this internal resistance, many Kuwaitis who were outside the country at the time of the invasion, or who subsequently escaped from Kuwait, engaged in active resistance. Again, it was a case of each person doing what he or she was most able to accomplish. For some this meant joining a special Kuwaiti Volunteer Army which was placed under training in Saudi Arabia; others continued to operate their diplomatic or political duties on behalf of the Kuwait government in exile, whose temporary headquarters were in Taif, Saudi Arabia. Others applied their administrative skills towards helping to coordinate planning for the liberation of Kuwait. Others organised their fellow citizens and the international community in their opposition to the Iraqi invasion. Thus was born the Free Kuwait Movement which played an active role in collecting and collating information about the invasion, liaising with the media, coordinating demonstrations and meetings, and in cooperating with international agencies concerning relief for Kuwait following its liberation.

On December 19th, following a lengthy meeting at which the Kuwait government presented evidence of human rights abuses in Kuwait, a United Nations General Assembly motion was carried by 144 votes to 1, with Iraq voting against. It was a resounding condemnation of Iraq's abuse of the norms of humanitarian law. The testimony concerning torture, summary executions, rapes and disappearances shocked delegates at the United Nations meeting. On the same day Amnesty International the interna-

The 3rd Egyptian Infantry Division with the coalition forces *(©1991 Jean-Claude Coutasse, Contact Press Images – Colorific!).*

tionally recognised human rights organisation, published a report stating that thousands of Kuwaitis
had been tortured, raped and killed since the August
2nd invasion. Six to seven thousand Kuwaiti troops
were reported to have been imprisoned in Iraq, and
Kuwaiti prisons were full of civilians including children as young as 13 years of age. The Amnesty
International report gave details of 38 cases in which
torture had been applied by Iraqis. Those who suffered in Kuwait knew that these reports represented
the 'tip of the iceberg'. The problem for those reporting on the situation was to find credible wit-
nesses who were still alive and were willing to talk.
It seems that the Iraqi approach was one of killing
third degree torture victims so that they would not
be able to provide evidence against their torturers.
Compiling evidence was therefore extremely difficult.

Impressive International Response

All Kuwaitis were confident that their country would
be liberated. Their only question was: 'when?'. The
international response to Iraq's unprovoked aggression was impressive in both its scope and extent. At
an early stage the United Nations Security Council
Resolutions identified Iraq's actions as illegal and
called for its immediate withdrawal. In order to add
teeth to its demands the world community first agreed

upon a strategy of sanctions which would isolate
Iraq and hopefully persuade its leaders to withdraw
from Kuwait. Everyone suffered as a result of these
sanctions. Vast quantities of food and medical supplies which had been stored in Kuwait were looted
at an early stage of the war and were transported to
Iraq. The Iraqi army had little interest in seeing food
supplies made available for Kuwaiti citizens and
during the course of the occupation it became increasingly difficult to obtain the basic food requirements for one's family. A measure of the extent to
which Iraqi citizens were also suffering from the
sanctions was given on November 20th when the
Iraqi National Assembly passed a bill which advo-
cated death sentences for people found to be hoard-
ing cereals. Sanctions thus hurt literally millions of
civilians in both Iraq and Kuwait.

Citizens were being starved from their homes in
Kuwait, denied food and with limited access to fresh
water and electricity. The Iraqis were intent on destroying public and private facilities in Kuwait and
many non-Kuwaitis joined in a rampage of looting,
theft, crime and destruction of property. Women
were at risk from rape by soldiers from both the
regular forces and the undisciplined 'Popular Army'
which Saddam Hussein unleashed on the country. It
was becoming plain to those who knew the true facts
of the situation in Kuwait that whilst sanctions might

eventually achieve the desired goal it would require many more months for them to do so, and would bring deep suffering to civilians in both Kuwait and Iraq. In the long run there was no firm guarantee that the sanctions policy would work, and it was felt that the longer it continued, the more ways the Iraqi leadership would find to circumvent the problem.

The only other solution was for military action against Iraq, forcing its government to withdraw its troops and to compensate both Kuwait and the international community for its actions. In order to accomplish the task of evicting Iraq from Kuwait a strong multi-national force was established. Thirty countries committed military support to the task. They were as follows: Argentina, Australia, Bahrain, Bangladesh, Belgium, Canada, Czechoslovakia, Denmark, Egypt, France, Germany, Greece, Honduras, Italy, Kuwait, Morocco, Netherlands, New Zealand, Niger, Norway, Oman, Pakistan, Qatar, Saudi Arabia, Senegal, Spain, Syria, United Arab Emirates, the United Kingdom and the United States.

Prior to actually committing troops to action every possible effort was made to achieve a negotiated withdrawal of Iraq from Kuwait. Some called this the 'peaceful solution', forgetting that the peace had already been broken by Iraq, and that Saddam's forces continued to wage war against Kuwait and its people on a daily basis. For these sufferers of the invasion there was no such thing as a peaceful solution, only perhaps the least painful return to freedom. The true extent of suffering by Kuwaiti citizens at the hands of Iraq's armed forces was not fully understood outside of occupied Kuwait.

The UN Security Council Resolution number 678 which had been passed on November 29th set an agreed deadline for Iraq to get out of Kuwait. After January 15th member states were authorised by the UN to 'use all necessary means' to force Iraq to withdraw its armed forces. As the cut-off date approached renewed efforts were directed towards persuading Iraq to withdraw, thus reducing the bloodshed which would result from allied military action. On November 30th President Bush announced that he was prepared to go "the extra mile for peace". He proposed that Tariq Aziz, the Foreign Minister of Iraq, should visit Washington in mid-December and following talks there James Baker would visit Baghdad. This proposal, perhaps wrongly interpreted in Baghdad as indicating a lack of resolve by President Bush to give the command for military action, was deliberately obstructed by the Iraqis. Their proposal to hold the Baghdad meeting between James Baker and Saddam Hussein on January 12th was rejected on the grounds that this would not leave sufficient time for the Iraqis to withdraw from Kuwait before

General Norman Schwarzkopf, Supreme Commander of the coalition forces in the Gulf (©1990 Dennis Brack, Black Star – Colorific!).

the UN adopted deadline. President Bush finally announced on December 18th that his efforts to arrange a visit by Tariq Aziz, between December 20th and January 3rd, had failed. He was still willing to send US Secretary of State James Baker to Baghdad to meet President Saddam Hussein but it was looking increasingly likely that the Iraqi President was determined to defy the UN ultimatum.

Build-up of the military coalition of forces against Iraq was impressive but planners knew that they were pitted against a very large Iraqi army which had been well trained in techniques of ground warfare. Military strategists claim that an attacking force should outnumber the defenders by at least three to one. There was no chance of achieving such a ratio in the time available since Iraq's army stood at around a million, with around 400,000 deployed in Kuwait. General Norman Schwarzkopf, who was commander of the multinational force, is reported to have calculated that far from attaining such numerical superiority, the fighting force at his disposal would not even allow him to achieve parity with the Iraqi army. In fact he believed that the ratio of front line troops would be closer to a three-to-one disadvantage and that he would have somewhat fewer tanks at his disposal than the Iraqis. Other books devoted to the war have dealt in great detail with the military aspects of the liberation of Kuwait and it is not our intention to repeat this information here.

Despite the apparent impasse, members of the UN Security Council were hoping that a way could be found to avoid taking the military option against Iraq. A French initiative failed to obtain any firm commitments from Iraq other than the vague promise of concessions "if there is a conference on Palestine". This linkage of the Palestinian problem to the current crisis was widely rejected as representing an attempt to cloud the issue concerning Iraq's illegal occupation of Kuwait. Two invitations to talks from the European Community were turned down by the Iraqis who apparently felt that the message they would hear would be exactly the same as that which the Americans would have delivered to Tariq Aziz had he gone to Washington: 'get out of Kuwait or face the military consequences'.

On January 9th Tariq Aziz met James Baker in Geneva. The meeting was seen by both sides as a final attempt to avert war. Secretary of State James Baker did his best to impress upon Tariq Aziz that the multi-nation coalition was determined to see through the task of removing Iraq from Kuwait. He handed the Iraqi Foreign Minister a letter from President Bush to President Hussein in which the American President reiterated his government's determination to seek compliance with the United Nations resolutions. Tariq Aziz read the letter carefully and then refused to accept it for delivery to Saddam Hussein. The Iraqi stance at this meeting was to call for a meeting to consider all the problems of the Middle East. Aziz also reaffirmed that Iraq would attack Israel if the coalition forces attacked them in Kuwait and Iraq. At the end of the six-hour meeting James Baker issued a statement in which he stated that he "had heard nothing new" and that Iraq seemed as determined as ever to hold onto Kuwait.

On January 12th both houses of the American Congress, the Senate and the House of Representatives, voted in favour of American military force being used to help liberate Kuwait. On the same day Javier Perez de Cuellar, Secretary General of the United Nations, arrived in Baghdad to meet with Saddam Hussein. The meeting was eventually held on the following day. It consisted of "a polite exchange of views" but led to no new conclusion or possible solution. Finally, on January 15th, the UN Secretary General made a statement to the world: "As... the world stands poised between peace and war, I most sincerely appeal to President Saddam Hussein to turn the course of events away from catastrophe and towards a new era of justice and harmony... If this commitment is made, and clear and substantial steps taken to implement (the UN)

resolutions, a just peace, with all its benefits, will follow." But it was not to be.

Desert Storm

President Hussein had been girding his troops for war. He called upon his soldiers to fight to the death to defend their occupation of Kuwait. Finally the coalition of forces, under joint command of General Norman Schwarzkopf and Prince Sultan ibn Abdul Aziz (Saudi Arabia's Minister of Defence), were directed to undertake the military action necessary to achieve the objectives of the international community: the liberation of Kuwait. "Operation Desert Storm" began just before midnight on January 16th.

The battle opened with sustained precision air attacks on carefully defined strategic targets in Iraq and Kuwait: command bases, air fields, military sites, chemical and nuclear facilities, electricity power plants. Cruise missiles were programmed to attack particular buildings in Baghdad, even to penetrate these through ventilator shafts. This was to be a modern war in which high technology SMART weapons would be used in order to minimise civilian casualties. Whilst the Iraqi ground forces mounted powerful air defences in the form of ground to air missiles and anti-aircraft fire, its air force remained hidden or else escaped across the border to Iran. Rather than risk the loss of these planes through their use in defending Iraqi ground troops, it appeared that Saddam Hussein decided to abandon any attempt to prevent allied air supremacy.

Over 30,000 sorties were flown in January and "carpet-bombing" by B52s of Iraqi emplacements along the southern borders of Kuwait was believed to have greatly weakened Iraq's defensive position. Unable to make any meaningful military response to the coalition's aerial bombardment, Iraq launched inaccurate SCUD missiles at Israel, Saudi Arabia and Bahrain, knowing full well that these were likely to kill civilians. During January, a total of 57 SCUDs were launched. Of these 10 landed in areas where they were able to cause damage, 17 landed where they had no impact on people, 30 were downed by Patriot missiles. The human toll from SCUDs during January was five people killed and 224 injured. Iraq continued to fire SCUDs right up to the end of the war but for the most part these were successfully destroyed by Patriot missiles. The one major exception occurred on the night of February 25-26th when a SCUD landed on a US army reserve barracks in Al Khobar, near Dharan on the Gulf coast of Saudi Arabia. It killed 28 US military personnel and wounded at least a hundred others.

Saddam Hussein appears to have been convinced that the Coalition forces, led by General

Schwarzkopf, were not prepared to face up to his ground forces. On February 15th Iraq announced that it was prepared to withdraw from Kuwait, complying with UN Resolution 660, but it attached a long list of unacceptable conditions to its offer. These were (1) a complete ceasefire; (2) annulment of all other UN resolutions regarding the conflict; (3) a complete withdrawal of all coalition forces from the region within a month of the ceasefire; (4) a withdrawal of Israel from "Palestine and the Arab territories it is occupying in the Golan and southern Lebanon" or that in the event that it did not do so that the UN should pass against Israel identical resolutions to those passed against Iraq; (5) a guarantee of Iraq's "historical rights" on land and sea; and (6) that the "political arrangements to be agreed" should be based upon the "people's will and in accordance with democratic practice". On top of all these conditions Iraq actually claimed war reparations for damage inflicted by the Coalition, together with the cancellation of Iraq's debts to Coalition countries as well as cancellation by the Coalition of debts from other countries in the region which had not joined the Coalition! Whatever else one wished to call this offer, it was certainly not unconditional. President Bush's description of it as a "cruel hoax" was somewhat nearer the mark.

Despite efforts by the Soviet Union to salvage something out of the situation, it was becoming clear that Saddam Hussein was prepared to force his troops into a bloody battle. Finally, on February 22nd President Bush issued his ultimatum: (1) begin withdrawing from Kuwait by noon on February 23rd New York time (8.00pm local time) and complete that withdrawal in seven days; (2) within the first 48 hours remove all its forces from Kuwait City and allow the prompt return of the legitimate government, and withdraw from all prepared defences along the Saudi-Kuwait and Saudi-Iraq borders and from Kuwait's portion of the Rumaillah oilfield; (3) release of all prisoners of war and civilian detainees within 48 hours; (4) remove all explosive and booby trap devices from Kuwait; and (5) cease combat air fire and aircraft flights over Iraq and Kuwait except for aircraft carrying troops out of Kuwait. President Bush promised that if these terms were met the Coalition would not attack retreating Iraqi forces.

It was already clear however that Iraq had no intention of agreeing to such terms. On the contrary the Iraqi army was busy setting fire to hundreds of Kuwaiti oil wells and other installations. The promised "scorched earth" policy was being carried out. There did not seem to be any point in further prevarication. Unfortunately the talks between Tariq Aziz and the Soviet government were seen as a cause to delay the ground offensive. Even on February 23rd, when it was clear that Iraq had sabotaged all of Kuwait's oil production capacity and had set about capturing large numbers of Kuwaiti men to use as hostages, President Gorbachev is reported to have called for more time so that negotiations could reach a compromise between the Gorbachev and Bush proposals. On February 24th, after all the destruction which had taken place in Kuwait, and after the Coalition ground offensive had begun to liberate Kuwait, the Soviet Foreign Ministry spokesman, Vitaly Churkin, read a statement indicating that the Soviet government regretted that "a real chance to solve the conflict peacefully and achieve the goals set by UN Security Council resolutions has been missed".

It was clear to everyone in the Coalition however that Saddam Hussein was playing for as much time as possible and that his forces would continue to destroy the country and continue to torture and kill its people until they were forced to leave.

The Coalition's Land Offensive

The final phase of the Coalition forces' joint action to free Kuwait began at four o'clock in the morning on February 24th. It was a brilliantly planned offensive in which land armies broke through Iraqi defences along a 480-kilometre front. For the most part Iraqi soldiers surrendered, but there were several instances of determined resistance.

We asked Colonel Salem of the 35th Brigade, whose forces had fought so bravely and successfully on August 2nd, to describe his role in the liberation of Kuwait. "After we retreated to Saudi Arabia early on the morning of August 3rd, we remained in Saudi Arabia until we re-entered Kuwait as part of the operation to free Kuwait on February 23rd 1991. Just before this date we joined up with the Saudi Arabian 20th Brigade and we came back to the same point at which we had originally crossed into Saudi Arabia. We started the battle to free Kuwait alongside the Saudi and Egyptians forces at Rumat al Sabah. We broke through the Iraqi lines with the 20th Brigade on the left. The Egyptians had their own mission. Ours was to go first to a place called Al Mitia and after that to re-occupy our own camp on the outskirts of Kuwait City. We were also instructed to secure the ammunition depot at Assad. On the 24th February, at three o'clock, we broke through and managed to reach our first objective. We kept going and on the 25th February, when we reached a point close to our camp we were told that the Iraqis were slaughtering people inside the city, they were gathering people in masses and taking them back to Baghdad, and that we should keep

Top: oil well fires choked the sky and killed plants and crops. Above left: an aerial view of a blazing oil well. Above right: sabotaged oil storage tanks. *(Ministry of Information)*.

moving forward. The message came from General Schwarzkopf that we should complete our mission until our last objective. We continued and we managed to re-occupy our camp at five o'clock that evening."

Although Colonel Salem had made the operation sound easy it was not without its dangers. They had been fired on whilst crossing the first minefield and came under very heavy mortar shelling just after crossing a major highway. "It was very heavy artillery which we met and I thought that our attack would fail because I was the one who was facing the full force of the bombardment. That day was cloudy and we had A10s flying on top of us but they couldn't see anything because of the low cloud. I called on the A16s and they managed to locate and stop the firing which was coming from the cover of a poultry farm.

"It was amazing that the Iraqis we captured did not seem to be under any stress. They were clean, shaved, in good health, and when we asked them how they had survived so well, they said 'Nothing happened here.' The shelling was in other areas but not in the area where we found them. The Coalition aircraft bombed along an axis and they didn't strike this area. We captured officers with all their maps and documents, and even their salaries... they had just received their salaries. Some were in the middle of their meals when we caught them. They were well supplied. We looked through their ditches and trenches. Some of them were like a house underground. Before the attack we had been checking on this area. In daytime there was no movement whilst at night at ten o'clock a car would come and give them their supplies and there would be very brief movement. I asked one of them how long he stayed in the trench. He said, 'The whole week, because we do not need to go out. We have everything, we have electricity, television, radios. At night our supply comes, sometimes we send our clothes to be cleaned. We have been living all this time down in the trenches'."

Colonel Salem and his men entered some of the trenches to see for themselves how they were constructed. "Believe me, the trenches consisted of a bedroom, living room, clothes room, kitchen and toilets. All the supplies were there and they could communicate through paths between the trenches so they could not be seen. They were very good in defence preparations, they had telephones, they had everything and they even had their mail. It was amazing because they stayed all the time there, nothing had been threatening them, and they used everything available... things that they could steal from the camps, from the country, from the people."

They may have been well organised when things were going their way, but Colonel Salem was disdainful of their lack of any humanitarian approach towards their own wounded. Recollecting his encounter with the Iraqi forces on August 2nd, he had this to say: "When it came to dealing with the injured, and trying to evacuate the casualties, they had nothing to send to evacuate casualties. If you are injured, if you are not capable of moving, you got one bullet and that's it. And it happened... they were running, they were asking for help, shouting... they paid no attention... they were running over some of them... in a very critical condition... we managed to evacuate one of them with our own injured... Those people have no regard for anything concerning injury or concerning help... some of their fellows, they were on the ground, injured, they ran them over with their APCs (armoured personnel carriers), in front of us. Or they destroyed a vehicle in which somebody inside was injured... they just came and destroyed everything in front of them".

The Battle of Al-Grain

But now the battle to free Kuwait was almost over. The Iraqis were on the run. For many of those inside Kuwait however the Coalition forces arrived too

An Arabic road-sign which reads: BUSH + MAJOR + MITTERAND = FREE KUWAIT. *(Peter Vine)*.

late. The big round-up of Kuwaiti men had begun on February 22nd and was still in full swing on February 24th. Iraqi soldiers were moving from house to house, ordering the men to board buses which took them to southern Iraq. A chance encounter between soldiers engaged in this operation and two members of the Kuwaiti resistance led to the battle of Al-Grain which left an unknown number of Iraqi soldiers dead and took the lives of twelve Kuwaiti resistance fighters.

We asked a member of the Kuwaiti Resistance to tell us precisely what happened on February 24th in the normally quiet and peaceful modern housing estate in a residential quarter of Kuwait City. "Our friends in the Al-Grain battle were planning to attack the Iraqi forces as they withdrew. They were planning for three kinds of encounters: street battles, or to hit them as they were withdrawing, or to provide support for the Coalition forces when the Iraqis clashed with them. We divided the Resistance Force into several groups, although we were all working together. The group which controlled Al-Grain area, where the battle took place, was known as the Group of Messila. The Resistance group controlling the Jabariya area of the city we now refer to as the '25th of February Group'. We prepared our plans before the 15th January and we believed that the air attack would be for not more than three or four days, and afterwards there would be a battle on the streets and elsewhere on land. We did not expect the air war to continue for more than a month. We had gathered information of where the Iraqis were concentrated, in the police stations, in the schools, and in the various other areas, and we had plans to attack them.

Above: a beach with Iraqi defensive trench
Below: an Iraqi arms store *(Ministry of Information)*.

We informed our government abroad about where the Iraqis were concentrating and sent them photographs.

"The Al-Grain battle took place on February 24th. We heard that there was a ground attack and all our comrades gathered in the house at Al-Grain. The plan was that they should gather at the house and then separate into small groups and go down to the expressway. One section of the group was to control the fifth ring-road. Nineteen men were gathered in the house that morning and the first group, led by Said Hadi al-Alawi, left the house in their full uniform with guns, and suddenly the Iraqi forces saw them. They ran back into the house. At the same time the Iraqi forces had surrounded the whole of Al-Grain area to kidnap all Kuwaiti males in order to take them to prisons in southern Iraq. When our three colleagues re-entered the house the Iraqis came and surrounded the house. Said Hadi had returned to the house to warn his colleagues so that they could rapidly disperse. It was around a quarter to eight in the morning. Unfortunately the Iraqis did not give them time to get away, they were already surrounding the house."

"A minibus with two members of the security force were the first to arrive at the house. They knocked on the front gate and of course nobody opened it. Inside the house the resistance group began to prepare to put up a fight, issuing themselves with weapons and ammunition. They saw that the Iraqis were going to jump over the wall surrounding the house, and Said Hadi, who was head of the group went to fire at them. His gun failed to work and another member of the group, Mohammed Yousef, attacked the Iraqis. When the other Iraqis in the area heard the gunfire, other members of the security force came, and afterwards the army. Around 50 or 60 soldiers came. To our group of 19 in the house it was not such a big group, they could fight with them. They started to exchange fire and whenever any Iraqis tried to approach the house they were killed by the resistance group inside."

"The battle was becoming more intense and the Iraqis were losing men. They called for more support... soldiers, tanks and artillery. This time, when they began the battle again, they had already gathered a large number of Kuwaiti men from the area to take them to Iraqi prisons. They freed them and every Iraqi soldier in the vicinity came to the house. At least 50 Kuwaiti men went free because of this battle. The force was growing so strong but still the Kuwaiti resistance group was fighting back. The Iraqis could not gain control of the house so they brought in an RBG anti-tank weapon. It looked like a bazooka but was very powerful.

Iraqi gun with Jordanian ammunition *(Peter Vine)*.

"The resistance group managed to divide up so that some went to an adjacent house. But the Iraqis were still not in control so they called for more support. Two tanks arrived outside the house at 10 o'clock in the morning, after two hours of intensive fighting. Inside the house an urgent discussion took place. It was decided that two fighters should sacrifice themselves by breaking away from the house, firing at the Iraqis and running to another area so that the pressure on the house would be eased and might give a chance for some others to escape. Two civilian members of the resistance group, Jassim Guloum and Mobarak Ali Sofer, agreed to make such an attempt.

As soon as they opened the door to get out, the Iraqi fire against them was intense and they were immediately critically injured. The leader of the group, Said Hadi, began to encourage the others , saying that this was their opportunity to defend their land, to defend their country, to defend the legitimate regime, and that they must fight on. They had not given up hope since they heard on the radio that there was a ground attack by the Coalition forces in progress and they were expecting that at any moment the ground attack forces would arrive to help them. They thought that they had only to keep up the fight for two or three hours and that then the ground forces would come to help them.

"But the battle at the house in Al-Grain continued and the resistance group began to run out of ammunition. They had never had that much ammunition... it had always been assumed that they would attack and run, attack and run, but not stay for a prolonged period to fight against a major Iraqi force. One military member of the group, Aamer Alenzi, had been particularly helpful to them in the battle since he had a 500 automatic weapon and he was very brave in using it. But the Iraqis finally hit him with a direct hit from their anti-tank RBG weapon. He was completely blown to pieces... there was nothing left of him except what was spread on the walls.

The house at Al-Grain – severely damaged – in which resistance fighters died *(Ministry of Information)*.

"After this, at around 12 o'clock, Said Hadi, the leader, said to his men that there was no way out for them except to sacrifice themselves. There was no help, most of the men had been badly injured, two had died. Said Hadi then went up on the roof and raised the Kuwaiti flag. He was the first man to raise the Kuwaiti flag since the country had been occupied. This action by Said Hadi made the Iraqis very angry… that someone had raised the Kuwaiti flag… and they asked for more help. After raising the flag, Said Hadi began throwing grenades at the Iraqis but he was shot by a tank. He was hit directly and killed.

"But the firing continued between the Iraqi forces surrounding the house and the men inside. It went on until around a quarter or half past five. Remember, it was February and at that time the light was short and it was becoming dark and there was no electricity. And the whole area was full of smoke. By that time most of the group had been killed or injured. At that stage Talal al-Haza, who was in the adjacent house, got out of the house, fired at the Iraqis whilst he was running, and he escaped. He ran right through the Iraqis, it was fantastic. If you watched it on television, like a Rambo film, you would never believe it! Two others managed to escape by running from the adjacent house, they were both members of the Kuwaiti military, Ahmad Alsaleh and Mshel Abdoula.

"But these were not the only survivors. In one house Sami Said Hadi and Jamal Albanai hid in the locker above the bathroom. In the other house Mohammed Yousef and Hazem Al-Saleh did the same. Sami Said Hadi had watched his father, leader of the entire group, die. He had been very seriously affected psychologically and his friend Jamal had helped him to hide. As the four men hid in their darkened recess above the bathrooms of each house, they could hear the Iraqis talking. An officer was encouraging a soldier to enter the house quickly, but the soldier said 'No, no, this is not Kuwaitis inside the house, it is Americans!' Our men fought so strongly, so bravely, so courageously…

"After five-thirty the Iraqis entered the house. They were quite frightened. There were dead and wounded Kuwaiti resistance fighters all over the house. Ibrahim Ali Sofer was lying among the injured on the floor. He knew that there were two of his colleagues hiding above the bathroom. He saw the soldiers hurl one grenade into a recess near the bathroom and he was afraid that they would throw another grenade into the place where the two men were hiding. Ibrahim suddenly started shouting and trying to fight with the Iraqis. They immediately came to him, caught him, and they left the others. He saved two people in this way.

"In the other house they looked for any survivors but they did not find them, and they were afraid. They wanted to get away from the house as quickly as possible. They were afraid because they could see how many of their friends had been killed. We believe there were at least a hundred between the injured and killed Iraqi soldiers. The Iraqis who entered the houses took all the injured and they left the house. The people who had been hiding in the house waited until about ten-thirty and then they crept out of the house. Each pair who had been hiding thought they were the only ones to survive. They made their escape from the house secretly and it was only later that they discovered they were not the only survivors! And Talal Al Haza, who escaped like Rambo, he thought he was the only one to survive. They escaped from house to house, they managed to pass around a checkpoint, and they escaped.

"The story of what happened to Talal al Haza, who we call Rambo, is very interesting. After escaping from the house and breaking through the Iraqi lines he entered another house where he changed his clothes and he stayed in one of the houses with another man, also in hiding. Later that evening, the Iraqis returned to the area and searched some of the houses. They found Talal with one other man. They took the two of them to Hadiya Police Station. They kept him inside the prison and there were instructions that on the following morning they were to be executed. That night, they knew that they were going to be killed and they wondered how they could escape. In the middle of the night it was really quiet, there was no movement, and they found an iron bar which they used to break the door of the prison. They managed to break out and to free everyone else in the prison. Suddenly the Iraqis saw them and wanted to get them back into the police station but the Kuwaitis escaped by running different ways across the desert… and they saved themselves.

"The Iraqis left the dead resistance fighters at the house but the injured were taken to the hospital. There they slit open their bodies, cut out various organs, and on the day of liberation their bodies were in the street, showing signs of torture…

"Our friends at the Al-Grain battle gave a very good example. They were prepared to defend dignity and their right to freedom, if necessary until they died. Many people do not have such a vision of the Kuwaiti people but our people have shown great courage. Those people who stayed in Kuwait and who fought in the resistance did so out of choice. We were prepared to resist right to the end."

During our research for this book we listened to many people describe their own experiences during the occupation of Kuwait. Thousands of people suffered and are still suffering. Many Kuwaitis have been killed and their families grieve for them. At the time of writing there are over 2000 unaccounted for Kuwaiti civilians and over 1000 members of the Kuwaiti military similarly classified.

Liberation

On the evening of February 25th the Iraqi army began pulling out of Kuwait in a state of mounting panic. The next day, February 26th, the de-facto withdrawal was made official by a broadcast given by Saddam Hussein. Even in total defeat the Iraqi President spoke of victory. By the evening of February 26th the Kuwaiti Resistance movement was in full control of the city.

On February 27th President Bush addressed the American people and the world in a televised speech delivered from the Oval Office of the White House. "Kuwait is liberated; Iraq's army is defeated; our military objectives are met. This is not a time for euphoria, certainly not a time to gloat, but it is a time of pride… This is a victory for all mankind and for the rule of law", he declared.

For the people of Kuwait it was a time of enormous relief.

Those who died and those who suffered all wanted one thing: the freedom of their country. The massive international effort which took place to fulfill that objective will never be forgotten by the people of Kuwait. Those who say that Kuwait has not learnt from the experience are wrong. Kuwait and its people will never again be the same as they were prior to Iraq's invasion. The aggression and cruelty which they witnessed has left an indelible mark. Many Kuwaiti people discovered during the crisis that they had courage and resources which had never before been put to the test. Today that enhanced self-reliance and confidence is helping them to forge a new future for Kuwait.

Above: graves of resistance fighters from the battle at Al-Grain. Photographs: *Peter Vine*.

Members of the resistance group who were killed in the house at Al-Grain on February 25th 1991

Further Reading

References to Natural History of Kuwait:–

Al-Attar, M.H. and H. Ikenoue, 1979. The production of juvenile shrimps (*Penaeus semisulcatus*) for release off the coast of Kuwait during 1975. *Kuwait Bulletin of Marine Science* (1).

Al-Attar, M.H. Description of larval, postlarval and juvenile stages of some penaeid shrimp found in Kuwait waters. KISR Technical Report No. MB–47.

Al-Rawi, A. 1987. Flora of Kuwait Vol.2. Compositae and Monocotyledoneae. Kuwait University.

Al-Sdirawi, F.A. 1985. Conservation and protection of the wildlife in Kuwait. Phase 1. Review and assessment of information on desert fauna. KISR report number 1927 submitted to Environment Protection Council. KISR.

Basson, P.W. et al. 1977. Biotopes of the Western Arabian Gulf. Marine life and environments of Saudi Arabia. ARAMCO.

Clayton, D. and K. Wells, 1987. Discovering Kuwait's Wildlife. Published by:– Fahad Al-Marzouk, Kuwait.

Clayton, D.A. and T.C. Vaughan, 1986. Territorial acquisition in the mudskipper *Boleophalmus boddarti* (Pisces: Gobiidae). *J.Zool.* Lond. (A), 209, 501–519.

Daoud, H.S. (revised by Ali Al-Rawi), 1985. Flora of Kuwait Vol.1. Dicotyledoneae. Keegan Paul International.

Eissa, S.M., 1979. Pattern and energetic cost of activity of the gerbil, *Gerbillus cheesmani* in Kuwait desert. *Bull. Fac. Sci. Cairo Univ.* 115 (48), 135–146

Eissa, S.M. and Y.S. El-Assy, 1975. Record of certain reptilian species found in Kuwait. *J.Univ. Kuwait (Sci)* 2. 123–146.

Euzen, O., 1987. Food habits and diet composition of some fish of Kuwait. *Kuwait Bulletin of Marine Science* (1987) 65–85.

Farmer, A.S.D. and J.E. Docksey, 1983. A bibliography of the marine and maritime environment of the Arabian Gulf and Gulf of Oman. *Kuwait Bulletin of Marine Science*. (4).

Farmer, A.S.D. and M. Ukawa, 1986. A provisional atlas for the commercially important penaeid shrimps of the Arabian Gulf. *Kuwait Bulletin of Marine Science*. (7) 23–44.

Fitzgerald, V.D., 1953. Notes on some rodents from Saudi Arabia and Kuwait. *Bombay Natural History Society* 51, 424–429.

Gunatilaka, A. and S. Mwango, 1987. Continental sabkha pans and associated nebkhas in southern Kuwait, Arabian Gulf. In Frostick, L. and Reid, I (eds.) 1987, Desert Sediments: Ancient and Modern. Geological Society Special Publication No. 35, pp. 187–203.

Hakim, S. et al., 1983. The Fisheries of Kuwait, 1982. KISR Technical Report (1053).

Halwagy, R. et al (eds.), 1986. Marine Environment and Pollution. Proceedings of the First Arabian Gulf Conference on Environment and Pollution. Kuwait University, Faculty of Science, Kuwait Foundation for the Advancement of Sciences and Environment Protection Council, Kuwait.

Haynes, P.R., 1979. Notes on the status and distribution of the birds of Kuwait. *Ahmadi Natural History Society Newsletter* 20, 1–34.

Hopkins, M.L. et al., 1984. An overview of Kuwait's fisheries including a preliminary economic analysis. *Kuwait Bulletin of Marine Science* (5): 37–59.

Hopkins, K. et al., 1986. Tilapia culture in Kuwait: A preliminary economic analysis of production systems. *Kuwait Bulletin of Marine Science*, 7, 45–64.

Jennings, M.C., 1981. Birds of the Arabian Gulf. George Allen & Unwin, London.

Jones, D.A., 1986. A field guide to the sea shores of Kuwait and the Arabian Gulf. University of Kuwait.

Khalaf, F.I. et al., 1984. Types and characteristics of the recent surface deposits of Kuwait, Arabian Gulf. *Journal of Arid Environments*, 7, 9–33.

Kuronuma, K and Y. Abe, 1986. Fishes of the Arabian Gulf. KISR. pp.356, 30 plates.

Lee, J.W. et al., 1986. Oceanographic characteristics of Kuwait waters in 1984. KISR Technical Report (1964).

Mathews, C.P. et al., 1986. Stocks of *Metapenaeus affinis* in Kuwait and Iraq waters MB–54 KISR (2231).

Mathews, C.P., 1986. Fin fish management project. Phase II. Final report. KISR (2177).

Michel, H.B. et al., 1986. Zooplankton diversity, distribution and abundance in Kuwait waters. *Kuwait Bulletin of Marine Science* (8): 37–105.

Stuart, B. and Pilcher, C. 1983. In:– Kuwait's Natural History – An Introduction. Birds. pp. 132–170. K.O.C.

Omar, S.A.S., 1985. Baseline information on native plants of Kuwait. KISR Technical Report No. AG–6.

Vaughan T.C., 1978. Distribution and relative abundance of rodents in Kuwait. *Congressus Theriol Int.* 2, 101.

Acknowledgements

Research and writing of this book involved the help and assistance of many organisations and individuals. The project was instigated at the request of Immel Publishing with the intention that the volume should form part of its Country Heritage series. We are grateful to the company for encouraging us to proceed and for staying the course throughout a difficult period of delays and text changes necessitated by the turn of events in Kuwait. We received considerable encouragement for our work, together with practical assistance, from His Excellency the Ambassador, Ghazi Al-Rayes, and his colleagues at the Kuwait Embassy in London. In Kuwait we were welcomed by the Ministry of Information and in particular by the Minister of Information, Professor Badr Jassim Al-Yacoub; and by Rida An Feeli and Mrs Amal Al-Hamad both of whom were actively engaged in coordinating arrangements for us. We should like to thank Kuwait Airlines for their help in travel arrangements.

Research on Kuwait's history and prehistory was greatly aided by members of Kuwait National Museum and particularly by Dr Fahed Al-Wohaibi. We are grateful to the Museum for providing photographs of certain artefacts held in the collection at that time. We also take the opportunity to express our deepest regrets that the Museum and its collection was so senselessly destroyed.

Our work on traditional aspects of Kuwait was aided by visits to the Al Sadu Centre and by discussion with its staff to whom we are most grateful. We also wish to thank the Arab Gulf States Folklore Centre for continuing to record aspects of traditional life throughout the Gulf countries and for providing us with necessary background information.

The natural history of Kuwait had been investigated by scientists at Kuwait University, KISR, the Environment Protection Department in the Ministry of Health, and by private individuals. We should like to mention Dr Mohammad Al-Attar at KISR, Ibrahim Hadi and Dr Mahmood Yousef Abdulraheem at the Environment Protection Department; Dr Mahmoud Shihab; Professor Colin Pilcher and Dr David Clayton. In addition to assisting with information, Dr Clayton very kindly allowed us to use some of his photographs of Kuwait's wildlife. We are also grateful to Dr Badria Al-Awadi, coordinator for the Regional Organisation for Protection of the Marine Environment, ROPME. Information gathering at KISR was greatly aided by Librarian Barbara Abu-Zeid whose efforts on our behalf we are pleased to acknowledge.

Our view of modern Kuwait was shaped in part by lengthy discussions with Dr Abdulhadi Alawadi, Undersecretary of the Ministry of Planning, and Coordinator of Kuwait's Five Year Development Plans. We also spoke with management personnel from Kuwait Oil Company and with many people involved in the country's impressive progress.

Information on the invasion, occupation and liberation of Kuwait was gathered by interviewing a large number of people who were directly affected by events in Kuwait. Some of these requested that their names should not be published. Others were reporting upon events which severely scarred their lives and the lives of many others. We feel therefore that it would be wrong to single out individual people for thanks in relation to the last two chapters of the book. We sincerely hope that they will find in these pages a source of happiness and pride in their country's achievement.